PANORAMA
OF A
PRESIDENCY

PANORAMA OF A PRESIDENCY

HOW GEORGE W. BUSH ACQUIRED AND SPENT HIS POLITICAL CAPITAL

STEVEN E. SCHIER

M.E.Sharpe
Armonk, New York
London, England

Library of Congress Cataloging-in-Publication Data

Schier, Steven E.
  Panorama of a presidency : how George W. Bush acquired and spent his political capital /
by Steven E. Schier.
      p. cm.
  Includes bibliographical references and index.
  ISBN-: 978-0-7656-1692-0 (cloth : alk. paper) — ISBN 978-0-7656-1693-7 (pbk. : alk. paper)
1. United States—Politics and government—2001- 2. United States—Foreign rela-
tions—2001- 3. Bush, George W. (George Walker), 1946- 4. Political capital—United
States—History—21st century. I. Title.

  E902.S425 2009
  973.931092—dc22   2008024989

Printed in the United States of America

∞

| BM (c) | 10 | 9 | 8 | 7 | 6 | 5 | 4 | 3 | 2 | 1 |
| BM (p) | 10 | 9 | 8 | 7 | 6 | 5 | 4 | 3 | 2 | 1 |

Dedicated to six people who have taught me much about American politics—

Jonathan Rauch
Larry Jacobs
John F. Harris
Barry Casselman
John McConnell
Tom Hauser

CONTENTS

PREFACE

Analyzing a contemporary presidency is no easy task. One is confronted with mountains of information and opinion through which one must trudge. Too much information, a common affliction nowadays, is as problematic as too little. In my efforts, I have been guided by the advice of Arthur Conan Doyle's Sherlock Holmes: "It is of the highest importance in the art of detection to be able to recognize out of a number of facts which are incidental and which vital. Otherwise your energy and attention must be dissipated instead of being concentrated" (*The Adventure of the Reigate Squire*). The reader can judge my success at identifying and analyzing the vital facts of the George W. Bush presidency.

My thanks go to the Faculty Grants Committee, President Robert Oden, and Dean Scott Bierman of Carleton College for granting me the time and financial support to finish this book. I also profited immensely from the opportunity to conduct Carleton's off-campus program in Washington in 2001, 2004, and 2007, when I was able to conduct many interviews and much useful research for this project. My student research assistants—Andrew Kaufman, Adam Smith, and Jill Rodde—provided invaluable help in bringing this project to fruition. Several political scientists who read and commented on earlier versions of this work, particularly Charles O. Jones, Justin S. Vaughn, and Ray La Raja, deserve my thanks. My colleagues in the Carleton political science department proved unfailingly supportive of my efforts. Patricia Kolb and her staff at M.E. Sharpe publishers have been able stewards of this project. My family—Mary, Teresa, and Anna—are due my greatest thanks for their abundant support and encouragement as I followed the many ups and downs of George W. Bush's time in the White House.

PANORAMA
OF A
PRESIDENCY

1 THE PRESIDENCY

George W. Bush's conduct of the presidency has spawned strong affirmative and negative evaluations. Discussion of this presidency in print and blogs touts him as a visionary president or denounces him as deserving of impeachment. The truth probably lies at a distance from either of these evaluative poles. What concepts help us understand this presidency? A consideration of four dimensions may help in appraising Bush's terms of office—his authority, power, skills, and the events occurring during his presidency. Does Bush's tenure fit a given "type" of presidency similar to those of some of his predecessors? Bush can be "typed" in terms of four aspects of increasingly narrower scope—the historical and institutional context of his presidency, Bush's response to the institutional challenges he confronted, his governing style in addressing institutional challenges, and Bush's presidential personality. Examining the dimensions of presidential authority, power, skills, and events will help us illuminate George W. Bush's presidential "type." We begin with the dimensions of broadest scope, those of presidential power and authority.

Power, Authority, and Regime Construction

The Bush presidency operated within the broad framework of American institutional development. A study of this development understands the political order as "the formative constructions of politicians in power" (Orren and Skowronek 2004, 92). At any given point in time, the decisions of power holders alter the course of institutional behavior and political alignments: "Political order is circumstantial, something that officials within government institutions will create or not, sustain or not, depending on their own interests, on the available resources and on the obstacles to change" (2004, 92). As political leaders create political order, they produce "constructions of broad consequence" to the political system (2004, 9). American presidents have great potential to maintain or disrupt the national political order. The grand ambitions motivating the George W. Bush presidency—creating a GOP electoral majority, pursuing a more militarily assertive foreign policy, and reconfiguring taxation and entitlement spending—aimed to create constructions of extensive consequence.

These big plans are best understood in terms of the power and authority a president seeks to exercise. *Power* involves the resources, formal or informal, that a president has in a given period to accomplish his goals. Success with power involves husbanding the resources of the office and deploying them strategically (Skowronek 1997, 18). Powers are both formal and informal. *Formal powers* are numerous and widely exercised by recent presidents, growing from constitutional authority, federal law, and court interpretation. They include the executive powers of appointment, budget preparation, and issuance of executive orders; legislative powers of the veto, pocket veto, and delivery of the annual State of the Union address; and judicial powers of appointment and pardons. The president's foreign affairs powers are vast, including duties as chief diplomat, negotiator of treaties and executive agreements, appointer of military and diplomatic officials, and commander-in-chief of the armed forces. The modern presidency, originating under Franklin Roosevelt in the 1930s and 1940s, has grown considerably in budget, staff, and formal powers.

Presidential powers are subject to variable application, and one source of this variance is the *theory of executive power* that a particular president adopts. Raymond Tatalovich and Thomas Engeman identified several approaches to the exercise of presidential power (Tatalovich and Engeman 2003). Early presidents often followed the Jeffersonian conception of the presidency, holding that presidents had no powers beyond those explicitly granted in Article II of the Constitution; no "implied" powers existed (2003, 33). Alexander Hamilton, in contrast, argued that the general grants of power to the president in Article II must include implied powers "because it is impossible to foresee or define the extent and variety of national exigencies, of the correspondent extent and variety of the means which may be necessary to satisfy them." (Hamilton, Jay, and Madison 1961, 147). At the furthest extreme from Jefferson lay the expansive theory of "prerogative power," first enunciated by political philosopher John Locke. Locke claimed that in emergencies, the prerogatives of office permit the executive to "act according to discretion for the public good, without prescription of law, and sometimes even against it" (Locke 1965, 422). The constitutional dangers of such an approach are conspicuous and no president has formally adopted it in practice. Twentieth century presidents frequently followed the "stewardship" theory of the presidency, first enthusiastically espoused and practiced by Theodore

Roosevelt: "My belief was that it was not only his right but his duty to do anything that the Needs of the Nation demanded unless such action was forbidden by the Constitution or the laws" (Roosevelt 1925, 357). George W. Bush consistently adopted the "stewardship" theory of presidential power, resulting in charges from critics that he had exercised power beyond the Constitution in a Lockean "prerogative" fashion.

In addition to formal powers, a president's informal power is situationally derived and highly variable. *Informal power* is a function of the "political capital" presidents amass and deplete as they operate in office. Paul Light defines several components of *political capital:* party support of the president in Congress, public approval of the president's conduct of his job, the President's electoral margin and patronage appointments (Light 1983, 15). Richard Neustadt's concept of a president's "professional reputation" also figures into his political capital. Neustadt defines this as the "impressions in the Washington community about the skill and will with which he puts [his formal powers] to use" (Neustadt 1990, 185). In the wake of 9/11, George W. Bush's political capital surged, and the public, the Washington political elites, and Congress granted him a broad power to prosecute a war on terror. By the later stages of Bush's troubled second term, beset by a lengthy and unpopular occupation of Iraq and an aggressive Democratic Congress, he found that his political capital had eroded. His informal powers proved variable, not stable, as is invariably the case for presidents.

Presidents usually employ power to disrupt the political order they inherit so as to reshape it according to their own agendas. Stephen Skowronek argues that "presidents disrupt systems, reshape political landscapes, and pass to successors leadership challenges that are different from the ones just faced" (Skowronek 1997, 6). Given their limited time in office and the often hostile political alignments present in Washington policymaking networks and among the electorate, presidents must force political change if they are to enact their agendas. In recent decades Washington power structures have become more entrenched and elaborate (Drucker 1995) while presidential powers—through increased use of executive orders and legislative delegation (Howell 2003)—have also grown. The presidency has more powers in the early twenty-first century than in former years, but also faces more entrenched coalitions of interests, lawmakers, and bureaucrats whose agendas often differ from that of the president. This is an invitation for an energetic president—and that description fits George W. Bush—to engage in major ongoing battles to impose his preferences.

At the center of the conflict lies the desire of presidents to create political "regimes" supported by popular approval and constitutional understandings

(Schier 2004, 3). A *regime* is a stable *authority structure* that reworks Washington power arrangements to facilitate its own dominance. Presidential power is intimately tied to presidential *authority*, defined as the "expectations that surround the exercise of power at a given moment; the perception of what it is appropriate for a given president to do" (Skowronek 1997, 18). Authority, to Skowronek, rests on the "warrants" drawn from the politics of the moment to justify action and secure the legitimacy of changes. The more stable a president's grant of authority, the easier his exercise of power. If a president claims more authority than he actually possesses, however, he invites challenges from rivals that can reduce his authority and power. During Bush's final years in office, Democrats energetically disputed his assertions of authority regarding Iraq war policy and his executive privilege power to shield aides from testifying before Congress.

Two of the consequential presidents in American history—Lincoln and Franklin Roosevelt—received large grants of authority from the dominant political regimes that they created in national government. A successful political regime can order events according to its own schedule, displacing the ability of permanent Washington to order events through its residues of power. It is a battle between presidential authority and other long-standing power centers in Washington. The ideal authority situation for any president is the entrenched dominance of a political regime in national politics and institutions with which he is affiliated. Dominant regimes in American history have invariably been partisan regimes.

George W. Bush's central project was the promotion of a conservative Republican(GOP) political regime. This seems a grandiose ambition and it is undoubtedly a big goal, best understood in terms of the following definition by Robert C. Lieberman:

> Regimes appear at a variety of levels, from formal institutions (such as the structure of Congress and the administrative state) to the social bases of politics (such as party alignments and coalitions and patterns of interest representation); from ideas (such as prevailing beliefs about the proper role of government) to informal norms (such as patterns of congressional behavior). Nested within these broadly defined institutional arrangements are commitments to particular policies that become the touchstone for political action and conflict for leaders and would-be leaders over the course of a generation or more. (Lieberman 2000, 275)

George W. Bush pursued "regime change" in all of these aspects. Politically, the administration sought persistent GOP electoral majorities through the tactic of ensuring high turnout among the party's base voters. This delivered a reelection victory for Bush in 2004. The 2006 election highlighted the shortcomings of this strategy, however, as many political independents deserted the GOP and facilitated a Democratic takeover of Congress. A second tactic of the Bush White House involved courting certain target groups in the electorate for conversion—in 2004, this included women, Latinos, African Americans, and Jews. The increased support from these groups in 2002 and 2004 melted away in 2006. Central ideas of the regime included an emphasis upon employing market forces in public policy (from market-driven environmental protection policies to private Social Security accounts), economic stimulus through recurrent tax cuts, and an aggressive foreign and military policy driven by a doctrine of preemption to forestall international terrorist threats. Institutionally, these policies would be facilitated by partisan GOP majorities in the House and Senate, and enhanced presidential control over the executive branch through expansive use of executive orders and reorganization, many spawned by national security concerns (Schier 2004, 3–4). The arrival of a Democratic Congress in 2007 greatly curtailed these policy and institutional activities of the administration's regime builders.

Could this broad regime initiative prevail? That turned on the magnitude of the impediments Bush faced with his project. Skowronek labels Bush an "orthodox innovator" who sought to finish the incomplete regime construction begun by Ronald Reagan in the 1980s. To Skowronek, Reagan's attempts to shape a regime "fell far short of the mark in revitalizing national government around his new priorities and opening a more productive course for development" (1997, 428). This was because of the "institutional thickening" that recent presidents have supposedly confronted, defined as "a pattern of greater institutional resilience in the face of these presidents' order-shattering authority, of an ever-thicker government that can parry and deflect more of their repudiative thrust" (1997, 413). The permanent Washington of law-makers, bureaucrats, judges, and interest groups was able to make Reagan's attempted conservative regime change more rhetorical than real. Further, as a "highly personalized candidate-centered politics" developed in the late twentieth century, the ability to maintain a dominant partisan electoral coalition also waned (Skowronek 2001, 15).

How successful was Reagan's regime building project? Answering this illuminates the results of George W. Bush's regime change efforts. At the mass level of partisan alignments, Reagan did not induce lasting GOP dominance, but Republican electoral successes beginning in 1994 did result from campaigns based on the Reagan agenda of strong defense, tax cuts, and governmental limitation. Reagan began, but did not complete, a conservative electoral transformation. He did alter defense policy and foreign policy greatly during his term. Though Democrat Bill Clinton pursued an alternative foreign policy approach in the 1990s, George W. Bush has adopted a national security approach based on heavy defense spending very much in the Reagan mold. Domestically, Bush has followed Reagan in cutting taxes, permitting large budget deficits and seeking Social Security reform. Both Reagan and Bush appointed conservative federal judges and Supreme Court justices in an attempt to broaden the institutional reach of a right-leaning regime. The policy continuities do reveal an underlying "orthodoxy" guiding the two presidencies. But did Reagan fall "far short" of regime construction, as Skowronek asserts, and were Bush's prospects limited as well?

Some evidence suggests that Skowronek overstated the institutional resistance that recent presidents have faced. A recent study by Daniel M. Cook and Andrew J. Polsky revealed aggressive and successful efforts by the Reagan administration to transform education and environmental policy, two areas accorded a relatively low priority by the White House. "We find that the Reagan administration made surgical use of the tools under its control to disrupt key targets in the old order and empower policy seekers within the Republican coalition . . . The record compiled under the Reagan administration contravenes the claim that contemporary American political institutions have so thickened as to be impervious to reconstructive episodes" (Cook and Polsky 2005, 600). These tools included budget control, personnel appointments, and reorganization through executive orders. Reagan's accomplishments, both within education and environmental policy and overall, suggest considerable progress toward constructing a conservative GOP regime, though not complete attainment of that goal.

Presidential regime construction becomes impossible only if institutional resistance to presidential initiatives grows as presidential powers do not. A major strategy of the George W. Bush presidency was the expansion of the formal presidential prerogatives regarding confidentiality and executive power. This approach was one of the pillars of the administration's regime construction efforts. The Bush administration made progress in creating a conservative political regime because the Reagan administration did not fall so "far short" in their regime construction endeavors that the project could not be resuscitated by a successor some twelve years later. Journalists by 2004 had identified several elements of a reigning conservative GOP regime—an alliance of business and socially conservative groups in Washington, a comparable coalition of economic and social conservatives in the electorate, strong and effective GOP partisanship in Congress, and a variety of administration strategies aimed at maintaining the regime's stability (Wooldridge and Mickelthwaith 2004).

So George W. Bush, in continuing efforts successfully begun by Ronald Reagan, had some early success at regime construction. The Reagan-Bush regime, like earlier regimes in American history—the Jacksonian Democrats, Civil War Republicans, 1896 Republicans, and New Deal Democrats—drew together "politicians, policy seekers, and segments of the mass electorate" (Cook and Polsky 2005, 580). How dominant was this new conservative GOP regime? Polsky and Cook provide a useful classification of the limits confronting such regimes. One type involves the *"endogenous limits* that stem from the nature of the political agreement that binds participants" (2005, 580). How well does the coalition stick together? Over time, once the central items of consensus are addressed, a fraying coalition is most likely. The George W. Bush presidency benefited from relatively few endogenous limits of this sort, from the crisis of 9/11 to the political difficulties of 2005—including controversial war management, a problematic response to Hurricane Katrina, multiplying scandals of the congressional GOP, and disputes within his coalition about Social Security and immigration reform. Artful coalition management and strong intra-coalition support for the president's national security policies contributed to coalition unity throughout most of the first five years of his presidency. But midway through his second term, Bush found his support among both GOP voters and national lawmakers receding.

Exogenous constraints, those arising from the political environment in which the regime operates, proved much more restrictive throughout Bush's presidency (Cook and Polsky 2005, 580–1). Bush encountered firm limits from these constraints. The administration's emphasis on the maintenance of its supporting coalition spawned partisan polarization in Congress and the electorate. This placed a low ceiling on Bush's job approval after the halo effect of 9/11 dissipated. It provoked Democrats to employ institutional rules like the filibuster and federal court challenges to impede the administration's agenda, and spawned grassroots liberal organizations like MoveOn to engage in ongoing media campaigns against the administration. In 2007 and 2008, the Democratic Congress aggressively investigated actions of the Bush administration and resisted his legislative proposals, imposing additional limits on Bush's ambitions.

The George W. Bush administration sought to continue the construction of a conservative political regime begun by Ronald Reagan. Its early successes resulted from an ability to minimize the endogenous challenges of regime construction. However, this effort actually increased the exogenous costs for the regime over time, placing limits on what could be achieved in the short run. To elucidate Bush's successes and failures at his regime project, it's necessary to focus on how he has responded to the challenges confronting him directly as president. To be successful, any president must deploy personal skills effectively in response to the wide variety of events during his term..

Events, Skills, and Challenges

At the heart of any presidency lie events and the political skills of the president and his administration. Presidents have discretion to create some events, but they also are subject to nondiscretionary events that "just happen" to them. Events create positive and negative political impact for presidents. A careful look at the major occurrences during the Bush presidency from this perspective reveals the rollercoaster ride of George W. Bush's time in office. Bush had two impressive years and then encountered big trouble, both self-created and from without.

By examining the chronicles of major events in three reputable reference sources—the World, Time magazine, and New York Times Almanacs—one can identify major trends of the Bush presidency from January 2001 to October 2007. Following Brace and Hinckley (1993), events involving Bush's presidency were included if at least two almanacs mentioned them. The events received classification as discretionary—happenings the president helped to create, or nondiscretionary—news foisted on the president from without. This analysis also classified the events as politically positive or negative for Bush in the short term. Multiple researchers checked the classifications, producing a reliable chronicle of Bush administration events and their political consequences.[1] Tables 1.1 and 1.2 depict the pattern of events. A complete list of the events is included in the Appendix.

The evidence reveals tremendous zigs and zags for this president. Despite a highly controversial election, the Bush administration got off to a very strong start, buoyed by savvy presidential actions and news from without that boosted the president. In 2001, the Bush administration produced twenty-six positive discretionary events and only one negative event; recall the tax cuts, major education reforms, an arms control deal with Russia, and military success in Afghanistan. In addition, nondiscretionary events ranked three to one positive for the administration, most notably including the 9/11 catastrophe that produced an upsurge of public support for Bush. The Bush administration's roll continued in 2002, but at a slower clip; it posted a 4.2 to 1 positive ratio in discretionary actions despite bad news on the economy. By the end of 2002, though, the Bush administration had already racked up 45 percent of all its positive discretionary events to October 2007.

The turning point in Bush's presidency was clearly the Iraq war. The suc-

Table 1.1

Bush Presidency Events: Presidential Discretion and Political Effects by Year

Year	Politically Positive Presidential Discretion	Politically Positive No Presidential Discretion	Politically Negative Presidential Discretion	Politically Negative No Presidential Discretion
2001	26 (24%)	3 (27%)	1 (3%)	1 (2%)
2002	21 (19%)	0	5 (15%)	2 (3%)
2003	15 (14%)	2 (18%)	4 (12%)	6 (10%)
2004	9 (8%)	0	5 (15%)	12 (20%)
2005	18 (16%)	4 (36%)	7 (21%)	7 (11%)
2006	11 (10%)	1 (9%)	3 (15%)	20 (36%)
2007 (to Oct. 15)	10 (9%)	1 (9%)	7 (21%)	11 (18%)
Column Total	110 (100%)	11 (100%)	34 (100%)	61 (100%)

Three researchers independently coded the event data, classifying events as discretionary and nondiscretionary and politically positive or negative in the short term. The Index of Agreement among the three coders was 95.7 percent. The few differences in coding regarding disputed cases were easily resolved in subsequent discussions among the coders. Event coding follows procedures in Paul Brace and Barbara Hinckley, *Follow the Leader* (New York: Basic Books, 1993), pp. 183–88. For more information on coding procedures, see the Appendix.

cessful invasion was just about the last good international news that the Bush administration received. From 2003 through 2005, negative fallout from the war buffeted the administration: the Abu Ghraib prison abuse scandal in Iraq, the Valerie Plame CIA leak controversy, no weapons of mass destruction (WMDs) found in Iraq, and no clear connection of Iraq with 9/11 revealed. In the event count, 2004 was clearly one of Bush's worst years; it contained 20 percent of all the major negative news events that buffeted the administration between January 2001 and October 2007. Twelve major news events from without were negative for the administration in 2004, none positive. One of Bush's greatest political accomplishments was winning reelection in such an ominous situation.

The administration compounded the bad news with its own errors as Bush's presidency proceeded. The first half of 2005 produced a small recovery in positive discretionary events for the Bush White House, but that was short lived. During 2004 to 2007, the administration incurred much lower positive to negative discretionary event ratios than it had in its early years. Unfavorable discretionary events included in 2005 the poor response to Hurricane Katrina,

Table 1.2

Bush Presidency Events: Positive to Negative Events Number and Ratio by Year

	Discretionary		Nondiscretionary	
	Number	Ratio	Number	Ratio
2001	26:1	26:1	3:1	3:1
2002	21:5	4.2:1	0:2	0:2
2003	15:4	3.75:1	2:6	1:3
2004	9:5	1.8:1	0:12	0:12
2005	13:4	3.25:1	1:3	1:3
2006	11:5	2.2:1	1:22	1:22
2007 (to Oct. 15)	10:7	1.4:1	1:11	1:11
Total	105:31	3:39:1	8:57	1:7.13

Three researchers independently coded the event data, classifying events as discretionary and nondiscretionary and politically positive or negative in the short term. The Index of Agreement among the three coders was 95.7 percent. The few differences in coding regarding disputed cases were easily resolved in subsequent discussions among the coders. Event coding follows procedures in Paul Brace and Barbara Hinckley, *Follow the Leader* (New York: Basic Books, 1993), pp. 183–88. For more information on coding procedures, see the Appendix.

failure at Social Security reform, and the aborted Harriet Miers Supreme Court nomination. That left the administration in a deep valley in 2006 with limited prospects for recovery. Much of the bad news in 2006 came from without. Troublesome nondiscretionary events multiplied greatly in that year, in the highest proportion of any year of his presidency—a 22 to 1 negative ratio. For example, controversies erupted over administration policies on wiretapping, the criminal prosecution and conviction of White House aide Lewis Libby, the resignation of House Majority Leader Tom DeLay, a possible sale of some US ports to Dubai, proposed immigration reform, and a continuing stream of bad news from Iraq. The White House also did not perform very well with events under its discretion in 2006, registering only a 2.2 to 1 positive ratio, one of the lowest annual scores of Bush's presidency. In November, Democrats gained thirty House seats and six Senate seats to take control of Congress for the first time since 1995. The first nine and one-half months of 2007 failed to produce improvement for the Bush White House, as it incurred a relatively low positive ratio of discretionary events (1.4 to 1, below the presidency average of 3.39 to 1) and a relatively high ratio of negative to positive nondiscretionary events (11 to 1, above the overall average of 7.13 to 1).

Event analysis reveals that the George W. Bush presidency turned on the Iraq war. Whether or not the United States involvement in Iraq ultimately yields success, the immediate political costs for Bush were heavy indeed, and the administration responded to this adverse environment with a series of costly political errors. The grand regime goals of the Bush administration—a political realignment and policy revolution benefiting conservative Republicans—were partially realized by 2002. After that, progress on those goals gradually eroded, undone by adverse events and the White House's unskillful response to the ensuing difficulties. Bush's plans were thrown into reverse by the Democratic Congress of 2007 to 2008.

Responding with skill to the challenges imposed by events is a concise definition of a successful presidency. A president's success or failure at this greatly determines his informal powers—his political capital—and thus his ability to employ formal powers effectively. In this regard, the passage of time is usually not kind to presidents. As challenges arise and decisions are made, presidents make enemies and deplete their public popularity (Brace and Hinckley 1993; Light 1983). Second terms in particular usually feature lower presidential popularity and success at governance, and the George W. Bush presidency proved no exception to this (Brace and Hinckley 1993; Zacher 1996). National crises may punctuate these trends with "rally" effects that produce a surge of popular approval of a president, temporarily expanding his political capital (Brody 1991). The post-9/11 "rally" for George W. Bush is the most long-lived in presidential history (Hetherington and Nelson 2003).

Wars, however, create great changes in national politics and can threaten a president's political capital. David Mayhew identified the two major effects of American wars on our national politics and public policy. First, wars produce "new issue regimes," defined by Mayhew as "new long-lasting highly public controversies within specific issue areas" (Mayhew 2005A, 475). Since September 11, 2001, those issues have involved national security from terrorist attacks and a related debate on the future of civil liberties. Second, wars can also create new political alignments. Bush and the GOP exploited concerns about terrorism to maximum partisan advantage in 2002 and maintained an important edge with those issues in 2004. Historically, parties in charge of major wars suffered big electoral reversals after the conflict's conclusion (Mayhew 2005A, 483). Larry Bartels and John Zaller also found that the drawn-out wars of Korea and Vietnam cost the party in charge a 4 percent loss at the polls in the 1952 and 1968 elections as the wars dragged on (Bartels and Zaller 2001). The Iraq war's 2006 electoral costs for the GOP place it firmly in the Korea/Vietnam category.

The impact of wars highlights the importance of elections as another category of crucial events in the course of a presidency. A few presidential elections have created lasting partisan regimes through an electoral realignment of groups of voters in stable support of a new majority party. The obvious cases are the rise of Republican dominance after the 1860 election and the appearance of the lasting Democratic New Deal coalition in 1932 (Mayhew 2002). Karl Rove, Bush's chief political aide, sought such a lasting transformation in the early elections of the twenty-first century. But lasting partisan realignments are by far the exceptions in American electoral history. Election outcomes are often prey to short term forces, such as the contingency of events, immediate political strategies of parties and candidates, and the presence of valence issues—those on which the public is overwhelmingly on one side—that advantage a particular candidate or party (Mayhew 2002, 147). A decisive valence issue in 2004, for example, was effective prosecution of the war on terror. The public was largely of one mind in support of this, and Bush was perceived by more voters as better able to pursue this than his opponent John Kerry (Ceaser and Busch 2005, 138). The valence issue of 2006 was corruption, costing the GOP control of Congress and consigning GOP realignment hopes at least temporarily to the dustbin.

One important consequence of elections is the presence or absence of a "mandate" that supports an energetic claim of authority by a newly elected president. Patricia Conley defines a mandate as a claim by presidents that their electoral victories provide "legitimacy for their efforts to shape the national agenda" (2001, 1) and notes that they occur rarely in electoral history. The most likely recent mandates included the elections of 1952, 1964, and 1980, when presidents won election with large popular support or with only moderate support while gaining congressional control of the president's party (2001, 77). In 2000, Bush gained no popular mandate, receiving fewer votes than his Democratic rival, Al Gore. In 2004, despite his historically narrow reelection victory for an incumbent president—the closest margin in the popular vote percentage ever—Bush claimed a mandate, given the increased GOP ranks in Congress. Despite his better electoral performance in 2004 than in 2000, events in his second term served to undermine informal powers, a fate that afflicted several of his predecessors in office. The 2006 election results ended any discussion of lasting realignment or of a 2004 mandate.

In the face of challenging events, presidents must demonstrate their personal skills. "Professional reputation" is an important aspect of a president's political capital (Neustadt 1990, 50–55). What are the component skills that create a strong *presidential reputation?* A president's public *rhetorical* skills can buoy public support and facilitate his dominance of national politics.

Ronald Reagan, the "great communicator," developed a public persona attractive to many Americans through his skilled use of rhetorical occasions. *Coalitional* skills require a president to maintain the support of fellow partisans while occasionally reaching beyond them to build broader public and congressional support for his initiatives. Coalitional skills involve both partisan maintenance and situational outreach beyond fellow partisans. Internationally, major initiatives on matters as diverse as military action against Iraq or international environmental protection require ability at coalition formation and maintenance. A related *bargaining* skill allows a president to bring together rival power holders to gain necessary support. This can involve splitting differences among lawmakers over taxation and spending or hammering out consensus language among differing nations about UN resolutions or international treaties. *Managerial* skills require clear lines of organization and accountability within the executive branch. The effective implementation of foreign and domestic policy is the consequence of able management. Finally, *heresthetic* skills involve a "deliberate attempt to structure political situations so that opponents will either have to submit or be trapped. There is also the possibility of redefining political conflicts to permit new coalitions to be created . . . [this is] the science of manipulation and strategy of winning" (Hargrove 1998, 32; Riker 1986). The ablest presidents have been able heberstheticians. Lincoln, for example, framed the slavery issue in a fashion to split his opposition and win the White House in 1860 (Riker 1986, 1–9).

Conflict and Disruption

A successful president must skillfully respond to events in order to pursue political conflict effectively. Stephen Skowronek notes that the presidency "has functioned best when it has been directed toward dislodging established elites, destroying the institutional arrangements that support them, and clearing the way for something entirely new" (1997, 27). Success through this "bettering ram" approach is difficult, however, given the characteristics of the contemporary presidency. A comparative view of the institutional traits of the presidency reveals the challenges confronting anyone new to the Oval Office. British observer Anthony King has identified several structural assets of national chief executives (1993, 415–52). A chief executive is more powerful if the national constitution assigns him important specific powers, if the office is directly elected by the people, if the executive enjoys a secure tenure in office, if he controls many appointments, and if his office is extensively staffed and is able to control or influence actions of civil servants. The

American presidency is strong in all of these regards. The main weakness of the American presidency, according to King, is "his lack of control over the legislative branch" (1993, 446). A president can overcome this weakness only in certain situations. If he is the effective leader of his political party, has a high degree of direct influence over congressional voting, and other politicians believe voters respond favorably to him, the president can mitigate his institutional weakness toward Congress (1993, 420–34). Overall, King argues that the presidency's powers consign the institution to "the middle rank of heads of government" unless a skillful incumbent can exploit situational advantages (1993, 446).

The growth of the institutional presidency in the latter half of the twentieth century, while providing important resources to the chief executive, also imposed some additional challenges upon the office. Hugh Heclo notes that the influence of individual presidents, by "becoming more extensive, scattered and shared," has "decreased by becoming less of a prerogative . . . less closely held by the man himself" (Heclo 1977, 172–73). An institutionally larger presidency has increased demands and expectations that no president can satisfy and is now beset by the shortcomings of large bureaucracies: "Aides and agencies abuse power, distort information, and become enmeshed in debilitating rivalries and intrastaff controversies" (Jacobs and Shapiro 2000, 499).

The George W. Bush presidency illustrated one great power of the institutional presidency—that of federal judicial nominations. Despite increasing discord over Bush within the GOP during his second term, his fellow partisans agreed that he had done their regime good service in his Supreme Court appointments of John Roberts as chief justice, replacing the deceased William Rehnquist, and Samuel Alito as associate justice, replacing the retiring Sandra Day O'Connor. The first 2007 term of the Roberts court produced a consistent stream of narrow 5–4 decisions yielding victory for conservatives (Lane 2007). On the lower federal bench, Bush also consistently appointed conservatives, compiling a record of success rivaling that of his mentor, Ronald Reagan (Yalof 2007, 200–202).

Bureaucratic management difficulties and rivalries with Congress are not the only challenges besetting the modern presidency. The national media has emerged as another rival institution, with great influence over politics and policymaking. Media resources are vital communication modes for political leaders: "newsmaking is now a central way for governmental actors to accomplish political and policy goals" (Cook 1998, 165). The media has become an important political institution sharing power in national politics and policymaking: "The news media . . . require aid and assistance from other political institutions to accomplish their task, but . . . in turn participate directly in the Washington politics of 'separated institutions sharing power'" (1998, 165). Media outlets and sources have proliferated with the rise of the Internet, further complicating presidential communications. In addition, rival voices are greater in number, as interest groups have proliferated in national government since 1960 (Rauch 1999).

Research has revealed that media coverage of recent presidents has been decidedly negative. Media coverage of the executive branch and national politics has a "pervasive negativism" in tone that can serve to promote "a pessimistic, if not cynical, perspective about government" (Farnsworth and Lichter 2006, 165; 166). The challenge for the White House in this is that "their good results will garner less attention than their bad results and that the American people will be given a quite misleading picture of their performance" (Niven 2001, 39). The Bush presidency employed an elaborate communications operation to counter these tendencies and enjoyed a period of positive news coverage after the 9/11 attacks. Later, a stream of bad news from Iraq and several administration miscues in 2005 and 2006 produced a steady pattern of negative coverage (Center for Media and Public Affairs 2006).

Presidents are now able to learn more about public opinion through private and media polls. But polling results often become a measure of presidential success. Bad poll numbers deplete a president's informal power of political capital. Poll support is notoriously difficult for presidents to manipulate, particularly on salient issues like the war in Iraq. Poll numbers also tend to get more media attention as presidential popularity declines (Groeling and Kernell 1998). Despite the Bush administration's recurrent efforts, public opinion soured on the war in the face of ongoing American casualties in 2005, shrinking Bush's job approval and political capital. A common strategy of political leaders in an era of pervasive polls is to adopt noncontroversial "valence" positions on salient issues and selectively polarize differences with opponents on less salient issues in order to shore up one's political base (Geer 1996, 165–66). George W. Bush pursued this strategy at times, trying to make his conduct of national security policy above criticism while pressing partisan differences on social issues such as gay marriage.

The political and institutional challenges confronting contemporary presidents are considerable. Able leadership of Congress and public opinion must situationally offset the weaknesses of the office. The institutional presidency can prove an impediment to performance unless managed well. The proliferation of groups and their demands can fragment a presidential agenda. The following paragraphs assess George W. Bush's response to these daunting conditions.

Responding to the Challenges of Office

Bush entered the presidency under unpromising circumstances, having lost the popular vote to Al Gore in 2000 while claiming a very narrow Electoral College victory. Charles Jones notes that in the 2000 election Bush ranked "dead last" among post World War II presidents in electoral and popular vote margins and—early the next year—in initial job approval level (Jones 2007A, 118). He was able to secure early in his presidency a "bargained mandate," defined by Patricia Conley as a situation in which a president's "party's strength in the House and the Senate adequately compensates for the narrow margin of his electoral victory." Presidents claim a mandate in such situations "because they are confident that Congress is in tune with their preferences, even if there is uncertainty about the state of public opinion" (Conley 2001, 117). Only the firmest of party-line support would sustain such a mandate, and congressional Republicans delivered this by providing the votes for passage of the administration's budget and tax cuts in the early months of Bush's first term. Thus, early on, Bush demonstrated party leadership and influence over the legislative branch, results that strengthened his presidency by vindicating his presumption of a mandate (Barshay 2002). Throughout his first term, Bush relied upon and more often than not received partisan support from Hill GOPers in ways that maintained his political influence. His administration's coalitional and bargaining skills during this time produced frequent success with Congress.

Still, by mid-2001 Bush's heresthetic and rhetorical efforts had not proven equally successful in winning over public opinion. His job approval rating remained stuck around 50 percent and Democrats disapproved of his presidency in large numbers. Then came the 9/11 crisis, an "exogenous shock" of the type that presidents often seize upon to bolster their leadership claims. "Presidents historically seek to provide leadership in exactly those policy areas in which some exogenous shock has resulted in a status quo that is . . . unstable and therefore susceptible to leadership" (Miller 1993, 303). The "rally" effect in public opinion began shortly afterward and lasted through the GOP successes in the 2002 elections up to the initial stages of the American invasion of Iraq in early 2003. During this time, Bush's approach to national security issues achieved "valence" status, as the public remained heavily supportive of his leadership. His high popularity allowed him to succeed with Congress on other policies as well, by deploying coalitional and bargaining skills to win approval of additional tax cuts and a Medicare prescription drug benefit. As the troublesome military occupation of Iraq dragged on without the discovery of WMDs, however, Bush's national security positions shifted from possessing a valence status in public opinion to being the subject of strong partisan contestation. That betokened a hard-fought and close reelection and ongoing problems with public support as his second term progressed. Events diminished the administration's coalitional, bargaining, heresthetic, and rhetorical success in winning over Congress and the public. Bad news weakens a president's professional reputation.

A fuller understanding of Bush's path in office requires a more thorough inspection of his actual governing style. With this topic, we move further from the institutional environment and closer to Bush as a decision-maker. What was the "type" of his personal approach to governance?

George W. Bush's Governing Style

Bush's extremely narrow victory in the 2000 election seemingly gave him small room for successful maneuvering in the White House. How he addressed these straitened circumstances provides insight into his approach to presidential governance. In Charles Jones' terminology, Bush entered office with a disputed electoral victory, limited Washington experience, and a sense of connection with GOP wins in Congress in 2000 (Jones 2005, 62). Bush surprised many observers with his initial approach to office. Given his seemingly meager list of power advantages from the 2000 election, he set out to govern in an assertive fashion, aggressively promoting policy proposals from the very outset of his presidency. Jones summarized Bush's style as "executive" in approach—as much as that of any of his predecessors in office. What is an "executive" style? One that is "proactive, hierarchical, contained, programmatic, resolute, and broadly accountable. Enterprise is the key to understanding this style" (Jones 2007A, 114).

Self-confidence characterized Bush's managerial style. The first MBA to win the White House, Bush applied several well-established management principles in shaping his administration. Donald Kettl described Bush as "the very model of an MBA president. He builds his approach to the presidency on teamwork, especially in his West Wing staff. He builds clear strategy and a business plan for implementing it. Unlike Bill Clinton, he has remained focused on a small agenda. He keeps his message sharp and focused" (Kettl 2003, 31). John Burke noted Bush's "active management role" that "set the tone and organizational culture of his presidency. . . . His level of involvement here stands in marked departure from that of his recent predecessors" (Burke 2004, 218). The president "has inspired a tremendous sense of personal loyalty in staffers" and the administration "wisely limits the number of people who regularly interact with the press" (Mayer 2004, 624). Bush's

White House evidenced great organizational and personnel stability during his terms of office.

The president's dependence on extensive delegation to subordinates, however, carried important risks. Donald Rumsfeld's increasingly controversial tenure as defense secretary during the Iraq occupation imposed political costs on Bush because of his great delegation of authority to the defense secretary. Rumsfeld's resignation on the day after the 2006 elections came long after the administration had incurred much political damage from its Iraq policies. Bruce Buchanan noted "Bush's biggest weakness is that he may not be in a position to discern the credibility of the options his advisors lay out for him" (Carney 1999). A disciplined staff can fall prey to "groupthink" that unknowingly excludes information and options (Kettl 2003, 150). This may have occurred in 2003 when the administration accepted flawed intelligence indicating that Saddam Hussein possessed weapons of mass destruction (Haney 2005, 299).

Bush also aggressively deployed his formal executive powers during his first term in order to exact maximum agenda impact without congressional consent. "Using a vast array of administrative tools, President Bush successfully dominated the policy process in both domestic and international affairs with minimal opposition from Congress. By using administrative tools and by exercising both inherent and implied constitutional authority, President Bush was able to implement numerous components of his campaign agenda without seeking legislative support" (Warshaw 2004, 101). Following the example of Reagan, Bush appointed ideologically conservative individuals to important subcabinet positions. He employed executive orders to change policies he opposed. For example, two days after taking office he reinstated a ban on federal funding for nongovernmental organizations engaged in abortion-related activities. Seven days later, he created by executive order the White House Office of Faith-Based Initiatives to pursue his social agenda (Warshaw 2004, 108). When Congress failed to approve major provisions of the administration's faith-based initiatives legislation, Bush implemented some parts of the policy through executive orders in December 2002 (Burke 2004, 144–45). The White House also altered administrative rulemaking to allow funding of a demonstration project permitting the Department of Health and Human Services to promote marriage among welfare recipients (Toner 2002, A1). Under Bush, the Office of Management and Budget's Office of Information and Regulatory Review, charged with oversight of bureaucratic regulations, received more staff and evidenced "a level of aggressiveness unmatched since the early years of the Reagan administration" (West 2005). In foreign affairs, Bush abrogated the Anti-Ballistic Missile Treaty and other treaties with which he disagreed, and removed economic sanctions against India and Pakistan after 9/11 to secure their assistance with the war on terror (Perlez 2001, A1).

Bush's narrow 2000 victory produced relatively low consensus on his administration's proposals, but that in no way deterred him from adopting an active approach to his agenda. His early successes with tax and education legislation were significant, but the rally effect generated by 9/11 inflated Bush's subsequent impact on the foreign and domestic agendas. Bush's governing style with Congress, save for the six months or so following 9/11, was hierarchical, managerial, and partisan. The White House took full command of a partisan agenda and relied on narrow GOP majorities to prevail on legislation. Bush in his relations with Congress did much to encourage the development of "responsible party government" at the national level. Gerald Pomper in 1999 noted how national political parties increasingly "bridge the institutional separations of national government" and "act cohesively under strong legislative leadership to reasonably fulfill their promises" (Pomper 1999, 252). Bush accelerated these trends by providing clear policy direction for congressional Republicans (Pomper 2003, 267).

Bush's strong popularity with the GOP public helped to produce very high levels of partisan support for his agenda from 2001 to 2005, particularly in the US House. Bush's agenda success with Congress during his first term was the highest since the landmark legislative presidency of Lyndon Baines Johnson in the 1960s ("Bush Finds Ways to Win" 2005, B-4). That does not mean that all went swimmingly for Bush. Partisan divisions on congressional floor votes reached very high levels ("Partisan Votes" 2005, B-8). The partisanship of the administration's governing strategy eventually polarized both Congress and the public, producing an unending flow of harsh words across a sharply defined partisan divide (Jacobson 2007B). This placed a low ceiling on Bush's poll ratings in his second term, limiting his influence within Washington. In addition, the Constitution's attempt to separate power remained successful in the US Senate. Despite a 55–44–1 majority in 2005, Republicans could not consistently work their will. Under Senate rules governing filibusters, only a sixty-seat majority provides the party in power with enough votes to end debate. Democratic unity in filibustering the nomination of John Bolton to be UN ambassador in 2005, for example, caused Bush to make Bolton a temporary "recess appointment" to the position. Bush's unrelenting conflict with Congress in 2006 to 2007 revealed the limitations of his partisan approach to the Hill. Though he at times prevailed in showdowns with congressional Democrats, as in the budget negotiations of late 2007, the White House's legislative agenda after 2006 was often stillborn and the administration's stance was defensive.

The strategy underlying Bush's aggressive use of formal executive powers and attempts at partisan domination of Congress involved less direct rhetorical persuasion of rival political actors than heresthetic manipulation of the choice situations he placed before his opponents. The underlying strategic goal for Bush was expansion of the GOP electoral coalition and entrenchment of GOP rule in governmental institutions. This required the use of heresthetics on important issues to divide and weaken the Democrats. Bush used the national consensus on the "war on terror"—a valence issue in 2002—as a weapon to defeat Democratic Senator Max Cleland in Georgia in that year's elections. Saxby Chambliss, his GOP opponent, charged, with White House support, that Cleland's vote against legislation creating the Department of Homeland Security was a retreat in the face of terror threats. Though Cleland disputed this, he was trapped. His defeat at the polls helped the bill to sail through Congress after the election, as other Democrats feared a similar heresthetic snare. Bush often advocated tax cuts in order to place Democrats in the position of having to defend "big government," a political trap indeed.

Another successful heresthetic manipulation that snared Bush's opponents involved the 2005 nomination of John Roberts to the Supreme Court. As political analyst Dick Morris put it: "By choosing a judge whom the Democrats confirmed unanimously when he was nominated for the D.C. Circuit Court—and whom they did not filibuster—Bush has made the Democrats impotent" (Morris 2005). Liberal journalist Ryan Lizza summarized the cleverness of the Roberts nomination: "Bush seems to be getting most everything he wants. He is nudging the Supreme Court to the right. His nominee is likely to have a relatively smooth confirmation process. His evangelical base won't revolt. Bush may even win some political capital to spend on the rest of his agenda" (Lizza 2005, 12). A trap indeed.

Several of Bush's heresthetic maneuvers, particularly during his second term, failed to produce success. Despite strong presidential coalitional and bargaining efforts, a bipartisan immigration reform bill failed to pass the Senate in 2006 and 2007. Many previously loyal GOP voters and activists rebelled at the possibility that the bill provided "amnesty" for illegal immigrants. Bush was unable to alter the situation with a persuasive heresthetic response. In 2005, Bush pressed for Social Security reform by arguing that his opponents' inaction threatened the future existence of the program. This heresthetic did not work because the public never fully embraced private accounts as the proper solution to Social Security's problems. Bush's heresthetic attempt to portray the Iraq occupation as vital to national security was undercut in 2005 and 2006 by disclosures of prewar intelligence errors and the occupation's increasing bloodiness. Bush's heresthetic failures were important setbacks to his ambitious governing style. What follows is a summary view of that style and its shortcomings.

One can sum up Bush's governing style as the pursuit of "strategic leadership" as defined by Erwin Hargrove and Michael Nelson:

> The essence of strategic leadership is the president's capacity to define the nature of a historical situation and to persuade others to support the courses of action he develops to deal with policy problems. Presidents must understand their times. Such leadership is best understood less as the acquiring of power than as an activity of clarifying ambiguous situations for people who would like a sense of direction. The acquisition of power serves the larger vision and the larger vision becomes the chief resource for the acquisition of power. (Hargrove and Nelson 1984, 124)

To achieve support for his larger vision, Bush energetically used the powers of the managerial presidency, asserted aggressively his constitutional powers, and employed party-line government in Congress to further his agenda. He sought a "presidency of achievement"—one that mobilizes the public to action, exerts White House dominance over the permanent government, seeks passage of an ambitious legislative program, and speedily pursues the presidential agenda as a chief necessity (Hargrove and Nelson 1984, 197). Earlier examples of such presidents, according to Hargrove and Nelson, were liberals Woodrow Wilson, Franklin Roosevelt, and Lyndon Johnson (1984, 67). In contrast, Bush pursued a conservative sort of "presidency of achievement," similar to that sought by Ronald Reagan. Hargrove and Nelson's description of Reagan's conservative "achievement agenda" fits Bush's agenda as well: "Legislative enactment was crucial to the success of his agenda, but the agenda itself was directed toward administrative change. . . . These goals permitted a strategy of tight presidential control of the departments and agencies from the outset, since management was the main objective" (1984, 264). The first MBA president had an ideology that suited his management orientation.

Two pitfalls obstructed Bush's pursuit of a "presidency of achievement." One grew from his support in Congress. The small partisan majorities supporting Bush in Congress from 2001 to 2006 meant that any slippage in his partisan support in either chamber risked stalemate (Hargrove and Nelson 1984, 214). GOP disunity on the administration's Social Security reform plans in 2005 produced exactly that outcome. After 2006, a Democratic Congress further curtailed Bush's legislative aspirations as stalemate became the norm. A related pitfall concerned public opinion. The strongly partisan profile of the administration's agenda inhibited public support for it as 9/11 faded from memory and the troublesome military occupation of Iraq produced a sour public mood (Jacobson 2007A). Polls during his second term revealed little public enthusiasm for Bush's agenda (PollingReport.com 2005). Bush in his second term risked a situation similar to that befalling William Howard Taft, in which "the president's agenda bears little resemblance to what the public is willing to accept" (Hargrove and Nelson 1984, 68). Bush's failure to sell his structural changes in Social Security placed him, on that issue at least, in Taft's situation. Bush's declining political capital in 2005 to 2006 also led to GOP fragmentation in Congress as lawmakers distanced themselves from an unpopular president.

Despite these shortcomings later in his presidency, Bush achieved much in its early years. Charles Jones notes that seventeen major legislative acts became law during his first two years in office, the second-highest total among first term presidents since 1945 (Jones 2007A, 122). His was very much a "mobilizing, entrepreneurial and managerial" presidency (Rockman 1984, 196). The "prime mover" of this regime change project was the president himself. What personal traits of George W. Bush caused him to pursue such an audacious presidency?

George W. Bush's Psychological Traits

Much ink has been spilled disputing the personal traits of George W. Bush. Most of the popular discussion about this involves caricatures of Bush written by authors with partisan and ideological motives. Careful analyses of Bush's personal psychology and behavior are few in number and suffer from a lack of direct access to the person analyzed. Still, some traits are evident from the limited number of examinations published so far.

Political psychologist Stanley Renshon (2004) has written the most thorough psychological analysis of George W. Bush. Early in his book, Renshon identifies the three traits comprising Bush's core psychology—ambition, character integrity, and relations with others. Renshon argues that Bush's ambition is unusually large, encompassing an attempt to transform the current paradigms governing both foreign and domestic policy. Big ambition marks Bush as "truly unique among modern presidents" (2004, 58). Writing from a perspective sympathetic to Bush, Renshon also argues that he possesses the three characteristics of character integrity—"fighting for your policy principles and risking real loss, not saying what your allies want to hear, and not supporting the policy they want" (2004, 64). In his relations with others, Bush maintains warm personal connections but he can "when necessary stand apart" (2004, 69). In combination, these traits produce a behavior pattern Renshon describes as *"right back at you.* It is at once defiant, but also affirmative of one's policy principles or convictions. It embraces conflict if it is not unavoidable. It is, importantly, one strong element in this president's psychology" (2004, 75).

Psychologists Steven Rubenzer and Thomas Faschingbauer present a similar if less sympathetic portrayal of Bush in their psychological analysis of all American presidents (2004). Rubenzer and Faschingbauer compare Bush to previous presidents and find he ranks relatively low in competence, intelligence, and tender mindedness, while ranking high in positive emotions, assertiveness, and lack of straightforwardness (2004, 35). In sum, they classify Bush as an extravert, a type of president encompassing some of the most colorful and successful characters to inhabit the White House, including Andrew Jackson (whom, they argue, Bush most closely resembles), Reagan, Clinton, Harding, William Henry Harrison, Franklin and Theodore Roosevelt, Lyndon Johnson, and Kennedy (2004, 74). These presidents "indulged their impulses and showed their feelings through their faces and body language. They did things extemporaneously and had a flair for the dramatic, but were not dependable or responsible. They did not take pride in being rational or objective, did not plan carefully before taking a trip, made decisions prematurely and acted without thinking" (2004, 75). This portrait suggests that Bush's *right back at you* approach described by Renshon can have a serious downside in governance.

Presidential scholar Fred Greenstein offers another personal inventory of George W. Bush that falls somewhere between Renshon's praise and Rubenzer and Faschingbauer's criticism. Greenstein gave Bush high marks for emotional intelligence, defined as having "emotions well in hand" (2004, 14). Bush's cognitive style demonstrated an ample intelligence but a tendency to be incurious (2004, 14). As a public communicator, Bush was effective, particularly with his "punchy vernacular" that works best with domestic audiences (2004, 15). He ranked high in organizational capacity due to his able management of strong associates, but could be shielded by a small ring of advisors at times (2004, 15). His political skills were generally sound but more effective domestically than internationally (2004, 16). Bush very much did have the "vision thing," "not because he is an aficionado of policy, but because he holds that if a leader does not set his own goals, others will set them for him" (2004, 16). This description resembles Rubenzer and Faschingbauer's discussion of Bush's assertiveness and Renshon's depiction of Bush's *right back at you* approach to conflict.

A composite view of Bush the person does emerge from these three analyses. All three suggest personal traits contributing to Bush's ambitious adoption of a wide-ranging "regime change" agenda. Renshon identified Bush's "unique" foreign and domestic policy ambitions, Rubenzer and Faschingbauer note his tendency to aggressiveness and Greenstein describes his possession of the "vision thing" regarding public policy. All three also identify Bush as possessing political skill—Renshon's discussion of "character integrity," Rubenzer and Faschingbauer's emphasis on positive emotions, and Greenstein's direct attribution of such skills to Bush. The assessments also reveal shortcomings in Bush's governing style, such as his incuriosity, the risk of his being shielded from important facts by a small group of advisors, and a possible lack of straightforwardness. Presidential traits shape the politics of the time. Bush's strong attitudes but limited expertise regarding policy helped to promote a "partisan and ideological politics" during his presidency (Kessel 2001, 243).

Bush's presidency seems quite consistent with Bush the person. It was highly organized, energetic and ambitious, aggressive toward partisan and ideological opponents, and not prone to internal dissention or introspection. This was a presidency bent upon large and lasting changes in politics and policy, led by the "Andrew Jackson" of the twenty-first century. Such a presidency took risks and sought large consequences.

Conclusion

The George W. Bush presidency had big impacts in both its broader regime construction efforts and everyday governing style. At the systemic level, George W. Bush energetically used his formal and informal powers in order to entrench a durable, conservative GOP regime, a stable authority structure that would persist for years to come. His ambitions were blunted through the exogenous limits imposed by partisan polarization that his regime construction efforts spawned. As difficulties mounted in his second term, additional endogenous limits to Bush's ambitions appeared. Declining public approval of Bush increased internal divisions within his governing party, greatly damaging the stability and durability of his governing coalition. The Democratic takeover of Congress in 2006, combined with Bush's persistently low job approval during his second term, ultimately frustrated Bush's regime ambitions.

Bush's governing style of "strategic leadership" in order to create a "presidency of achievement" at times successfully created situations of heresthetic advantage for the White House. But as Bush's political capital eroded in his second term, fewer heresthetic successes became possible. His strong management orientation at times fell prey to the risks of flawed advice from subordinates, notably regarding the Iraq occupation and response to Hurricane Katrina. Bush's focus on maintaining the support of his partisan base limited his ability to court the approval of rival partisans and nonpartisan citizens. His partisan governing style put a ceiling on his public support. The price of such polarization was particularly evident in Bush's second term, when unfortunate events and unskillful administration responses to them even cost him the approval of many fellow partisans.

This variable record reflects the contrasting traits of George W. Bush himself. His large policy ambitions led to an audacious presidency, furthered also by his aggressive behavior in office. This led to a partisan and ideological presidency involving big stakes, big disruption of established policies and institutions, and large successes and failures. Bush reconfigured tax, energy, and education policy, enforced a dramatic new doctrine asserting the preemptive use of force in foreign policy, oversaw a string of GOP electoral successes, imposed strong management controls on the executive branch, and aggressively employed the institutional powers of the presidency in pursuit of a large regime change project. The only presidents who really rival his impact in recent decades are two other extraverts who pursued "presidencies of achievement"—Lyndon Johnson and Ronald Reagan. Each of these presidents' accomplishments, however, fell short of their most ambitious plans. Johnson's pursuit of "guns and butter" foundered over growing opposition to the Vietnam War and rising inflation and unemployment. Reagan's conservative regime ambitions never produced a GOP Congress during his presidency.

George W. Bush fell short of his largest goals as well. The following chapters of this book explain how this happened in popular politics, Washington governance, foreign and domestic policy. The specifics in each chapter conform to a single narrative arc involving the four dimensions of power, authority, skills, and events. During Bush's first term, 9/11 presented Bush with a policy and political opportunity upon which he effectively capitalized. From September 12, 2001 through the 2004 election, events boosted Bush's formal and informal powers and regime authority. Further, his administration demonstrated skillful use of the opportunities provided by this situation to promote Bush's foreign and domestic policy agenda, his expansion of presidential authority, and his entrenching of a conservative GOP political regime.

Bush's second term involves a very different trajectory. Adverse events—Katrina, Iraq—were frequently addressed unskillfully by the administration. This undermined the president's formal and informal powers and limited the effectiveness of his skills, thus weakening his professional reputation.

All this emboldened his opponents and undercut his attempts to create the lasting authority structure of a GOP political regime. Ultimately, the successes and failures of the Bush presidency leave the presidency with an ambiguous potential in American politics. Can lasting regime construction by presidents still occur? That seemed more possible in 2001 to 2004 than in 2007 to 2008. More on this point comes at the end of the book, after we explore these themes through several aspects of the George W. Bush presidency.

Note

1. Three researchers independently coded the event data, classifying events as discretionary or nondiscretionary and politically positive or negative in the short term. The Index of Agreement among the three coders was 95.7 percent. The few differences in coding regarding disputed cases were easily resolved in subsequent discussions among the coders. Thus the reliability of the analysis rivals that of Brace and Hinckley's event study of previous presidents (1993, Appendix A).

2 PUBLIC POLITICS

A conspicuous aspect of presidential government is the pursuit of electoral success, public support, and interest group backing. Contemporary media culture thrives on political horse races, opinion polls, and disclosures about lobbying and interest group influence. As noted in the previous chapter, a central imperative of the Bush White House has been the establishment of a dominant electoral coalition that could pursue its policy agenda in government. To explore this, we need to examine the administration's strategy for mobilizing public and interest group support during elections and when in office. Holding such support through skillful management of events would prove crucial to its pursuit of presidential power and authority.

"Strategy" is a commonly used word in politics, encompassing many aspects. One main component of strategy in public politics is managerial. An administration must manage its public outreach, interest group relations, and electoral efforts well in order to prevail. Electoral management is itself multifaceted, composed of voter registration and "get out the vote" efforts, advertising campaigns, and constant fundraising. The Bush presidency devoted great time and attention to all such managerial tasks, with variable results.

Another important aspect of strategy is heresthetic and rhetorical. Rhetoric involves the "persuasion value" of statements, attempts to phrase arguments about candidates, issues, and policy in a way that magnifies support (Riker 1986, x). But success at popular politics requires both rhetoric and strategic manipulation, or heresthetics. Heresthetics can be understood as an effort to maintain popular support by manipulating the policy or electoral alternatives that other people encounter. As William Riker puts it:

> It is true that people win politically because they have induced other people to join them in alliances and coalitions. But winners induce by more than rhetorical attraction. Typically they win because they have set up the situation in such a way that other people will want to join them—or will be forced by

circumstances to join them—even without any persuasion at all. And this is
what heresthetic is about: structuring the world so you can win. (1986, ix)

Presidents, given their institutional powers and command of media attention, can have great rhetorical and heresthetic impact on popular politics.
Certainly the Bush White House strove constantly to maximize that impact. Its
success, however, depended greatly on the environment in which its strategies
operated. Exogenous elements of situations often shaped how skillful the
administration could be. In turn, these characteristics shaped the endogenous
attributes of the coalition the White House sought to construct. The political
environment molded the ability of the Bush presidency to "bind" people to
its coalition (Cook and Polsky 2005, 580).

The particular circumstances of any political situation are not just the
sum total of the actions of politicians enmeshed in them. Events matter. In
the case of the Bush presidency, two primary events matter—9/11 and the
onset of the Iraq war. New facts make new politics, requiring politicians to
adapt rhetorically and heresthetically to altered circumstances. 9/11 was a
true "shock from without," but the Iraq war resulted directly from a presidential decision. Each event reconfigured the focus and debate over issues
and alternatives in the context of the national agenda. The Bush presidency,
then, presided over a complex new "issue regime" regarding terrorism in
which it had to seek public support (Mayhew 2005A, 475). In 2002, the
recent events of 9/11 and military success in Afghanistan promoted the
political success of the administration in that year's elections. In the 2004
and 2006 elections, the administration repeated this strategy with steadily
less effectiveness due to ongoing difficulties with the Iraq occupation. The
administration's ability to heresthetically structure voters' choice situations
depended greatly on events.

The following pages further examine the rhetorical and heresthetic
strategies, consequential events, and shifting environment of public politics
during the George W. Bush presidency. These occurred in a time of strong
political polarization that had predated Bush's election but to which the
political strategies of his White House and his own actions as president
contributed.

Growing American Political Divisions in the Late
Twentieth Century

Vociferous political differences characterized national politics during much
of the Bush presidency, but such partisan and ideological conflicts had

been growing for decades before he took office. Political scientists discovered among the American public a growing relationship between party identification and ideology—Republicans becoming more preponderantly conservative and Democrats more liberal in their views. This trend began in the 1970s and grew steadily through the 1980s and 1990s. Writing in 1998, Alan Abramowitz and Kyle Saunders found that the parties themselves became more ideologically distinct, a situation that then produced a clearer ideological and partisan divide among the public: "Clearer differences between the parties' ideological positions made it easier for citizens to choose a party identification based on their policy preferences. The result has been a secular realignment of party loyalties along ideological lines" (Abramowitz and Saunders 1998, 636).

Why did this happen? Morris Fiorina and Matthew Levendusky call this a simple matter of party "sorting," in which "a tighter fit is brought about between political ideology and party affiliation" (Fiorina and Levendusky 2006, 53). James Campbell and Abramowitz make a broader argument that, beyond sorting, the "center" in American politics has shrunk as well, creating polarization at both the mass and elite level. Campbell finds that, as ideological differences among partisans grew, the number of self-described moderates and those claiming not to know their ideology declined from 1972 to 2000 (Campbell 2007, 27). Polarization has also grown in Congress, where ideological divergence between the two parties increased steadily from the 1970s to the twenty-first century (McCarty, Poole and Rosenthal 2006, 23–34).

Certainly the elite narrative of American politics was fraught with polarization in the 1990s, a point upon which scholars agree. Recall the many partisan controversies besetting the presidency of Bill Clinton. Upon taking office, a conflict erupted about administration policy concerning gays in the military. The 1994 elections brought GOP control of Congress. The most notable GOP congressional leader, House Speaker Newt Gingrich, led partisan challenges to many Clinton policies, featuring a shutdown of the federal government over a budget stalemate in 1995. After a period of bipartisan cooperation producing welfare reform and approval of the North American Free Trade Agreement, the final years of the Clinton presidency brought forward institutional warfare between president and Congress over Clinton's legal transgressions in testimony concerning his extramarital affairs. The House impeached the President but the Senate failed to convict. Clinton retained high job approval but was personally unpopular with the public (Harvey 2000, 130–40). A certain amount of "Clinton exhaustion" gave the GOP a shot at the presidency.

The 2000 Elections

America in 2000 was in the late stages of an economic boom that had begun in the mid-1990s. The nation's military involvement in the Balkans had been concluded with some success and no American casualties. Salient public issues were those on which Democrats long had an advantage: education, health care, and the environment (Abramson, Aldrich and Rohde 2003, 132). Yet certain elements of the situation gave Republicans hope. Public concern about "ethics in government," fueled by the scandals surrounding Clinton, presented rhetorical opportunities. History also held some ominous lessons for Albert Gore, the likely Democratic nominee. Only twice previously had incumbent vice presidents won the White House after their party had held the executive mansion for two terms—Martin Van Buren in 1836 and George Herbert Walker Bush in 1988. Both of them had lost their bids for reelection. Gore, an articulate and intelligent candidate, lacked Clinton's warmth and charisma.

All this set the stage for the emergence of George W. Bush as a presidential candidate. During his second term as governor of Texas, his staff began serious planning for a White House run. What strategy to pursue? Two general directions presented themselves. One option involved clinging to the political center, as Bill Clinton had done as a "new Democrat" candidate in 1992. Another was to mobilize the conservative GOP base while making only limited, necessary appeals to the center in order to win an Electoral College majority. Karl Rove, strategic mastermind of the 2000 Bush campaign, was originally inclined toward centrism, until presented with a memo by strategist Matthew Dowd indicating that the number of true swing voters had shrunk dramatically in recent presidential elections (Edsall 2006, 50–52). The Bush approach then shifted toward a "base plus" strategy instead of a "center out" approach.

The rhetorical embodiment of this approach was entitled "compassionate conservatism," conservatism, yes, but not of the dangerous or extreme variety. Bush frequently joined the themes, as in this stump speech in Iowa in 1999: "Is compassion beneath us? Is mercy below us? Should our party be led by someone who boasts of a hard heart? . . . I am running because my party must match a conservative mind with a compassionate heart." The candidate also particularly emphasized his interest in education reform, a policy area seldom highlighted by previous GOP presidents or candidates. For his party's base, however, Bush promised tax cuts and conservative federal judges. Accompanying this message was an emphasis on the candidate's personal honor and probity, reflected in Bush's concluding line in many of his speeches: "When I put my hand on the Bible, I will swear to not only uphold the laws of our land, I will swear to uphold the honor and dignity of the office to which I have been elected, so help me God." This is an appeal to "ethos," identified by Aristotle in his *Rhetoric* as "persuasion achieved by the speaker's personal character when speech is spoken as to make us think him credible" (Aristotle 2007). Heresthetically, Bush sought to shift the terrain of choice for voters by emphasizing the quality of the candidate's character and promising no radical discontinuity in the issues discussed during the Clinton presidency, when domestic issues far superseded foreign policy on the public agenda. This message of "safe change" was delivered clearly in the candidate's convention acceptance speech.

Managerially, Bush campaign ads early on featured talking head presentations of the candidate on various issues. Only when confronted by a strong primary challenge from Senator John McCain of Arizona did the campaign go negative, though coupling its criticisms of McCain with a new message about Bush, repackaging him as "a reformer with results." The Bush campaign was able to fund its race for the nomination thoroughly, amassing $106 million in funds for the primary season and expending all of them by the national convention. In raising such large amounts, Bush became the first candidate since 1980 to exercise his option to fund his campaign outside of the federal system providing partial public finance of nomination campaigns. That system fixed a maximum expenditure limit at less than half of Bush's total. Given the steadily rising costs of campaigning, the Bush campaign gained strategic resources and flexibility from this choice, while offending few GOP primary voters, who as a group tend to be skeptical of public campaign finance. For the fall campaign, Bush accepted $67.5 million in public funds, as did his opponent. In all, the Bush campaign had significantly more funds in 2000 than did Al Gore, amassing $192.6 million to the Democrat's $132.8 million (Center for Responsive Politics 2000). Consistent with his compassionate conservative emphasis, many of Bush's ads in the fall targeted traditional Democratic issues like Social Security and education. Bush's choice of Dick Cheney, former White House chief of staff, GOP Congressman, and secretary of defense, sought to signal his commitment to governance. Cheney of Wyoming, however, did not broaden the ticket's geographical appeal.

In contrast to the consistent strategic message of the Bush campaign—on compassionate conservatism and personal integrity—the campaign of Albert Gore featured variable themes. A central strategic quandary involved Gore's relationship with the personally unpopular Bill Clinton. Gore throughout 2000 sought to distance himself from Clinton. The managerial calculation about this was straightforward; Clinton was unpopular with swing voters in key states needed for victory. But what should be his strategy for defeating Bush? Gore locked down the nomination early in the primaries; though he limited his overall spending by taking matching funds he easily dispatched his rivals, the most prominent of whom was former Senator Bill Bradley of New Jersey. During the summer, Gore tried three different strategic approaches—as attacker of Bush, affirmer of the Clinton-Gore economic record, and populist reformer (Ceaser and Busch 2001, 119–25). His successful convention speech affirmed the populist approach for the fall campaign: "together, let's make sure that our prosperity enriches not just the few, but all working families. . . . I want you to know this: I've taken on the powerful forces, and as president, I'll stand up to them and I'll stand up for you." Gore's campaign advertising employed a variety of themes—on traditional Democratic issues such as Social Security and the environment—seeking to warn about the consequences of a Bush presidency. He received a boost in the polls from his choice of centrist Democratic Senator Joe Lieberman of Connecticut as his vice presidential nominee and from an energetic if lengthy convention acceptance speech.

The major events of the autumn were the three campaign debates, a prime heresthetic and rhetorical opportunity for each candidate. The personal performance of the candidates—ethos again—featured prominently in public perceptions and media coverage of the events. Each debate featured a different Al Gore persona, from haughtily condescending (debate one) to deliberately low-key (debate two) to aggressive and articulate (debate three). As Gore himself put it, his debate performances were "too hot, too cold and just right." In contrast, Bush doggedly stuck to his message of unthreatening conservative reform, illustrated in these concluding remarks from debate one: "I understand the limited role of the federal government, but it could be a constructive role when it comes to reform, by insisting that there be strong accountability systems."

Gore, considered by many observers as a superior debater, found himself on the media defensive during the debates. Reporters noted his often condescending tone and a penchant for exaggeration in some of his rhetorical examples both in the debates and campaign speeches. Bush, in contrast, benefited from low expectations and made no serious mistakes during the exchanges. He emerged from the debates with a narrow lead in the polls. Bush further benefited from more positive media coverage than Gore during the national conventions and final phase of the campaign (Kern 2001; Project for Excellence in Journalism 2000).

Opinion polls showed a close race with a slight Bush lead after the debates until a bombshell hit in the final week of the campaign. Revelations of Bush's previously undisclosed drunk driving arrest—which occurred decades before, when he was in his twenties—threatened to undermine his claims to probity and character. Persuasion and manipulation of preferences becomes far less effective in the face of such disclosures. That, coupled with a superior get out the vote (GOTV) effort by Democrats masterminded by organized labor, may explain why Bush finished behind in the popular vote on election night. Rhetorically, managerially, and heresthetically, Bush and Gore had finished in a near tie, with Gore receiving 50.3 percent and Bush 49.7 percent of the national vote won by the two major parties. Overall, Gore's popular vote margin was some 543,000 votes, placing him ahead by a very narrow margin of 48.38 percent to 47.87 percent.

But the Electoral College result varied from that. On election night, Gore had won 267 electoral votes, three short of victory, with Bush amassing only 246. Gore had carried most northeastern and far western states, along with the populous states of America's northern tier. Bush swept the southern and Rocky Mountain states. The race to an Electoral College majority all came down to the popular vote result in Florida, with its 25 electoral votes. The initial count there had put Bush ahead by only 527 votes. The presence of a third candidate, Ralph Nader of the Green Party, on the Florida ballot may have siphoned enough votes from Gore to produce this result—a classic heresthetic example of how the structure of a choice situation can determine its outcome. In a bizarre twist on election night, Gore first called Bush to concede but then called again to retract the concession. What followed was a six-week legal tussle involving recounts in certain counties, and conflicting decisions in state and federal courts. The US Supreme Court in *Bush v. Gore* settled the matter in December by overruling a statewide recount ordered by the Florida Supreme Court. The court held that the recount procedures mandated by the Florida court violated Fourteenth Amendment equal protection standards for counting all votes consistently. The court further ordered that the recount be stopped because it could not be completed before the December 12 "safe harbor" deadline in federal law for states to select electors free of possible congressional preemption (*Bush v. Gore* 531 U.S. 98 2000).

Bush never trailed in any of the vote counts, but the controversy over the final outcome marked his presidency from its first days. A substantial minority of Americans believed he had not legitimately won the election. In a Gallup poll in December 2000, only 18 percent of Democrats, 7 percent of blacks and 48 percent of all respondents thought Bush had won the election "fair and square." By inauguration day, Bush's Gallup job approval rating was only 57 percent; one of the lowest since polling on this question began in 1945. Bush faced a strongly divided nation from the outset of his presidency. Political polarization was more entrenched than ever.

The 2000 election featured an evenly divided electorate. Neither candidate had scored a great electoral victory. Still, Bush's performance was well above that predicted in the election models developed by political scientists, most of which forecasted a Gore popular vote victory of 53–55 percent (Weisberg and Wilcox, 2003). Though by this standard Gore underperformed, he did win the popular vote. A possible flaw in his strategy may have cost him the election. Some evidence suggests he might have fared better if he had placed himself closer to the successful aspects of the Clinton record (Abramson, Aldrich, and Rohde 2003, 191). How well did Bush fare in his "base plus" strategy? Karl Rove noted after the election that the GOTV effort on the GOP side had been inadequate. Approximately four million conservative Christians, whom the Bush campaign had been counting on, did not turn out to vote (Kirkpatrick 2004). Of those Christian conservatives who did vote, however, 80 percent supported Bush (Cable News Network 2000, 1). Bush had some success in courting the political center, winning the independent vote 47 to 45 percent while losing moderates by 52 to 44 percent (Cable News Network 2000, 1). "Base plus" thus had some success in the center, but fell short regarding turnout with the base itself. This was a central conclusion of the Bush strategists after 2000, which led them to extensive research and experimentation on how to enlarge the turnout of their base voters (Hamburger and Wallstein 2006).

The 2000 Bush coalition did involve some gains over Bob Dole's performance in 1996 with various voter groups. Bush improved the GOP performance with Catholics, working class, and southern white voters. These all reflected secular trends of these groups toward the GOP over the decades. Bush did well with certain Republican base voter groups, capturing 87 percent of highly religious Protestants, 66 percent of high income voters, and 68 percent of southern whites (Abramson, Aldrich and Rohde 2003, 109–118), but not well enough to win the overall popular vote. "Base plus" would benefit in the future from better managerial execution.

The closely contested presidential results had a counterpart in the 2000 congressional elections. The GOP lost two seats in the House (dropping from 223 to 221 seats) and four seats in the Senate (from 54 to 50 seats), retaining effective control by a very narrow margin. Similar closely divided results occurred in the states, with the GOP losing one governorship and adding seventy state legislative seats nationwide. All this suggested to many observers that George W. Bush would need to govern in a bipartisan "centrist" fashion in order to succeed as president. He did not take that advice, as we will see in chapter three. Operating from a unified GOP congressional base, Bush sought to persuade the public to support his agenda through an expansive public outreach program.

The 2002 Elections

It would be difficult to overstate the contrast between the political environments of the 2000 and 2002 elections. The 9/11 attacks produced a surge in popularity for Bush that persisted through most of 2002. The Gallup poll reported that his job approval mushroomed from 51 percent in early September 2001 to 90 percent two weeks later. Bush's high popularity persisted through 2002, with Gallup reporting Bush at 63 percent job approval just before the 2002 elections. This became a considerable political resource for the GOP in those elections, and strategically they made much of it.

Still, in the autumn of 2002 it was not obvious that the congressional elections that year would benefit the GOP (Dionne 2002). It was difficult to determine how Bush's job approval would affect the House and Senate races, each featuring specific candidates and their campaigns. Political scientists have identified presidential popularity as an influence on midterm election results (Jacobson 2003, 3). That year, however, other traditionally important factors, such as a sluggish economy with unemployment near six percent, did not necessarily portend GOP success. Any slight trend, it seemed to observers, could prove determinative. Republicans held a slim six seat majority in the House, while the Democrats controlled the Senate by a single seat. The playing field was also narrow. Reapportionment following the 2000 census created many safe incumbents in the House. Money and media attention ended up concentrating disproportionately on races in five competitive states—New Hampshire, Minnesota, Iowa, Tennessee, and Georgia (Sabato 2003B, 263–4).

The Bush White House sought to make the war on terrorism the dominant issue of the election. This opportunity presented itself because "Bush's job approval ratings were detached from the economy," centered instead on support for his response to 9/11 and initiation of military action in Afghanistan (Jacobson 2003, 8). Karl Rove stated the strategy succinctly: "We can go to the country on this issue because they trust the Republican party to do a better job of protecting and strengthening America's military might and thereby protecting America" (Edsall 2002A). Heresthetically, by structuring electoral choices around the theme of "security," voters might well move in a GOP direction. Bush enunciated this theme in his 2002 State of the Union address: "Our first priority must always be the security of our nation." He then invoked "three great goals for America: We will win this war; we'll protect our homeland; and we will revive our economy." The Republican advantage on security issues was very large. A Gallup poll in early 2002 gave the GOP a 56 to 30 percent advantage over Democrats as the party best able to handle foreign affairs and a 65 to 23 advantage on national defense and military issues.

Terrorism was not the only issue on the public's mind. The economy's unimpressive performance gave Democrats a strategic opening. Since 9/11 had damaged the economy, it was not clear that the public would hold Bush and the GOP accountable for this in November. Bush did reduce public concern surrounding the collapse of the Enron Corporation by signing into law a corporate reform bill in the summer. In the autumn of 2002, two issues emerged that allowed the administration to shift the focus from the economy. First, the White House pushed for a congressional resolution supporting a war with Iraq. Second, the administration also attacked Senate Democrats for holding up a bill establishing a Department of Homeland Security. At issue was a provision regarding security personnel at airports. Democrats wanted labor law to fully apply to the hiring and firing of these workers, but Bush argued for greater presidential discretion in such matters. Both controversies, given Bush's popular support as a national security manager, placed Democrats on the defensive.

The national GOP campaign, spearheaded at the White House under Karl Rove's direction, attempted several managerial innovations in the 2002 elections. Republicans succeeded in raising substantially more funds than Democrats for the 2002 electoral cycle, $527.4 million compared to $323.7 million (Edsall 2002B). The main innovation of 2002, however, was the institution of new get out the vote efforts, pioneered by national party strategists under the supervision of Karl Rove. One initiative, the "72 hour campaign," replaced phone bank contact with personal contact and calls to potential voters. This was related to an effort by House Majority Leader Tom DeLay (R-TX) to recruit volunteers to work on turnout in competitive House districts (*Roll Call* 2002, 13). GOP turnout efforts outstripped those of the Democrats. In a final effort to boost GOP voting, President Bush embarked on a whirlwind tour during the final two weeks of the campaign. Presidential stops were chosen a few days in advance in response to the latest polling in the states. Such presidential attention to a midterm campaign was unusual in its length and thoroughness.

Democrats had some initial hopes of gaining seats in both congressional chambers in 2002. The economy, though recovering from recession, still featured high unemployment—just below six percent during the campaign. Further, midterm elections had historically almost always cost the president's party congressional seats (Busch 1999). Democratic heresthetic strategy involved directing voters to choose on the basis of domestic issues like the economy and health care, regarding which Democrats traditionally fared well in the polls, while neutralizing national security issues by largely agreeing with the President's thus far successful approach. Rhetoric representative of this approach came from Senate Majority Leader Tom Daschle (D–SD) in early 2002. Praising the "superb job" by President Bush and his "national security team," he then critiqued the economic plan of the president, claiming that "When it comes to our second battle, our economic battle, I think most Americans would probably agree that the news hasn't been so good lately. But there's no reason we can't win both of our battles." Democrats evidenced managerial continuity in their voter turnout efforts and campaign advertising at a time when the GOP was energetically implementing several turnout innovations. Ultimately, it was not successful: "The Democrats appeared to lack a message not because they had nothing to say, but because the Republicans, led by the White House, articulated their message of security so effectively" (Todd 2003, 40). As the election neared, the structure of the choice situation favored the White House.

Democrats encountered increasing heresthetic and rhetorical disadvantages as the 2002 campaign progressed. One central impediment was their inability to command public attention for their attempts at persuading and structuring the choices of voters. Media coverage regarding the campaign was skimpy, magnifying the GOP cash advantage in communication (Jurkowitz 2003, 48). That, combined with high job approval for the president and his active role in the conclusion of the campaign, obscured the Democratic message. The public remained more focused on international problems than the economy. An October Gallup poll revealed that 42 percent of respondents viewed international issues, terrorism, and war as the top issues facing the country, with 37 percent identifying the economy as the central national problem. Further, Gallup found that 71 percent trusted the government to handle international problems, hardly a "throw the bums out" sentiment that might work against the current administration.

Election night 2002 produced a historic gain in congressional seats for the Republicans. They added six House seats, raising their majority to 229 Representatives, and two Senate seats, retaking a slim majority of 51 seats. For the first time since the New Deal midterm of 1934, the president's party had gained in both chambers. The GOP also added 175 state legislative seats to hold a majority of those seats nationwide for the first time since 1952. Still, the magnitude of the GOP victory can be overstated. Democrats picked up three governorships, though the GOP retained a majority of twenty-six of those offices. The margins of national congressional control remained quite narrow, hardly rivaling 1934, when Democrats won large congressional majorities.

What role did President Bush play in securing this narrow but unusual victory? Bush's main successes were heresthetic, defining choices for voters, and managerial, assembling and targeting considerable resources: "creating an environment where being associated with him was not detrimental to candidates and using the fundraising prowess of the White House to ensure that no potential Republican vulnerability lacked resources or attention" (Schweers 2003, 74). Another key influence on the U.S. House vote was the pattern of reapportionment. One group of scholars estimated that GOP success at reapportionment had cost the Democrats five House seats in 2002 (Abramson, Aldrich, and Rohde 2003, 264). The overall pattern of reapportionment very much aided House incumbents; only four House challengers won their races (Jacobson 2003, 11).

Surveys at the time of the election revealed that Republicans had improved on their 2000 performance with voters, increasing their vote from 2 to 5 percent among most demographic categories (Sabato 2003A, 11). The pattern of partisan support remained similar to that of 2000. Rural voters, white males, and white Protestants remained strongly Republican. Unlike 2000, the GOP narrowly won Catholics, baby boomers, and senior citizens. African Americans remained 90 percent Democratic and Latinos almost two to one Democratic (Sabato 2003A, 11). Despite the GOP victory, polarization characterized national politics, as Gary Jacobson noted at the time: "Deep party divisions in Washington are firmly rooted in electoral politics, and they reflect divisions in popular opinion on most domestic issues. The elite and popular consensus supporting the president's war on terrorism and, by extension, confrontation with Iraq remains strong but narrowly focused; it has not spread to issues that divided the parties before September 11" (Jacobson 2003, 18–19). Sound campaign skills and favorable events had created only a small margin of victory for the GOP.

An emboldened President Bush pressed his advantage. He had gained congressional authorization for military action against Iraq during the 2002 campaign season. After the election, Congress agreed to Bush's version of the previously controversial airport security legislation. The president also secured another round of tax cuts in 2003 and enactment of a Medicare prescription drug benefit for seniors. Bush chose to invade Iraq in early 2003, producing a quick military victory over Saddam Hussein. But the increasingly controversial course of the Iraq occupation would most clearly set the context for the 2004 election. Democrats by then had learned how to improve their voter turnout operations, taking lessons from the surprisingly bad news on that front in 2002. All this portended a highly competitive presidential race in 2004.

The 2004 Elections

The consensus surrounding Bush administration foreign policy had evaporated by 2004. The invasion of Iraq, launched in March 2003, produced an immediate victory in the toppling of the Saddam Hussein regime. Then the trouble began. The administration had hoped for a relatively quick exit from Iraq, but mushrooming sectarian violence and a persistent Al Qaeda presence prompted a lengthy military occupation. This led to a steady flow of American casualties over the months and years with little improvement in the country's security. Iraqis demonstrated courage by voting in large numbers for a constitution and government, but headway in establishing a functional national military and government was slow. In the spring of 2003, a furor developed over American soldiers' mistreatment of detainees at Abu Ghraib prison. By mid 2004, it was clear that no weapons of mass destruction, the presence of which was a key administration justification for the invasion, could be located. Allegations of mismanagement of Iraq reconstruction efforts arose that year alongside the continuing violence in that country.

This stream of bad news took its toll on George W. Bush's job approval ratings. In Gallup polls, he fell from 68 percent approval just after the 2002 elections to 47 percent by July of 2004. Iraq became the nation's "most important problem" in April 2004 and remained at that ranking consistently until 2008, when economic problems rose to the forefront. Democrats became overwhelmingly opposed to the Iraq occupation, with Republicans stalwart in support, and independents, a crucial group of swing voters, hovering somewhere in between. Bush's reelection was very much in question. The heresthetic problem for the administration was a large one. It faced declining public support over the top issue of the day, making it difficult to restructure voter choices around another issue. A redefinition of the problem more advantageous to the White House was needed. The reframing would entail a strong rhetorical defense of current policies combined with an emphasis on the personal deficiencies of the Democratic nominee as a possible commander in chief. An outstanding managerial effort regarding fundraising, advertising, and voter turnout also would be essential to electoral success.

Alongside Iraq, the economy loomed as a major issue. On this, the news was mixed. Economic growth in the two years preceding the second quarter of 2004 had averaged 3.5 percent, higher than in the election years of 1992 and 1996, but lower than 2000 (Campbell 2005, 229). The unemployment rate, however, remained above 5 percent throughout the year. This "half empty, half full" situation prompted both major presidential candidates to use the issue to their advantage. The president's job approval numbers hovered around 50 percent in the polls for most of the year, suggesting that the election would be a close one. For the Bush campaign, a closely divided country, coupled with a stream of bad news about Iraq, meant that there was little margin for error.

The Bush campaign managers, fashioning a script similar to the success-ful one of 2002, tied Iraq to the broader war on terror. Regular attention to improving aspects of the economy was invoked as well. A central heresthetic strategy, however, involved shifting the terrain of choice toward unattractive aspects of their opponent, Senator John Kerry of Massachusetts. According to Bush strategist Matthew Dowd, this focus targeted both Kerry's overall acceptability as an alternative and "his ability to make an argument about us" (Dowd 2006, 25). By using ethos against Kerry, Bush could structure an effective defense. The criticisms would come through a variety of persuasive appeals: a wave of television ads as well as direct comments from campaign surrogates and the president himself. The first great wave of ads criticizing Kerry came in March 2004, shortly after he had clinched his party's nomi-nation. This failed to put Kerry decisively behind, as the Bush campaign had hoped, but did augur future heresthetic and rhetorical themes that the campaign would employ.

Alongside these heresthetic and rhetorical strategies existed an expansive managerial operation to ensure a high turnout. As in 2002, the approach was two-pronged: create a large GOP base vote and carefully target appeals to particular sorts of swing voters. Dowd identified those voters as "suburban married working women; younger working-class males; and Hispanics" (Si-mon 2004). The efforts to bring GOPers to the polls were unprecedented, involving the expenditure of $120 million, six times the budget of 2000 (Hamburger and Wallstein 2006, 140). A central tactic involved "microtarget-ing" small groups of likely GOP voters through elaborate, computer driven targeting analysis employing the Voter Vault database. Teams of volunteers engaged in sequential contact with likely GOP voters as the election neared. This turnout operation yielded, according to the national party, a network of 1.4 million active volunteers (DuHaime 2006). The party was aided by the election activities of an independent organization, the Progress for America Voter Fund, which spent $19 million on commercials in eleven states and sent many pieces of mail and emails to potential voters (Justice 2004, A18). In all, the Bush campaign, the Republican Party, and supportive groups would spend $1.14 billion in securing his reelection, the highest total in American history to that point (Edsall and Grimaldi 2004).

The goal of a narrow win in an evenly divided country was much more modest than the White House had originally envisioned for 2004. A sweeping partisan realignment, comfortably placing the GOP as the nation's majority party, seemed out of reach. Bush's partisan governing style in 2003 to 2004 had limited opportunities to win over Democrats in Washington or the electorate, most of whom now bitterly opposed the president. His policy initiatives during early 2004—support for a constitutional amendment on same-sex marriage, talk of additional tax cuts—catered to his party's conservative base. A survey in October 2004 found partisan polarization regarding Bush to be more pronounced than for any president ever before in polling history (Jones 2004).

Thus the identity of the Democratic nominee loomed large in the Bush camp's strategizing. John Kerry had dispatched his main rivals for the nomination, former Governor Howard Dean of Vermont and Senator John Edwards of North Carolina, by early March of 2004. Like Al Gore in 2004, Kerry attempted a variety of thematic approaches during the remainder of the 2004 campaign. He complained about slow job creation, criticized Bush's Iraq management, and emphasized traditional Democratic issues such as Social Security and Medicare. A Kerry strategist, Bill Knapp, argued that the campaign had to present arguments via speeches and ads on two fronts: first, national security and terrorism, and, second, a variety of domestic issues on which Kerry had an advantage over Bush (Knapp 2006, 68). Strategically, this was a very tall order. The heresthetic and rhetorical approach in this scattershot campaign was, however, never consistent. Kerry complicated the task with his variable and overly subtle pronouncements on Iraq and terrorism, epitomized by his comment about an Iraq funding bill: "I actually did vote for the $87 billion before I voted against it." Despite the thematic problems, his effort was well funded. Kerry's campaign, the Democratic Party, and its supportive groups spent $1.08 billion in his presidential effort, just $60 million less than the total expended by the Bush effort (Edsall and Grimaldi 2004).

Democrats undertook an unprecedentedly ambitious turnout effort. The national party allocated $60 million, twice the 2000 level. The Democrats' turnout operations, more than those of the GOP, were augmented by the activities of supportive groups. One such group, Americans Coming Together (ACT), claimed to have raised $125 million, employed 2,500 workers to register and mobilize new voters, and sent millions of mailings, fliers, and phone calls. The AFL-CIO planned to spend $45 million in sixteen key states (Justice 2004). One key managerial difference between the parties involved their methods of voter contact. Democrats relied on hired workers, but the GOP emphasized contact by volunteers from particular voters' neighborhoods. The yield from the latter approach would prove greater on Election Day, probably because messages arriving from a familiar source are more likely to be trusted by voters.

Republicans gained a scheduling advantage by placing their convention in early September, one month later than the Democrats. Since both campaigns accepted $76.9 million in optional public financing for the fall campaign, the amount would have to fund a thirteen-week campaign for the Democrat but only a nine-week effort by the incumbent. Kerry's convention speech was heavily autobiographical, referring frequently to his service in Vietnam. His opening sentence reflected this: "I'm John Kerry and I'm reporting for duty." This rhetorical approach yielded trouble for Kerry. He received no post-convention "bounce" in the polls and failed to emphasize the prospective reasons for a Kerry presidency. Shortly after the convention, an anti-Kerry group, the Swift Boat Veterans for Truth, began what would become a $13.8 million ad campaign attacking his Vietnam record and qualifications to serve as commander in chief (Center for Responsive Politics 2004). While the ads ran during the otherwise slow news weeks of August, the Kerry campaign failed to respond quickly to the attacks. When Kerry did respond later in the month, voters could be forgiven for wondering why Vietnam had become the top issue of the 2006 election. All of this pushed the Kerry campaign off stride.

The GOP convention, held in New York to evoke 9/11, went smoothly, with Bush reprising his war on terror themes as well as introducing an agenda for his second term: tax simplification and reductions, medical liability, and Social Security reform. As he put it in summary: "I'm running for President with a clear and positive plan to build a safer world, and a more hopeful America." Though he emerged from the convention with a small bounce in the polls and narrow lead over Kerry, all would not go smoothly for the president in the coming weeks. A major turning point, which proved to be a great opportunity for John Kerry, lay ahead in the presidential debates.

Before the three presidential debates, John Kerry tried to move beyond his previously nuanced position on Iraq. In late September, he bluntly declared the Iraq war a mistake, terming it "the wrong war, in the wrong place, at the wrong time." The new position increased his contrast with Bush, but Kerry continued to face a heresthetic problem when he addressed the Iraq issue: "As he moved left on Iraq, Kerry was more likely to tap into dissatisfaction with the war, but he also ran the risk of becoming too closely associated in the public mind with activists" on the left opposed to the war and seeking immediate withdrawal (Ceaser and Busch 2005, 128). This activist position remained at the edge of public debate over the war in 2004, with polls indicating a public closely divided on the conduct of the war and whether it was worthwhile. Kerry's new position did not move the horserace poll numbers, which showed Bush with a small lead.

The first presidential debate, however, allowed Kerry to seize a rhetorical opportunity and improve his image with voters. Focused on national security and foreign policy issues, Kerry provided concise and assured responses as the president seemed to grow more exasperated during the course of the exchange. He scored points on the Iraq war, quoting the president's father as having "said our troops would be occupiers in a bitterly hostile land. That's exactly where we find ourselves today." Polls revealed that Kerry had improved his image with voters in the debate and had emerged as the clear winner. Bush fared better in the last two debates, particularly when he shifted his ethos argument about Kerry in the third debate. Instead of painting his opponent as a flip-flopper, Bush portrayed Kerry as an out-of-step liberal: "Your record is such that Ted Kennedy, your colleague, is the conservative senator from Massachusetts." Bush filled in the policy details on Kerry's liberalism during the course of the debate. By the end of the debates, Kerry's impression among voters was better, and the race, according to a *New York Times* poll, was a dead heat with Bush at 47 percent and Kerry at 46 percent (Nagourney, Elder and Backus 2004). The race was up for grabs with two weeks of campaigning to go.

The final phase of the campaign involved an intense advertising air war and voter mobilization ground game. The Bush campaign clearly won this round managerially, rhetorically, and heresthetically. As the election results would reveal, the campaign's expensive system of volunteer contacts out-stripped Democratic turnout efforts. Two particularly effective ads in the final phase of the campaign reemphasized the national security framing of the Bush campaign. "Wolves," distributed by the Bush campaign, argued for resolution in the face of gathering terrorist threats, highlighting Kerry's record on defense and concluding "weakness attracts those who are waiting to do America harm." An affiliated group, Progress for America, pitched both the national security issue and Bush's ethos in describing a child's reaction: "He's the most powerful man in the world and all he wants to do is make sure I'm safe, that I'm okay." Together with the Swift Boat Veterans for Truth commercials, these were found in studies to be the most effective ads of the fall campaign (Birnbaum and Edsall 2004). In presenting specific arguments to structure voter choices, the GOP effort proved more effective by the end of the campaign.

In contrast to Bush's disciplined effort, the Kerry campaign tried a variety of different themes on the stump and airwaves. Kerry himself began the last week by emphasizing a range of domestic issues, but was forced to change his approach when news disclosures about Iraq and a new videotape by Osama Bin Laden dominated the media. One advantage for the Kerry campaign was favorable coverage by major news media. A study by the Columbia School of Journalism found that 36 percent of stories about Bush during the campaign were negative, compared to only twelve percent regarding Kerry. Thirty percent of Kerry stories were positive, compared to 20 percent of Bush stories (Parsons 2005). By the end of the campaign, however, Kerry's ethos problem had not disappeared. A post election survey of Kerry's likeability level by the National Election Study of the University of Michigan found that his "feeling thermometer" rating from voters was the lowest of any Democratic nominee since 1972 (Gopoian 2005). The Kerry forces had high hopes for the variety of turnout operations underway by the Democratic Party and affiliated groups. Unlike the GOP, however, which ran a unified turnout operation under national party control, Democratic efforts involved a variety of separate unions, affiliated groups (such as ACT), as well as the national party. This coordination problem, along with voter contact by impersonal employees as opposed to volunteer neighbors (the GOP approach), would help to spell the difference on Election Day.

George W. Bush won a narrow victory over John Kerry in both the popular and Electoral College vote. The president accrued 50.7 percent of the popular vote among the two parties to Kerry's 48.3 percent and 286 electoral votes to Kerry's 252. Turnout spiked to 60.3 percent, more than a five percent increase over 2000, a testament to the effectiveness of turnout operations by the campaigns. Bush's popular vote victory margin was three million votes, a substantial improvement over his popular vote loss of 2000. Republicans also enjoyed gains in congressional elections, adding four House seats, largely as a result of a controversial mid-decade redistricting in Texas, and four Senate seats. The GOP now commanded 232 votes in the House and 55 in the Senate. Down ballot, however, Democrats gained sixty state legislative seats nationwide to narrowly outnumber GOP lawmakers in statehouses (by a mere two seats), and no net change in party control occurred in gubernatorial races.

Gerald Pomper's summary reflects the closely-fought results: "The dominant characteristic of the 2004 election was the stability of the vote over four years. The geographic pattern virtually replicated that of the earlier election. . . . Bush's areas of support in the two elections were almost identical, yielding an astonishing correlation of +.97, the highest statistical association between successive elections in American history" (Pomper 2005, 42–3). The national Republican victory, as in 2000 and 2002, was a narrow one, yielding less than overwhelming majorities in Congress and a close partisan balance across the states. Superior campaign management, effective rhetoric, and canny heresthetics had delivered victory to the president and his party, but had hardly sealed the GOP's place as the majority party.

Continuity characterized the presidential candidates' performance with particular parts of the electorate. As in 2000, Bush received strong support from GOP base groups, drawing 65 percent from high income voters, 66 percent from southern whites, and 70 percent from highly religious Protestants (Abramson, Aldrich, and Rohde 2007, 109–110). Certain groups targeted by the Bush campaign also produced considerable support for its candidate, including suburbs (53 percent, a 9 percent increase since 2000) and working class whites (55 percent support, about the same as 2000) (Abramson, Aldrich and Rohde 2007, 109–110; Cable News Network 2004, 1). A particularly notable targeting success was the increase of Hispanic support for Bush, which rose in the exit polls from 35 percent in 2000 to 44 percent in 2004 (Cable News Network 2004, 3). Some scholars have argued that these results exaggerate the increase in Hispanic support for Bush, but a variety of surveys and analysis yield the general conclusion that Hispanic support for Bush did increase over 2000 (Kenski and Tisinger 2006).

Bush was competitive with centrist voters but lost two such groups, albeit narrowly, to John Kerry. Bush captured 48 percent of the independent vote to Kerry's 49 percent and 45 percent of moderates to Kerry's 54 percent (Cable News Network 2004, 3). Kerry could also claim success in attracting voters under thirty, carrying them by 54 to 45 percent, a considerably larger margin than Gore's 48–46 edge in 2000 (Cable News Network 2004, 1; Cable News Network 2000, 1). That trend augured well for the future prospects of the Democratic Party in an election featuring little other good news for them. Though Democrats had increased their turnout in many areas, the GOP had simply outperformed them at this game.

What explains these results? Superior campaign heresthetics, management, and rhetoric certainly contributed to Bush's victory. Kerry's only clear edge emerged in the debates, but the final two weeks of the campaign restored Bush's lead. The Bush attack on Kerry's ethos also played a role, effectively labeling him as too vacillating and too liberal. Polls at the end of the campaign found more voters labeled Bush as a strong leader, and more found Kerry to be too liberal than found Bush too conservative (Campbell 2005, 238–40). These are, however, very much victories at the margins. In fact, America remained almost evenly divided and strongly polarized in 2004. George W. Bush had a large impact on that phenomenon in the 2004 election: "The single largest effect on the surge in participation between the two elections was the increase in candidate-based polarization. . . . The deep divide between those who were attracted to George W. Bush and those who were repulsed by him appears to have motivated the largest share in the increase in turnout and especially in activism between 2000 and 2004" (Abramowitz and Stone 2006, 151). It really was all about George.

The 2006 Elections

Key swing voters in 2004 gave their votes to George W. Bush, believing that he was a strong leader who would effectively manage national security matters. By 2006, this perception was far less prevalent among those casting ballots. New facts make new politics, and the facts had been adverse for the Bush presidency from late 2004 to Election Day 2006. The American military presence in Iraq was foremost among those troublesome facts. Though elections had been held and an Iraqi government formed, sectarian violence continued to flare and American casualties continued to mount, raising doubts about Bush's competence as a national security manager. The response of the national government to Hurricane Katrina's assault on New Orleans and the gulf coast also raised questions about the administration's ability to handle national crises. By the fall of 2006, Bush's job approval ratings had fallen below 40 percent in all national polls, a dangerous level in an election season.

The GOP controlled Congress contributed to the "brand problems" for the national party in 2005–6. The Congress accomplished little. Among the major issues receiving limited congressional attention were Bush's ambitious Social Security proposal, immigration reform ideas, tax simplification plans, and ethics legislation. Congress did not even pass most of its 2006 appropriations bills until after the November election. Scandals plagued the Hill GOP as well. Most notably, House Majority Leader Tom DeLay of Texas announced his resignation in 2006 in the midst of his prosecution on corruption charges in Texas. DeLay was one of several GOP lawmakers associated with Jack Abramoff, a GOP lobbyist charged with influence buying. In all, thirteen GOP House members found themselves mired in scandals as the election approached (Best 2006). By October of 2006, a Gallup poll reported that only 23 percent of respondents approved of congressional job performance.

Scholars identify presidential job approval, the number of congressional seats held by the president's party, and the performance of the economy as central factors in explaining midterm election outcomes (Jacobson 2007B, 154–70). The economy, alone among these factors, promised good news for the GOP. The stock market hit new highs in 2006, personal incomes increased, and unemployment moved downward toward 4 percent. Would voters reward Bush and the Republicans for this prosperity? That would depend on which issues were uppermost in voters' minds. The central challenge for the president, then, was again heresthetic—to convince voters to accept an election agenda fashioned by his administration. The White House's rhetoric in autumn 2006 was deployed toward this end, with results quite at variance from those of 2002 and 2004.

The GOP did enter the 2006 elections with several structural advantages in the congressional races. First, the Republican Party's usual voters are distributed more efficiently across House districts and states than are Democratic voters. In 2000, for example, George Bush lost the popular vote but carried 240 of 435 House districts and won thirty states to Gore's twenty (Jacobson 2007A, 2). Second, compared to Republicans in their takeover year in 1994, Democrats in 2006 had substantially fewer vulnerable seats held by the opposite party to target (Jacobson 2007A, 4–5). Third, George W. Bush was not on the ballot, so some GOP lawmakers might be able to distance themselves from Bush in order to secure reelection.

In this troublesome situation, the White House again resorted to its war on terror heresthetic. By structuring choices around a dire threat of a global terror war in which Iraq was a central front, the administration hoped to again place Democrats on the defensive. Karl Rove told the Republican National Committee in early 2006 that the GOP held a "post 9/11 worldview," but that the Democrats embraced a "pre 9/11 worldview," one that was "deeply and consistently wrong" (Balz, 2006). On the stump, Bush claimed that the country was safer under his policies and that Iraq was no distraction from the war on terror but rather "the central battlefield where this war will be decided." The administration presented much rhetoric to this effect surrounding the fourth anniversary of 9/11. In the short term, the heresthetic seemed to be working; a Gallup poll in mid-September showed Bush's job approval had risen to 44 percent and favorable evaluations of America's efforts in the war on terror had also edged upward. It seemed that the heresthetic employed by the administration might be as effective as it had been in 2002 and 2004.

New facts then quashed those White House hopes. In late September came disclosures that Representative Mark Foley (R-FL) had sent sexually suggestive emails to male House pages. Foley immediately resigned, but the scandal had legs, producing defensive responses from the House GOP leadership about their prior knowledge of the emails. The scandals took time and resources away from the war on terror heresthetic as Republicans played defense. The House and Senate passed ethics bills in response, but could not agree on common language before the election, leaving the issue ripe for Democratic picking.

Another issue of the fall split the GOP internally. Though the White House, under Karl Rove's aegis, had long been targeting Hispanic voters for inclusion in the GOP coalition, many strongly conservative Republican lawmakers objected to the "path for citizenship" extolled by Bush in his recent immigration reform proposal. As with the ethics bill, the House and Senate could not agree to a compromise version of the immigration legislation before the election. This left many conservative activists upset with the administration for its supposed weakness in enforcing current immigration laws. One issue that the GOP had hoped would motivate their voters in 2006 was a constitutional amendment banning same-sex marriage. This failed to receive majority support in the Senate. Senate Majority Leader Bill Frist (R-TN) then brought up proposals to repeal the estate tax and ban flag burning, but they failed to pass as well. GOP attempts to structure the agenda did not gain much ground during the campaign season.

Managerially, the GOP did not have the large cash advantage it had enjoyed in previous years. The National Republican Senatorial Committee raised fewer funds than did their Democratic counterpart, a marked contrast to 2002 and 2004 (Rothenberg 2007, 77). On the House side, the National Republican Congressional Committee amassed only 22 percent more funds than the Democratic Congressional Campaign Committee, down from a 47.5 percent advantage in 2004 and a whopping 59.7 percent advantage in 2002 (Wasserman 2007, 109). As the number of competitive races proliferated in the fall, both parties found they had inadequate cash to fully fund their involvement in all such races, a highly unusual position for the GOP (Abramson, Aldrich and Rohde 2007, 286). The vaunted GOP turnout machine was likewise countered by energetic Democratic efforts by national and state parties, trade unions, and other pro-Democratic groups. President Bush himself was in less demand by candidates of his party than he had been in 2002. Ads featuring Bush were run by Democrats this time, accusing their GOP rivals of being too close to the president.

Sensing great opportunities, Democrats recruited candidates aggressively, raised competitive amounts of contributions and devised a sound heresthetic strategy for the 2006 elections. Second midterms have usually not gone well for presidential incumbents. The events of the last two years had given Democrats many rhetorical opportunities to attack the administration's competence and policy positions. A central Democratic topic was Bush's unpopular Iraq policies. Senate Minority Leader Harry Reid (D-NV) highlighted this theme in a speech in September 2006: "These are the consequences of staying the course in Iraq: we're less safe, facing greater threats and less prepared to meet them." Focusing voter choices on Iraq, the top issue commanding public attention in opinion polls in late 2006, was a happy and easily accomplished heresthetic maneuver for Democrats. House Minority Leader Nancy Pelosi (D-CA) also hit at another GOP weakness by invoking the phrase "culture of corruption" to characterize Republican rule in Congress. Both messages figured prominently in Democratic campaign ads across the nation. Backed by a proportionately greater share of campaign funds and extensive turnout operations, Democrats had grounds for optimism. Though Democrats could not fund all of the competitive congressional races in which their candidates found themselves in 2006, this was a fate shared by their GOP rivals for the first time in several election cycles.

George W. Bush correctly termed the 2006 election a "thumpin'" for his party's candidates. Congressional control shifted to the Democrats, thanks to a GOP loss of thirty House and six Senate seats. For the first time in midterm history, every incumbent congressional Democrat on the ballot won reelection. Democrats increased their share of the national House vote by 5 percent, from 46 to 51 percent of ballots cast. The election produced a Democratic pickup of six governorships, raising their total to twenty-eight. Democrats also picked up 322 state legislative seats, giving them control of ten additional state legislative chambers; Democrats after 2006 controlled twenty-three legislatures to the GOP's fifteen. This was truly a Democratic sweep, but congressionally, at least, the margins remained narrow, with Democrats holding 232 House seats, a fifteen seat majority, and a very slim fifty-one to forty-nine seat majority in the Senate.

Historically, the election resembled the "war midterms" of Truman in 1950 (twenty-eight House seats and five Senate seats lost for the president's party) and of Lyndon Johnson in 1966 (forty-seven House seats and four Senate seats lost). "In all three of these elections, the economy was in decent shape but voters were unhappy with the president . . . because of increasingly unpopular wars . . . and the president's party suffered" (Jacobson 2007A, 22). David Mayhew notes that a war can bring electoral contests about whether it "should have been fought in the first place" and over the possibility of "incompetent management" (Mayhew 2005A, 480). Both debates occurred in 2006.

The election results revealed a clear shift away from the GOP by many voter groups since the 2004 election. Those swing voters, independents and moderates, voted decisively for Democrats by margins of 57 to 39 percent and 60 to 38 percent, respectively, a drop of 7–8 percent in GOP support in two years. The GOP lost Catholic voters by 55 to 44 percent, a large shift since Bush carried them with 52 percent support in 2004. Hispanics also shifted decisively to Democrats by 60 to 39 percent, compared with their approximately 40 percent support for Bush in 2004. The strong opposition to immigration reform by conservative Republicans in Congress may have cost the party support with this group. Voters under thirty also went Democratic by 60 to 38 percent in 2006, compared to their narrower 54 to

45 percent preference for Democrats in 2004 (Cable News Network 2004; Cable News Network 2006).

2006 can only be described as a year of heresthetic failure by George W. Bush and the GOP. Voters' views of events failed to agree with the arguments presented by the party and its president. Good economic news helped Republicans very little and issues of Iraq and congressional corruption, framed to GOP disadvantage, carried the day with a decisive majority of voters. Managerially, the Democrats, after several frustrating election cycles, had matched or exceeded the GOP in fundraising and turnout. The "elephant's edge" in the heresthetic, rhetorical, and managerial aspects of national politics vanished in 2006. How lasting are the GOP losses? One could argue that they resulted from short-term factors. Corruption scandals come and go and the American occupation of Iraq will not last forever. Still, for Republicans to rebound, new facts and new issues must crowd out those concerns. Improvements in management, heresthetics, and rhetoric would have to accompany those new issues and facts. That is a strategy based on hope, not the most reliable roadmap for future politics.

The nation remained strongly polarized in the wake of the 2006 election, but in a fashion that did not favor GOP prospects. A postelection poll by the *Washington Post* revealed that independents were highly dissatisfied with the Iraq war and leaned heavily toward Democrats (Balz and Cohen 2007, 11). A survey by the Pew Center in 2007 revealed that 50 percent of the public identified or leaned toward Democrats while only 35 percent aligned with the GOP, a marked contrast to the even 43–43 percent split between the parties in 2002 and 37–37 split in the 2004 exit polls (Pew Center 2007, 1). This led some GOP strategists to decry their party's "damaged" brand: "The voters' judgment on the GOP was based almost entirely on job performance. Unfortunately, it's not just one area in which the voters think we came up short. No, the damage spans the entire brand." (On Message 2006, 3). George W. Bush could not avoid some of the blame for that damage.

Persuading the Public

The Bush White House directed its heresthetic, rhetorical, and managerial resources to courting public opinion in the many months between fall election campaigns. As recent presidencies have done, the administration devoted great time and resources to persuading the public and structuring choice situations so that public opinion was likely to favor the president. George W. Bush spent large amounts of his own time attempting to persuade the public to embrace his problem definitions and proposed solutions. Samuel

Kernell calls such presidential efforts "going public" (Kernell 2007, 1). Recent presidents have engaged heavily in this personal persuasive activity. "It is a strategy by which a president promotes himself and his policies in Washington by appealing directly to the American public for support" (Kernell 2007, 1–2). Why go public? According to Kernell, Washington politicians are now more independent, and presidents cannot succeed by bargaining with an elite group of Washington insiders. Influence over policymaking is now too far flung for that. "Presidents quickly discovered they needed to trade with many more participants . . . It is an unmanageable prospect, one that guarantees overload and multiplies the chances of failure" (Kernell 2007, 32). So a president instead should try to reach fellow Washington politicians through the public, by heresthetically structuring popular choices and presenting rhetorical arguments. As an agenda item receives a favorable popular reception, fellow D.C. politicians will take note and follow the president's lead.

This is no small task. The White House engages in three activities to effectively go public. First, there are activities by the president himself, including public addresses, appearances, and political travel. Second are the broader White House communications operations, including media management, press briefings, and public events involving administration officials. Third, outreach to sympathetic interest groups occurs that can assist in any public campaigns on behalf of presidential initiatives. This last activity also provides vital maintenance of the president's supporting coalition of interests. We'll consider each of these in turn.

A president's time is one of his scarcest resources, so agenda decisions about how to deploy the chief executive are some of the most strategically important of any presidency. Kernell argues that the conditions for success at this enterprise are stringent. First, a president must accurately convey his preferences. Second, citizens must then form their opinion based on this message. Third, citizens must also convey their support for the president to other decision makers whom the president hopes to influence. Lastly, those decision makers then must align themselves with the president because of the citizen communications they have received (Kernell 2007, 193). The White House can really control only the first activity, and then must hope for the best with the others. It's the persuasive equivalent of a triple bank pool shot.

Early in Bush's first term, he barnstormed in favor of major agenda items such as tax cuts and education reform, usually targeting constituents of Democrats in states like South Dakota, for example, who might support the president's agenda. In 2003, he campaigned in states of moderate Republican senators in order to secure their support for his second round of tax cuts.

Social Security was the topic of his lengthy schedule of public appearances at the beginning of his second term. The president consistently pursued a partisan strategy in his public persuasion. Why? "A president determined to make nonincremental policy changes for which no broad public support exists, and with only a narrow congressional majority, almost certainly had little choice but to pursue the partisan strategy," going public to ensure "support from his base and perhaps also . . . blunting the effects on the general public of opposition attacks" (Sinclair 2007, 185).

Early in each of his terms, Bush went public on only a few of the most important issues he had stressed in each campaign, reflecting the persistent issue discipline of the Bush White House. By focusing tightly on his own priority issues via a partisan strategy, the president did encounter certain costs of going public. These costs became more apparent when the president's job approval numbers slumped in his second term, making him appear less formidable to his opponents. Going public discourages compromise, because a president pushes particular formulas in public rather than negotiating them in private. It is antideliberative, making policy an exercise in heresthetic manipulation and rhetorical persuasion, not a bargain about details. It is adversarial in that it seeks to defeat opponents of the president's positions through public arguments. It therefore makes coalition building in Washington more difficult. (Edwards 2007, 284–288)

The clear example illustrating the costs of going public was the president's Social Security reform proposal in 2005. Though broad agreement existed that the popular retirement program faced long-term fiscal problems, there was no such consensus on how to alter its financing to address those problems. Further, Bush's proposal for "personal accounts" (opponents called it "privatization") drew much opposition from backers of the traditional program, who saw great risk to individual account holders in such arrangements. The president undertook "60 Stops in 60 Days" to explain his personal account ideas. Alongside the president, some 31 administration officials made 166 stops, visiting 40 states and 127 cities, and gave more than 500 radio interviews (Edwards 2007, 233). Affiliated groups ran supportive ads on cable news networks.

Heresthetically, the president structured choices for the public around themes of "necessary action" for "personal accounts." His rhetoric followed this structure. At his tour's first stop in Fargo, North Dakota (home of two Democratic senators who were targets of persuasion), he stated: "Look, here's the thing. The threshold question is whether there's a problem that needs to be solved. And if there is, then who can come up with solutions that will work." He went on to explain how his proposal would resemble the current thrift federal employee savings plan, which he believed worked well. These were personal accounts, not part of privatization, a "trick word" according to the president, intended to "scare people." This carefully managed campaign—crowds for presidential forums were carefully prescreened—involved much presidential and staff time through early 2005 (Edwards 2007, 230).

But after a spring of attempted persuasion, public opinion in June remained no more supportive of Bush's ideas than before his administration launched its rhetoric. Polling revealed that once Bush's name was attached to the proposal, Democrats became far less supportive of it (Edwards 2007, 262–3). Thus had Bush become a contributor to the political polarization whose onset predated his presidency. It did not help the White House that bad news from Iraq impeded the president's attempt to structure choices about Social Security. By the summer of 2005, it was clear that Congress would take no action on the president's proposals.

This failure was a case of overgrown ambition. The public was not ready to embrace wholesale restructuring of a large and popular government program. The president, in an evenly divided country, could not coax Democrats into joining him in a politically risky reform effort. So the administration strategy remained a partisan one throughout the persuasion campaign. It was a strategy involving considerable political risk for GOP lawmakers, given Democrats' intransigence. In this case, going public did not promote compromise, deliberation, or broad coalition building, and did not defeat the president's opponents. This is a dangerous strategy best deployed selectively, for failure can disable a presidency. Unskillful heresthetic and rhetorical efforts can undermine a president's political authority, as it did in this case. Skill involves determining what public appeals have a chance to succeed, and the Bush White House miscalculated its prospects with Social Security reform in 2005. Bush attempted no public campaign of similar magnitude for the remainder of his presidency.

Managing the Media

Also deployed in assisting the Social Security reform effort was the considerable communications apparatus of the White House, including the Office of Communications, the Press Office, the Office of Media Affairs, the Speechwriting Unit, the Office of Political Affairs, and the Office of Public Liaison. The ongoing duty of these offices was the courting of the media, public opinion, and interest groups on behalf of the Bush administration. Karl Rove explained the underlying premise of these operations: "Look, if you don't believe a president can affect public opinion, then it really doesn't matter what the president says, does it? Or how he says it. I find it hard to believe you can't" (Kumar 2004, 76).

Several of these offices were engaged in ongoing management of the volatile relationship between the White House and reporters, a relationship that daily shapes public views of the president. Early in the Bush presidency, the administration took a disciplined and distant approach to the press. Bush's communications skills did not rival those of the "great communicator," Ronald Reagan. His speeches often featured stiff presentation and his unscripted comments in press conferences and with reporters did not employ smoothly flowing syntax. As journalist Ken Auletta put it: "More than any President in recent memory, Bush is uneasy in the spotlight—especially in front of television cameras" (Auletta 2004, 53). Bush also believed that most reporters had liberal agendas, a charge not without foundation (Pew Center 2004), which further encouraged his personal distance from reporters.

White House staff pursued an approach similar to that of their boss. Communications director Dan Bartlett stated: "The vast majority of people in this building—the press doesn't believe this—don't want to talk to the press. They want me to do their job" (Auletta 2004, 55). It was not a leaky White House. This is not to say that the Bush administration paid little attention to message management. Senior staff meetings planned out daily and weekly issues of focus for their communications efforts, and pursued this schedule with a resolute intensity. What this did not involve, however, was personal cultivation of reporters individually or in groups. This approach worked reasonably well during Bush's first term as high job approval ratings soared after 9/11. But as adverse events dented presidential popularity during the second term, shortcomings in the administration's handling of the media became apparent. The White House found itself playing defense, and that required a tactical fleetness that its hierarchical methods were incapable of supplying: "Its operation was poor at listening, slow in responding to problems and weak at taking advantage of unanticipated opportunities" (Kumar 2007, 381). In response, the communications operation became more flexible. Bush appeared in settings beyond press conferences in which he responded to the questions of others and more administration members were employed in explaining policies (Kumar 2007, 377).

The press, for its part, tended to give predominately negative coverage to the administration. This was not a new trend. Bush's father and Bill Clinton had likewise endured preponderantly negative coverage during their presidencies (Farnsworth and Lichter 2006, 29–58). The nonpartisan Center for Media and Public Affairs, in its content analysis of evening network newscasts, found that only during the crisis period of 9/11 to the end of 2001 did coverage register strongly positive (63 positive to 37 percent negative). For most of his presidency, the tone of coverage was in ratio between two and three to one negative (Center for Media and Public Affairs 2006, 5). The Bush White House had planned a disciplined, hierarchical communications strategy, but that was no solution to negative press coverage, if such a solution exists. The key variables in altering that strategy were adverse events and declining presidential popularity. That forced a tactical flexibility in operations, but did not alter negative press coverage or cure the president's popularity doldrums.

A similarly focused undertaking was the Bush White House's effort to maintain cooperative and informative relationships with interest groups in its coalition. Groups can help deliver votes in elections and move public and congressional opinion. This effort was led by the White House Political Office and the Office of Public Liaison, under the supervision of Karl Rove for most of the Bush presidency. The supportive interests involved in this relationship included large and small business, social conservatives, gun owner groups, and antitax advocates. GOP efforts to reorganize the Washington interest group community to the party's advantage predated the Bush presidency. After the GOP takeover of Congress in 1994, antitax advocate Grover Norquist of Americans for Tax Reform, with the help of House Minority Leader Tom DeLay, launched the "K Street Project," aimed at encouraging "business associations and corporations to hire as lobbyists philosophical fellow travelers instead of left-leaning Democrats" (Hamburger and Wallstein 2006, 106). Their efforts, accompanied by an increase in the overall number of Washington lobbyists, brought a new and larger group of conservatives to positions of prominence in the D.C. lobbying community. Along with the arrival of the Bush administration, this produced important changes in national policymaking patterns, producing a "Republican-corporate merger" involving "a jointly produced legislative and regulatory agenda backed by major interests as well as by the White House, by the leadership on Capitol Hill, and by the formal institutionalization of business lobbyists as key shapers and promoters of legislation" (Edsall 2006, 131).

Mark Peterson describes the resultant pattern of interaction between the Bush White House and sympathetic groups as one of "liaison as governing party" in which the breadth of group interactions was "exclusive" and the purpose of group interactions was "programmatic" (Peterson 2007, 296). In this relationship, the White House restricts its interaction to groups of "like minded allies" that are encouraged to use their resources to "enact the president's policy agenda" (Peterson 2007, 297). The Carter and Reagan administrations also employed a similar approach to interest groups. The White House orchestrated the heresthetic, rhetorical, and managerial activities that would propel electoral and policymaking success. Groups were to play a compliant and supportive role.

Group spending on advertising and membership mobilization played a part in early administration legislative and electoral victories, but became less helpful during Bush's second term as events and public opinion turned against the president. Efforts by interest groups were viewed by the administration as necessary, but by no means sufficient, components in efforts to change the direction of national policy. In the White House's view, the margin was narrow and all necessary resources had to be employed to pass its agenda:

> In the eyes of the Bush team, America is a polarized country, one where there are fundamental divisions worth fighting over. A president—and a party— should not worry about slender margins of victory or legislative control. The goal is to accumulate just enough power to use the energies and passions of the base to effect ideological change in the nation's laws and institutions. (Peterson 2007, 324)

Conclusion

The Bush presidency's many efforts at coalition maintenance, in elections, and in policymaking all aimed at a sweeping transformation of national politics. If these efforts were successful, electoral realignment could give the GOP a lasting edge as the nation's new majority party. Domestic policy would be governed by the twin goals of social conservatism and a market-oriented effort to install a new "opportunity society" in health care and retirement programs, accompanied by lower taxes. A strong national security regime, successfully prosecuting the war on terror, could induce the necessary electoral support to maintain power, while supporting interest groups would help in elections and press particular policies through Congress. The White House would be the strategic center of this far-flung operation, with strong executive leadership managing a big mix of policies to maintain a persistent majority coalition among interest groups and within the electorate. This would be an executive-dominated policy and political realignment, with the president managing both his endogenous partisan coalition and the broader, exogenous political environment.

All this depended upon pursuing this grand design through the president's able use of formal powers and his maintenance of abundant informal powers, the political capital of popular approval and a strong professional reputation in Washington. Regime change ultimately depended upon strong presidential power and authority. Adverse events and unskillful administration management of new circumstances, conversely, would weaken presidential power and authority. As presidential successes evaporated after 2004, so did the plausibility of this political overhaul.

The administration successfully extended its regime change efforts from 2001 through 2004 by artfully deploying a national security heresthetic that convinced just enough voters to deliver narrow GOP victories. When the Iraq war turned against the administration, its primary strategy for electoral success vanished. In heresthetic terms, the public increasingly no longer saw the facts about the war fitting the administration's frames. This made the administration's rhetoric, based on these frames, less persuasive, and rendered White House attempts at political management less consequential. Concurrently, other aspects of the administration agenda did not go over well with the public, foremost among them the president's approach to Social Security reform. Bush himself had become a strongly polarizing figure, not the best salesperson for his proposals. An improving economy helped the White House's political ambitions little during 2005–2007. Voters' minds were focused elsewhere. By 2008, growing economic problems gave many an additional reason to disapprove of Bush and the Republican party.

In these circumstances, the Bush White House began to lose support among the voters it had targeted as critical for the GOP's electoral future— Hispanics, Catholics, moderates, and independents. Perhaps in the future these voters will become stable elements in a Republican majority coalition, but this won't happen anytime soon. The GOP, after Bush's time in the White House ends, may have future opportunities to court them. As of the end of the Bush presidency, though, the unpopular war in Iraq, widespread questions about the competence of the administration, and revelations of GOP corruption in Congress had made consolidation of a majority coalition impossible. Bush and the GOP were, by the end of his presidency, in a defensive position, unable to create policy and electoral opportunities for themselves. This was far from the original hopes of George W. Bush and Karl Rove at the outset of their time in the White House.

3 WASHINGTON GOVERNANCE

In the aftermath of his razor thin victory in 2000, many in Washington assumed George W. Bush would be limited to a timid governing style. The controversy surrounding his election, coupled with the very small GOP majorities in the House and Senate, would require Bush to pursue a cautious, centrist agenda in the fashion of his predecessor, Bill Clinton. Thomas Mann of the Brookings Institution stated shortly after the 2000 election that Bush would "face enormous difficulty keeping many of his campaign promises: the burden will be on the victor to reach across the aisle and mend the other party's wounds before he can govern effectively" (Mann 2000, 2). Bush did nothing of the sort, evidencing from his first days in office an aggressive executive style well described by Charles O. Jones as "proactive, hierarchical, contained, programmatic, resolute and broadly accountable. Enterprise is the key to understanding this style" (Jones 2007A, 114).

Enterprise, indeed. George W. Bush demonstrated in office an unflagging desire to expand the power and authority of his office. The power goal of Bush administration governance involved increasing presidential prerogative under federal law and the Constitution. In pursuing this, Bush followed a trail blazed by many of his twentieth century predecessors, beginning with Theodore Roosevelt, who first enunciated a stewardship theory of the presidency: "My belief was that it was not only the president's right but his duty to do anything that the needs of the Nation demanded unless such action was forbidden by the Constitution or by its laws" (Roosevelt 1925, 357). The Bush White House adopted a particularly expansive version of this view of a president's formal powers. Labeled the "unitary executive" approach, it had its origins in the Reagan administration, and would involve the Bush administration in no shortage of legal controversies.

Bush also sought to boost the authority of the presidency by making it the central force in a ruling GOP political regime. The president's enterprising efforts to structure and dominate the national agenda sought to produce favorable congressional action, a durable majority electoral coalition supporting the GOP, and Republican superiority in office holding at the national, state, and local levels of government. This involved an energetic use of his informal powers—political capital resulting from popular approval and a sound professional reputation in Washington—as well as his formal powers. For Bush, a lot was riding on this presidency. Success or failure at Washington governance would have enormous consequences.

Such a strong emphasis on presidential leadership—for purposes of increasing formal executive powers and arranging a new, ruling governing regime in national governance—would necessarily demand much of the president himself. A central resource for the president as prime mover was the position of chief executive itself: "Position is the key source for the executive-oriented president. It provides occupancy at the very pinnacle of the executive hierarchy" (Jones 2007A, 117). To bolster his position, Bush sought to assemble a team of tight-lipped loyalists to direct his White House, because "organizational support may contribute to exceeding expectations" (2007A, 117). An emphasis on hierarchical position, however, meant less focus on the "collaborative dimensions of policy and lawmaking" (2007A, 118).

In accordance with Jones' analysis, this chapter will reveal Bush's governing style toward the executive branch to be hierarchical, orderly, and disciplined. His approach to Congress was directive, demanding strong party loyalty when the GOP had majority control, allowing Bush to govern in a neoparliamentary fashion. Conversely, when confronting a Congress with Democratic majorities, Bush was combatively defensive as he defended executive prerogative and his policy agenda. He sought to dominate the judiciary through two strategies. First, presidential appointments provided an opportunity to stock the judiciary with judges likely to sustain his administration's constitutional interpretations and policy initiatives. Second, the administration could win constitutional endorsement of its expansive approach to executive power through argumentation in federal courts. This was, in sum, not the cautious, centrist administration some savants expected, but rather a presidency intent on expanding formal executive power in order to dominate national policymaking and transform American politics. Big ambitions and audacious actions characterized the Bush approach to Washington governance—along with a scorn for the advice of Washington insiders who urged him to not "push the edges of the envelope" as much as his administration did.

A Guiding Theory: The Unitary Executive

The Bush administration's drive for dominance of Washington governance grew from its embrace of a controversial theory of executive power. Known as the *unitary executive theory,* it had its roots in Theodore Roosevelt's view of the executive as possessing powers beyond those strictly enumerated in Article II of the Constitution. The unitary executive approach made particularly ambitious claims about executive power. The theory draws from three sources within the Constitution. First, Article II states: "The executive Power shall be vested in a President of the United States of America." To proponents of the unitary executive, this means that only the President may exercise the executive power and that the President may act in ways not evident in the powers delegated in Article II. Second, the "oath clause" directs the president to "faithfully execute the Office of the President and to preserve, protect and defend the Constitution of the United States." Unitary executive theorists hold that this protects the president from "enforcing things he independently determines are unconstitutional" (Kelley and Barilleaux 2006, 13). Third, the "take care" clause requires the president, with the advice and assistance of subordinates, to "take care that the laws are faithfully executed." Unitary executive theory holds that this obligates the president to be sure executive agencies are executing the law according to the president's wishes, "as opposed to some independent policy goal" (Herz 1993, 252–53).

The central elements of unitary executive theory derive from an expansive reading of these constitutional grants of power. Three "integral components" of the theory are: "The president's absolute power to remove subordinate policy-making officials; the president's authority to direct the way in which subordinates exercise discretionary executive power; and the president's power to veto or nullify those officials' exercise of discretionary executive power" (Kelley and Barilleaux 2006, 11; Yoo et al. 2001, 7).

The first of these tenets was ceded to the president by the Supreme Court in 1927, while the last two claims remain controversial. During the George W. Bush presidency, Congress and the courts involved themselves in controversies surrounding claims of the Bush administration regarding presidential power over executive branch subordinates. Many of these controversies concerned "the ability of the president to control the executive branch—whether it is to control information from outside actors, such as the Congress, the news media, or public interest groups or to control the regulatory process so that it benefits presidential policies of key constituencies" (Kelley 2005, 40).

Unitary executive theory had its origins in the Reagan White House as it sought to roll back a resurgence of congressional power that began in the 1970s with the fall of the Nixon presidency. In this sense George W. Bush was again operating as an orthodox innovator in furthering the attempted constitutional reconstruction pioneered by the Reagan administration. But

Reagan's immediate successors, George Herbert Walker Bush and Bill Clinton, also attempted to expand presidential prerogatives in ways consistent with unitary executive theory, as the following examples reveal.

Presidential Signing Statements

Presidents since Reagan have employed signing statements, issued by presidents as they sign legislation, to expand executive prerogative. Signing statements can serve several functions. Most often throughout American history they have merely rhetorically extolled the merits of the legislation about to be signed. But other uses of the statements can involve greater consequences for governance. Presidents can present their own understanding of the new law in order to influence future federal court interpretations. Specific presidential preferences on the implementation of the law can serve as guidance for executive branch bureaucrats. Presidents also can use signing statements "to signal the president's refusal to enforce or defend a provision or the provisions of law that he deems unconstitutional" (Kelley and Barilleaux 2006, 23). In recent decades, presidents have increasingly employed signing statements for uses beyond the merely rhetorical. The number of signing statements defending executive branch prerogatives mushroomed from 75 from the years 1789–1976 to 322 from 1977–2004; the number instructing executive branch agencies on implementation rose from 34 before 1976 to 74 from 1977–2004. The George W. Bush presidency was emphatic in its use of signing statements (Kelly 2005, 31). From 2001 through 2006, Bush made 117 declarations in signing statements defending the president's constitutional prerogative, in comparison to 78 by Bill Clinton during his two terms in office, 117 by Bush's father (emphatic like his son), and 87 by Reagan (Kelley and Marshall 2007, 26). George W. Bush, however, issued purely rhetorical signing statements far less often than did Reagan, his father or Clinton (2007, 26).

Two examples, one regarding sharing of sensitive information with Congress and another relating to executive branch appointments, illustrate the Bush administration's expansive constitutional claims in signing statements. The first concerns the statement accompanying Bush's signature on the Homeland Security Act, a wide-ranging bill passed in the wake of 9/11 which, among other provisions, created a new cabinet-level Department of Homeland Security. One provision prohibited federal employees from sharing "critical infrastructure information" with any entity other than Congress without written permission from bureaucratic superiors. The Bush administration considered this congressional exemption a violation of executive prerogative, stating that it did not view this disclosure provision as a requirement and that it would construe it "in a manner consistent with the constitutional authorities of the President to supervise the unitary executive branch and to withhold information the disclosure of which could impair foreign relations, the national security, the deliberative process of the Executive, or the performance of the Executive's constitutional duties" (Bush 2002, 2092–3). This is just one of some 126 mentions of the "unitary executive" in Bush administration signing statements during the president's first five years in office, a total far beyond that of any previous administration (Kelley and Barilleaux 2006, 24).

The administration also claimed broad discretion over executive branch appointments. In 2003, Bush rejected seemingly binding provisions in legislation setting qualifications for officials (Cooper 2005, 528). In the Century of Aviation Reauthorization Act, the administration chose in its signing statement to treat requirements in the law as merely advisory: "Congressional participation in such appointments is limited by the Appointments Clause of the Constitution to the Senate's provision of advice and consent with respect to presidential nominees. The executive branch shall construe the provisions concerning qualifications in section 106(p)(7)(B)(iii) as advisory, as is consistent with the Appointments Clause" (Bush 2003, 1796). Claims of far-reaching formal presidential power over information and appointments, central to the unitary executive theory, are evident in these examples.

What is the practical consequence of signing statements? Some scholars see them as de facto "line item vetoes," allowing the president to ignore portions of laws he signs while upholding and implementing those with which he agrees (Cooper 2005, 530–532; Rudalvige 2005, 176). This charge has merit if we can identify concrete empirical consequences from the signing statements. Do the statements produce government action consistent with the signing statement rather than the law as passed by Congress and signed by the president? If so, we have a significant constitutional problem on our hands. The Government Accountability Office (GAO), an agency of Congress, undertook a rigorous examination of the effect of the George W. Bush administration's signing statements upon actual policy implementation by the executive branch. Analyzing eleven 2006 appropriations bills that had received a Bush signing statement, the agency examined nineteen specific objections registered by Bush in his signing statements. After gathering evidence from the agencies charged with implementation of these provisions, the GAO found that ten provisions were implemented as written and six were not (three involved circumstances in which compliance didn't arise as an issue). Though 31 percent of the provisions involved noncompliant implementation, the GAO concluded that "Although we found that some agencies did not execute the provisions as enacted, we cannot conclude that agency noncompliance was the result of the president's signing statement" (Government Accountability Office 2007, 20).

Controversial Prerogative Claims

It remains possible that presidential signing statements in practice constitute line-item vetoes not allowed under the Constitution, but so far that charge has not been proven. What is clear is that the George W. Bush administration has pushed prerogative claims through signing statements more insistently and expansively than did its predecessors. This led the administration into conflict in federal courts on several occasions. One particularly controversial case involved control of information about the administration's energy policy task force, the National Energy Policy Development Group, convened by Vice President Cheney in 2001. This controversy reached the Supreme Court, producing an important decision about executive power.

In early 2001, President Bush appointed his vice president to formulate an energy policy for the administration. Media reports soon indicated that the task force had always met in secret with representatives of major energy producing companies. This prompted two Democratic representatives, Henry Waxman of California and John Dingell of Michigan, to request from Cheney information about the membership and activities of the task force. Specifically, the lawmakers asked the GAO to investigate the group. The vice president's counsel refused to comply with a sweeping request from the GAO for information about the task force's composition and activities. The vice president followed up with a letter claiming that the GAO had power only to evaluate the results of public programs, not their formulation. The GAO then narrowed its request to include only the task force's membership and dates of its meetings. Cheney continued to refuse, claiming that doing so would "contribute to a further eroding of executive branch prerogatives" (Rozell 2006, 99).

The GAO then brought suit in Federal Court, and was joined by two interest groups, the conservative Judicial Watch and the liberal Natural Resources Defense Council, in seeking information about the task force. Their argument was that the provisions of FACA—the Federal Advisory Committee Act—applied to the task force and that disclosure of its membership and minutes was therefore required by law. The Bush administration responded that the Constitution grants the president "a zone of autonomy in obtaining advice, including with respect to formulating proposals for legislation. . . . Congress does not have the power to inhibit, confine, or control the process through which the President formulates the legislative measures he proposes or the administrative actions he orders" (Olson 2004). If FACA interfered with this process, the administration claimed, it was unconstitutional.

The dispute reached the Supreme Court, which ruled in favor of the Bush administration. The court held that a presidential claim of executive privilege, employed by the president to protect the confidentiality of important consultations, was not necessary in this case, because the request for information did not have the constitutional "urgency or significance" presented by a criminal trial at the center of a previous case involving executive privilege, *U.S. v. Nixon* 418 U.S. 683 (1974). The Court instead sent the case back to lower federal courts with instructions that they employ "a deferential eye toward protecting executive prerogatives. The Court did not address the broader point of FACA's constitutionality" (Rudalvige 2005, 191). The administration's unflagging defense of prerogative also appeared in its approach to running the executive branch, a job given unusual significance by George W. Bush.

Managing the Executive Branch

The public perception of the Bush administration's direction of the executive branch varied greatly during its time in office. The conventional wisdom about this aspect of his professional reputation soared and sank over the course of his presidency. In the wake of 9/11 and the successful invasion of Afghanistan, views of the administration's competence soared and admiring books about Bush's management style appeared (Kettl, 2003). With the onset of the difficult military occupation of Iraq and the fumbled response to Hurricane Katrina, however, studies appeared decrying the administration's conduct of the executive branch (Aberbach 2007; Pfiffner 2007). The truth is more complex than either of these summary statements would suggest. Bush's MBA background and strongly executive approach to his office made management a high priority for him. Aggressive management comported well with the unitary executive view that the administration took toward the Constitution. It also produced considerable controversy. One source of dispute was Bush's executive assertion of wartime powers after 9/11 involving detainees and secrecy, discussed later in this chapter. Another was the administration's effort to change many long-standing relationships involving "permanent Washington"—the networks of administrators, congressional committees, and interest groups.

George W. Bush and his administration had little regard for "permanent Washington" and thus sought to assert control over an executive branch that might not always see things the president's way. In this, Bush resembled his avowed mentor, Ronald Reagan. Bush emulated the Reagan approach to the bureaucracy regarding several important processes—executive branch appointments, White House cabinet and department relations, review procedures for administrative regulations, contracting for federal services, and program performance evaluations. Beginning with Bush and his White House staff and working outward, we next explore how Bush's pure "executive style" manifested itself in the operations of the executive branch.

George W. Bush began his executive branch preparations early, before the battle over the Florida election results had been resolved. He announced Andrew Card as his chief of staff on November 26, and his top White House staff had been appointed by early December. His top aides had long experience working with him. Almost 30 percent of initial EOP (Executive Office of the President) staff was from Texas, and more than 80 percent of that EOP staff had worked on the 2000 Bush campaign. Bush was following the pattern of many recent presidents in surrounding himself with long-time political associates at the upper levels of the White House staff. Foremost among these were Karen Hughes, chief spokesperson for the 2000 campaign, and Karl Rove, head campaign strategist. Hughes served as counselor to the president and de facto head of the communications operation; Rove headed a new Office of Strategic Initiatives. Condoleezza Rice, a former aide of Bush's father, led the National Security Council, and Margaret Spellings, an education aide to Bush during his time as governor, directed domestic policy formulation. Alberto Gonzales, a former Texas Supreme Court judge appointed by then-Governor Bush, became White House Counsel.

Early in the George W. Bush presidency, it became clear that Card was not serving as a palace guard, controlling all access to the president. Instead, all of the White House staff people mentioned above had direct access to the president, as did Bush's influential vice president, Dick Cheney. In formulating and boosting the administration's initial agenda, these top staff people, with firm ties to the president, engaged in a wide ranging strategic and substantive conversation. Leading figures in the cabinet, including Defense Secretary Donald Rumsfeld and Secretary of State Colin Powell, also had regular access to the president, which allowed them influence over the administration's agenda. Rumsfeld came strongly recommended by Cheney, and Powell had served in the first Bush presidency as head of the Joint Chiefs of Staff. Bush's long time personal friend and head of the 2000 campaign, Don Evans, became commerce secretary.

9/11 produced a great exogenous shock to this system, and resulted in the creation of a new Office of Homeland Security, headed by former Pennsylvania Governor Tom Ridge. As an office, the organization had little bureaucratic clout, with no control over budgets or personnel. These powers were increased in late 2002 when the organization was expanded to become a cabinet department. In the second term, many of Bush's long-time staff people were promoted to cabinet positions. Alberto Gonzales became attorney general; Condoleezza Rice, secretary of state; and Margaret Spellings, secretary of education. With the rise of political difficulties in the second term, Bush reached out beyond his original "zone of comfort" for senior staff. Joshua Bolton, a long time Washington hand, moved from director of the Office of Management and Budget to head of the White House staff upon Card's resignation in 2005. Fred Fielding, a veteran of the Reagan White House, replaced Gonzales as White House counsel in 2007 to help fend off challenges from the newly Democratic Congress. When Gonzales resigned in mid-2007, he was replaced by Federal District Judge Michael Mukasey, chosen in part because of his ability to be confirmed by the now Democratically controlled Senate.

What goals are evident in Bush's staffing decisions at the highest levels of the presidency? Andrew Rudalvige describes them as a staff and issue management style marked by "strong politicization and centralization" (Rudalvige 2007, 148). Strong politicization meant Bush's use of staff and approach to issues aimed to further an agenda of pressing executive prerogative—through a unitary executive approach—in order to maximize the formal power of the president himself. Further, management of a GOP coalition from the White House would enhance presidential regime authority. Centralization of power and authority was the essential means for successful politicization of the executive branch.

This twin emphasis on politicization and centralization appeared early on in the administration's appointment process. The new administration developed an appointment process in the mold of that employed by the Reagan White House, which had sought to gain political control over what it viewed as a hostile bureaucracy upon taking office in 1981. In the George W. Bush administration, senior White House staff were appointed first, so that they could give "clear direction" to subsequent cabinet appointees. Subcabinet appointees resulted from a process in which the White House staff played a large role, so as to maximize prospects for centralized White House control of cabinet departments. During his presidency, Bush at times resorted to recess appointments for controversial appointees who were unlikely to receive Senate confirmation. Recess appointees, named when the Senate is in recess, can serve without confirmation until the end of the next session of Congress. UN ambassador John Bolton, who had served as policy director on the 2000 campaign and in the State Department before taking the UN position, was a prominent recess appointee who was not confirmed by the Senate (Aberbach 2007, 116). More than a third of the initial executive branch appointees had worked on the 2000 Bush campaign, 43 percent worked in the first Bush presidency, and another 20 percent came from trade associations and lobbying firms (Rudalvige 2007, 140). This led to a sort of "team Bush" approach among the president's appointees, many of whom viewed themselves as the president's agents within the executive branch.

Though this approach did boost presidential control, some negative effects resulted. Perspectives beyond the consensus positions of "team Bush" were unlikely to gain serious consideration over time, an accusation leveled at the administration regarding its decision to initiate war with Iraq and its conduct of the subsequent occupation (Woodward 2006). Aggressive politicization also led to great rows over the administration's use of scientific information. Critics argued that the "echo chamber" of the Bush administration ignored important evidence on a variety of scientific issues (Mooney 2005). The firing of eight US attorneys for supposedly insufficient loyalty to the White House drew a congressional investigation in 2007, leading to questions about Attorney General Gonzales' testimony under oath and eventually to his resignation (Johnston and Lipton 2007).

The Office of Management and Budget and Federal Regulation

The George W. Bush administration also followed the Reagan example in employing the Office of Management and Budget (OMB) as a means for shaping federal regulations in accord with the president's agenda. This OMB power had its origins in executive orders issued by Ronald Reagan. Executive Order 12291 required that "major" federal regulations—those with an economic impact of more than $100 million annually—be submitted to OMB's Office of Information and Regulatory Affairs (OIRA) sixty days before the publication of the initial notice of the regulation in the *Federal Register* and then again thirty days before the publication of the final rule. Non-major rules also had to be submitted to OIRA during a shorter screening period. The executive order gave OIRA power to stay the publication of a regulation, require the issuing agency to respond to OIRA's criticisms, and recommend withdrawal of the regulation if OIRA was not satisfied with the revised regulation. A second executive order, 12498, further enhanced OIRA power by requiring agencies to submit to OIRA any regulations they might consider in the coming year (Executive Order 12498).

Bill Clinton replaced these orders with Executive Order 12866, which revised the review process but kept OIRA's role largely intact. OIRA employed cost-benefit analysis in reviewing regulations, a form of policy analysis that allowed OIRA to substantively review all federal regulations. Since the head of OIRA was a presidential appointee, this new process amounted to a growth in presidential oversight and coordination over vast areas of federal regulation, enthusiastically continued in the George W. Bush administration. Bush appointed Dr. John Graham of Harvard's Center for Risk Analysis as head of OIRA. Graham instituted comprehensive cost-benefit analysis in regulatory review: "setting new requirements for reviewing the costs and benefits of regulatory proposals, establishing a higher threshold for reaching scientific certainty in regulatory decisions, and creating new opportunities for outside experts to challenge the government's conclusions about the dangers that a rule was designed to mitigate" (Singer 2005, 903). This aggressive regulatory review produced its share of controversy. The *New York Times* in the summer of 2004 devoted a series of articles to linkages between OIRA and the parts of the business community that seemingly resulted in regulatory outcomes benefiting those business interests. For example, the "Administration, at the request of lumber and paper companies, gave Forest Service Managers the right to approve logging in federal forests without the usual environmental reviews" (Brinkley 2004). The administration also used the Data Quality Act, which allowed anyone to challenge any federal regulation as based on unreliable science, and to question many proposed rules. This led a number of scientists to accuse the administration of politicizing science (Union of Concerned Scientists 2004). Such controversies reflected the effectiveness of the Bush White House in inserting its preferences into the federal regulatory process.

The arrival of a Democratic Congress in 2007 prompted the Bush administration to revise Clinton's Executive Order 12866 in order to increase presidential control over regulation writing. The revised order strengthened the administration's regulatory review over agencies in several ways. First, the order required agencies to submit to OMB and submit for public comment any regulatory changes having an impact of $100 million or more on the economy. Second, agencies were required to state in writing the "specific market failure" that they intended to cure with new regulations. Such failures, according to OMB, might be insufficient competition or insufficient product labeling (Skrzycki 2007). Third, regulators would have to estimate the total annual costs and benefits of new regulations issued each year and the regulation writing process must be overseen in each agency by a political appointee (Skrzycki 2007). Congressional Democrats and public interest groups voiced great displeasure with this new extension of administration power. Democrat Henry Waxman, chair of the House Committee on Oversight and Government Reform, declared: "The executive order allows the political staff at the White House to dictate decisions on health and safety issues, even if the government's own impartial experts disagree. This is a terrible way to govern, but great news for special interests," but Jeffrey A. Rosen, general counsel of OMB, termed the order "a classic good government measure that will make federal agencies more open and accountable" (Pear 2007). To circumscribe regulatory battles with Democrats in Congress, the administration, in the words of Columbia Law School professor Peter L. Strauss, achieved "a major increase in White House control over domestic government" (Pear 2007). These changes appeared at the outset of a confirmation battle with the Democratically controlled Senate over the nomination of Susan E. Dudley to replace John Graham as head of OIRA. Dudley, like Graham, opposed regulation unless a major market failure needed correction. Facing a hostile Senate, Graham's appointment died in committee in 2006. Bush named Dudley a recess appointment in April 2007. The timing of her appointment permitted her to serve as head of OIRA until the end of Bush's presidency without Senate confirmation.

New Departures in Federal Contracting and Performance Evaluation

Beyond a conservative redirection in federal regulation accomplished by an expansion of White House control over regulators, the Bush administration sought to restructure the employment practices within the executive branch. One major initiative concerned "competitive sourcing," which is the use of private contractors to perform government duties. The number of these contractors employed in such activities grew considerably during the administration, "Creating something of a blended workforce in areas ranging from information technology to military interrogation" (Rudalvige 2007, 140). Contractors billed the government some $400 billion in 2006, a sharp rise from the $207 billion billed in 2000 (Shane and Nixon 2007). The outsourcing initiatives met with strong resistance from public employee unions and sympathetic Democrats in Congress, fueled by controversies over the effectiveness of contracted operations in repairing the damage from Hurricane Katrina and in assisting in the post-invasion occupation of Iraq (Aberbach 2007, 128).

Another administration management initiative, the Program Assessment Rating Tool (PART), attempted to include program performance information in the annual budget preparation process. PART ambitiously sought to determine whether programs were effective by "systematically assessing program management and actual results" and by attaching "budgetary and management consequences to programs that cannot demonstrate their effectiveness" (Breul 2007, 24). Alongside this system, the administration installed a "traffic light" grading system, the Executive Branch Management Scorecard, to track progress at management improvement for each major department and agency. Every ninety days, the OMB published revised traffic light scores—red for poor, yellow for intermediate, and green for good—available for public viewing over the Internet. At the outset of this initiative early in the Bush presidency, 110 of 130 scores were red; by late 2008 the number of red scores had shrunk considerably, indicating management progress by OMB's standards. The comprehensiveness of this evaluation process was unprecedented and reflects Bush's particular emphasis on government management. Further evidence of this lay in the appointment of Clay Johnson, a top aide of Governor Bush, as head of management initiatives early in the new administration.

Management Shortfalls: Katrina and Iraq

Despite the Bush administration's emphasis on management, public attention on these matters was mostly drawn to severe deficiencies during the Hurricane Katrina response and the Iraq occupation. This led at least one commentator to suggest that much of the blame for Bush's declining public support during his second term resulted from the public's view of incompetent government management by his administration: "Voters' complaints about George W. Bush . . . are more about competence than ideology. . . . Iraq. Katrina." (Barone 2006). No doubt much of the administration's management legacy will be shaped by the Katrina and Iraq episodes. What were the administration's shortcomings in each instance? Significant indeed; but in important respects, not entirely due to the administration's own handling of the matters. In Iraq, the new and less than fully competent Iraqi government complicated administration of the postwar situation. The Katrina response involved significant coordination problems with state and local governments, particularly in Louisiana.

Problems with the Iraq conflict are well known—faulty intelligence about weapons of mass destruction and the relationship of Saddam Hussein with Al Qaeda; a difficult and protracted military occupation—expensive in both money and lives—and mismanagement of funds allocated to the Iraqi government and to US government contractors in Iraq. The sources of these problems are multiple, but many of them fall under the category of unanticipated outcomes. Could so many large and unanticipated outcomes be due to management shortcomings at the highest levels of the White House? The original battle plan devised by General Tommy Franks and Defense Secretary Donald Rumsfeld, which proved quite successful, apparently did not receive widespread commentary during its formulation. So far so good, despite the narrow process (POLO STEP 2007). Broader perspectives about the overall Iraq occupation, however, seem to have been subject to a similarly constricted review. Alternative analysis existed to that employed by the administration in shaping policy. Extensive, high cost estimates by the State and Defense Department analysts concerning the Iraq occupation and proposals for a larger troop presence for the Iraq occupation urged by many uniformed officers received little presidential attention (Waas 2006). Andrew Rudalvige suggests that "the president either did not heed, or did not seek out, competing arguments on a variety of questions central to the conduct of the war and its aftermath" (Rudalvige 2007, 153). If true, this was a serious management deficiency producing great political costs for the administration. As the Iraq occupation proceeded, the president's political capital steadily shrank.

The Katrina response involved all three levels of American government—federal, state, and local—and blame for management shortfalls must be accordingly dispersed. The flooding problems in New Orleans, scene of the most celebrated disaster, grew from a legacy of prior dredging and the construction of inadequate dams by the Army Corps of Engineers, which left the city quite vulnerable to flooding. Journalist Michael Grunwald defined the situation this way: "Unfortunately, America has concluded that what went wrong in Katrina was the government's response to disaster, not the government's contribution to the disaster. . . . The devastation of Katrina was a direct result of America's water resources policy, which is not a policy at all but an annual scramble for appropriations" (Grunwald 2006, 33). Local and state officials approved water projects around the city to facilitate shipping at the expense of public safety. The problems in New Orleans were decades in the making, involving public officials at the local, state, and national levels of government (Pfiffner 2007, 16). The response of New Orleans local government and Louisiana state government before and after Katrina hit New Orleans was far less than resolute and contributed to the magnitude of the disaster.

But personnel and program deficiencies in the Federal Emergency Management Agency (FEMA) also plagued the Katrina response. FEMA had recently been placed in the new Department of Homeland Security, and its mission had been broadened to include responses to future terrorist attacks. Budget and personnel were shifted from traditional emergency relief operations. In the midst of this redirection, none of FEMA's top three positions were occupied by people with any disaster relief experience (FEMA the Feeble, 2005). Michael Brown, FEMA director, was among these and received harsh criticism for the tardy FEMA response. The president, for his part, did not handle his public response to the calamity well. On vacation when the hurricane hit, he waited before visiting the scene of devastation, preferring instead to "fly over" the area two days after Katrina's arrival on the way back to Washington, D.C., after speechmaking in California. Among his initial public comments was praise for Michael Brown's work: "Brownie, you are doing a heck of a job." Within two weeks, Brown had resigned in the midst of a sluggish FEMA response to the disaster, which had cost one thousand lives and $100 billion in damage (Brinkley 2006).

As in other areas of his presidency, George W. Bush's management efforts engendered both conflict and controversy. James Pfiffner claims "his deficiencies as a manager have undermined his policy victories. These deficiencies include his lack of systematic deliberation over policy alternatives and his failure to weigh sufficiently the judgments of military and other public administration professionals" (Pfiffner 2007, 17). Certainly these shortcomings manifested themselves in important instances: during the Iraq occupation and in the response to Katrina, as noted above. But the broader management record of the Bush administration requires more nuanced assessment. Bush centralized management power through his initiatives at OMB and sought to systematically grade and improve management performance.

The measured response to 9/11 and the well conducted 2001–2002 military operations in Afghanistan (Pfiffner 2005; Woodward 2002, 2006) must be counted as management successes alongside more celebrated failures. In the months after 9/11, the Bush White House engaged in wide ranging consultations that produced advocacy of multiple possible courses of action. But these successes occurred early in the Bush presidency. The later responses to Katrina and the Iraq occupation included a more constricted flow of information and alternatives to the president, which served to inhibit good management of these admittedly difficult situations. Over the long term, will the celebrated management calamities of Iraq and Katrina constitute the Bush legacy in government management? That seems unlikely. The Bush administration engaged in aggressive centralization and politicization of management duties, a legacy that his White House successors may well be inclined to continue. That suggests a broader and more consequential management legacy than that suggested by just Iraq and Katrina.

An Executive-Centered Approach toward Congress

The most conspicuous evidence of George W. Bush's pure "executive style" as president can be found in his relations with Congress. Charles Jones notes that the executive style "is less attentive to the collaborative dimensions of policy and lawmaking," instead defining "the job proactively by tasks rather than by constraints" (Jones 2007A, 118). Bush conceived of his relations with the legislature in hierarchical, managerial terms, not dissimilar to his approach to the executive branch. For most of the time during his first term, a Republican-controlled Congress accepted its role as a junior partner in an executive-led national GOP regime. Bush's operating style with the legislature preferred some leadership skills over others. The task with the legislature was conceived as primarily managerial, which also involved partisan coalitional and heresthetic skills. Public rhetorical skills and bargaining skills were deemphasized. The signal task for Bush with the legislature involved designating a limited but clear agenda for congressional action. But agenda formation did not entail much initial bargaining within the administration or with Congress. As Bush early on told chief administration lobbyist Nick Calio "we will not negotiate with ourselves, ever. . . . People will move toward us and continue to move toward us" (Brownstein 2007, 230).

Though the administration did seek Democratic support for its proposals, as time passed that became less available and the White House engaged in partisan coalition management, depending on unified GOP floor votes to narrowly pass its agenda into law. The White House then framed its agenda primarily for GOP consumption and heresthetically structured alternatives in ways GOP lawmakers could use to their benefit, often at the expense of Democrats. This coalition-enhancing heresthetic was most successfully employed in the 2002 elections, but became steadily less successful in subsequent elections as exogenous events—particularly the bad news from the Iraq occupation—made administration frames less appealing to voters who were not GOP true believers. Rhetorical creativity, more important for public persuasion than in moving legislators, received correspondingly little emphasis in dealings with Congress. In meetings with legislative leaders, Bush would often repeat his public statements, which often left lawmakers unimpressed. Bargaining, when it occurred, would happen only when absolutely necessary (Brownstein 2007, 243).

Bush's approach to Congress, then, focused heavily on endogenous constraints within his own partisan coalition. When he sought reforms that failed to unite GOP lawmakers—on Social Security and immigration—he failed with Congress. Through mid-2005, this approach produced a considerable record of legislative accomplishments. A central paradox of the Bush presidency, however, lay in the mounting exogenous costs of Bush's distinctly endogenous focus upon his partisan coalition in Congress. The exogenous costs were several. First, as Bush racked up a series of partisan victories on the House and Senate floors from 2001 to 2005, he created increasing enmity among Democratic lawmakers and party activists. This meant future accomplishments relying upon Democratic support would be impossible. Second, certain administration agenda items proved popular with the GOP base but not with moderate and independent voters, such as the intervention in the Terri Schiavo case in early 2005, when Congress ordered court review of a controversial end-of-life decision for an incapacitated woman (Cook 2005, 173). Third, the insular White House management of the war on terror facilitated strong Democratic attacks on the Iraq occupation as its course became more difficult. Cumulatively, the record of the Bush administration with Congress is one of self-limiting successes culminating in a Democratic takeover of Congress in 2006 that extinguished prospects for any further legislative breakthroughs.

The Bush administration's partisan approach, based on hierarchical management of a compliant GOP congressional coalition, did rack up many successes in its heyday. The tactical sequence of its operation was ably summarized by Bertram Johnson: "First, drive a metaphorical 'stake in the sand' by pressing for swift passage of a House bill that is close to the president's ideal proposal; second, place pressure on pivotal senators to toe the administration line; and, third, be willing to compromise if necessary, particularly with respect to social policy" (Johnson 2004, 174–75). House rules allow a majority party to work its will regarding the legislative agenda, but the Senate is a much different matter. Sixty votes are required to stop filibusters—unlimited debate—and the GOP never commanded more that fifty-five votes during the Bush presidency. This allowed minority Democrats to employ filibusters on certain controversial issues, including an unprecedented use of extended debate regarding some federal district court nominees. Tax and many budget bills, however, were not subject to filibusters under Senate rules, and the administration scored major victories with them from 2001 to 2005, including two large tax cuts and annual passage of a budget acceptable to the administration.

The Roots of Party Government

Analysts of national legislative-executive relations had not seen such a unified partisan coalition in action in recent decades. Several observers termed the process as "parliamentary" or "neoparliamentary," reflecting the ability of the executive in such systems to routinely receive legislative endorsement of his major party proposals. (Owens 2006; Schier 2005; Pomper 2003). British observer John Owens summarized the characteristics of "American-style party government" from 2001 to 2005 under George W. Bush. First, the two congressional parties "present meaningful and commonly agreed legislative agendas," second, "they are ideologically homogeneous and act cohesively under strong centralized and coordinated leadership, especially when in the majority" and third, "majority leaders of the respective chambers and the same party coordinate their actions with the president, and typically accept his leadership . . . in order to implement the most important priorities on their party agenda" (Owens 2006, 133–34).

This is an extraordinary set of circumstances. The roots of such an unusual set of institutional relationships lie far beyond the Bush White House. Changes at the mass level helped make this institutional behavior possible. As noted in the previous chapter, party "sorting," in which a tighter fit appeared between party identification and ideology, has been ongoing for decades (Fiorina and Levendusky, 2006) creating greater ideological homogeneity among identifiers of both parties. That produced primary electorates more likely to nominate liberal Democrats and conservative Republicans. Add to this the possible polarization of the electorate involving a shrinkage of the number of voters in the ideological and partisan center (Campbell 2007; Abramowitz, 2007), and you have an electorate more inclined to accept partisan extremes. Concurrent with this has been a rise in straight-ticket voting (Barone 2006), which is more likely to produce party government. Also, highly partisan redistricting has produced many districts with strongly one-sided partisan and ideological profiles that elect liberal Democrats or conservative Republicans to the US House (Jacobson 2006).

All these trends gave George W. Bush a partisan group of legislators ready to follow his lead in 2001. As Representative Tom Davis (R-VA) put it, the feeling was "he's our leader, let's get behind the team leader" (Brownstein 2007, 272). To the Bush administration, a largely partisan approach seemed sound strategy, for several reasons. First, major administration initiatives were likely to receive uniform GOP support, making retreat unnecessary on policy specifics in order to bargain a compromise. Second, Democratic voters strongly disliked Bush because of the circumstances of his 2000 election, making the possibility of substantial Democratic support low. Third, reaching out to Democrats could produce divisions among GOP lawmakers as the administration bargained on policy substance. Fourth, Bush himself was disinclined to bargain and had large policy ambitions that he believed he could satisfy with GOP support. In the short term, the partisan approach surely seemed the right row to hoe.

Add a White House strongly committed to partisan governance to the forces facilitating polarization in Congress and it is no surprise that partisan voting reached nearly unprecedented levels from 2001 to 2006. Keith Poole and Howard Rosenthal discovered that political polarization in congressional roll call voting climbed every year from 2001 to 2006, reaching the highest levels of polarization in 120 years in 2005 to 2006 (Poole and Rosenthal 2007, 5). The trend toward increasing polarization, evident since 1970, actually accelerated during the George W. Bush presidency. Within this overall trend, however, lie a variety of specific variations in interbranch relations, detailed in the following paragraphs.

Patterns of Presidential-Congressional Relations

With Bush entering the White House during a time of political polarization and after a highly controversial election, it's not surprising that his relationships with Congress usually involved what Charles O. Jones terms "competitive partisanship" (Jones 2007B, 408 onwards). This "is typified by the parallel development of proposals at each end of Pennsylvania Avenue or by the two parties in each house of Congress. Often these proposals represent different approaches to the problem, with participants in both institutions having sufficient support and expertise to be credibly involved" (Jones 2005, 27). The White House and Hill GOP aligned themselves on a common approach, and Democrats, touting rival alternatives, would attempt to derail GOP initiatives or, if possible, induce compromise bargains. Given the remarkable GOP unity behind Bush's major agenda items (detailed below), Democrats from 2001 to 2006 often had to be content with obstructing or merely voicing displeasure at inevitable partisan outcomes. One brief cooperative period during the Bush presidency existed in contrast to such partisan battles. That occurred after 9/11 and primarily concerned national security legislation. In this period and on these issues, bipartisanship reigned, defined by Jones as "active and cooperative involvement of Republicans and Democrats in several phases of the lawmaking process, from problem definition to program approval" (Jones 2005, 29). Even in this period, however, Bush sought to dominate congressional lawmaking, successfully inducing Democratic consent on a number of measures, such as the Patriot Act and Authorization of Force resolution concerning Iraq, that later in his presidency became topics of intense partisan contestation.

Prior to 9/11, 2001 consisted of much competitive partisanship involving president and Congress, with the advantage in the competition shifting with control of the US Senate. Before May 1, Republicans controlled a 50–50 Senate with the vote of Vice President Cheney as presiding officer. The defection of Senator James Jeffords of Vermont from the Republican Party at the end of April, and his willingness to caucus as an independent with the Democrats, effectively shifted partisan control on the chamber. During these shifts, partisan voting diverged greatly on major issues on which Bush took a position. Congressional Quarterly's "Key Votes" during the pre-9/11 period provide evidence of this. Key votes have been found to be "a very parsimonious (that is, consistent) measure of congressional support for [Republican] presidents" (Shull and Vanderleeuw 1987, 573). During the first nine months of 2001, Bush's positions on key votes received the support of 89.4 percent of House and 92.9 percent of Senate GOPers. Democrats lined up overwhelmingly on the other side, with Bush garnering only 15.8 percent support in the House and a tiny 8.5 percent in his favor in the Senate.

9/11 immediately induced more bipartisanship in floor voting on key votes. GOP support for Bush rose even higher in the twelve months after the crisis, to 94.5 percent in the House and 93.1 percent in the Senate. The big shift, though, came through increasing Democratic support for Bush. House Democrats supported him on key votes 25.8 percent of the time and Senate Democrats greatly increased their voting for Bush, backing him 53.8 percent of the time. The largest Democratic support came on security-related votes. Almost all Democrats backed Bush's position on the Patriot Act, for example. Democratic support for Bush's position on key votes strongly correlated positively (+ .59 at the .05 level of significance) during this period, for the only time during his presidency. This was a time when Bush, riding high in the polls in the wake of a great national security crisis, had much political capital. Democrats were loath to challenge him on national security measures.

The result was an unusual spurt of legislative productivity, producing by David Mayhew's calculation, seventeen major laws, the highest total for a new president in his first two years since 1945 (Jones 2007A, 122). These measures included one of the largest tax cuts in American history, a major reform of federal education policy, the Patriot Act creating new domestic security measures, a bailout of national airlines, an airport security law, a use of force resolution for Afghanistan and another for Iraq, creation of the Homeland Security Department, fast track trade authority for the president, corporate accounting reform, election reform, and $40 billion in emergency aid to New York City in the wake of 9/11. On only one major piece of legislation during this time, campaign finance reform in 2002, did Bush sign legislation to which he had major objections. That bill passed in bipartisan fashion and Bush was loath to buck the popular reformist consensus.

As 9/11 faded, partisan differences on many issues reasserted themselves in Congress. The 2002 election, involving aggressive use of national security issues by the president to boost GOP prospects, deepened the distrust across party lines and ensured that competitive partisanship would reemerge in congressional-presidential relations. From 2002 to 2005, congressional Republicans continued to offer Bush resounding support on key votes, at levels of 86.5 percent in the House and 89.9 percent in the Senate. Democratic backing for the president's position declined significantly from the post 9/11 unity period, with Bush garnering only 18.4 percent support in the House and 32.3 percent support in the Senate. Despite the increased polarization, Hill Republicans were able to achieve a string of important legislative victories for Bush during this time; twenty-four major laws were enacted, by David Mayhew's calculation (Mayhew 2008). These included a major Medicare prescription drug benefit, an additional $350 billion tax cut, a partial-birth abortion ban, and unborn victims of violence law (making death of a fetus a murder) in 2003. In 2004, Congress passed important overhauls of intelligence gathering and corporate taxation. The year 2005 saw reforms of bankruptcy statutes and class action lawsuits become law, along with an energy bill and the Central American Free Trade Agreement. In 2006, Congress passed a revision of military commissions laws, port security legislation, a seven hundred mile fence on the Mexican border, and an agreement to share civilian nuclear technology with India. During 2001 to 2006, Bush and his GOP Congress had passed into law 41 major measures, an average of 6.8 per year. That is above the average of major legislation passed from 1946–2000 as compiled by David Mayhew (2005B). During that period, 317 major laws went on the books, an average of 6.2 per year (Mayhew 2005B, 121).

The Costs of Partisan Achievement

The Bush administration's record of partisan achievement was not without its costs. It produced an increasingly intractable congressional minority party that, upon becoming the majority party in 2007, forcefully resisted presidential leadership. Before the 2006 elections, under the emphatic partisan direction of House Minority Leader Nancy Pelosi (D-CA) and Senate Minority Leader Harry Reid (D-NV)—chosen as leaders in the wake of the Democrats' bitter 2002 election defeat—Hill Democrats issued increasing rhetorical and procedural challenges to Bush as his public popularity slowly declined from the heights of 9/11. Just seven Democrats in the House and two in Senate, for example, supported the 2003 tax cut. No more than four Senate Democrats supported any of Bush's controversial first-term appointments to federal appellate courts. Senate filibusters supported by virtually every Democrat blocked Bush's medical malpractice bill and delayed his class action reform proposals in 2003. "Overall, in Bush's first term, Democrats voted together in the House more often than they did under Clinton; in the Senate, Democrats equaled the unprecedented level of party unity they had achieved under Clinton" (Brownstein 2007, 235). Long-standing congressional norms of reciprocity and accommodation across the two parties weakened as battle lines hardened.

The 2006 elections, ushering in a Democratic Congress, tilted competitive partisanship against the president. Bush encountered the costs of partisan rule in 2007 to 2008, when Pelosi became Speaker and Reid Majority Leader. Bush's legislative agenda suffered during the last two years of his presidency. On key votes, Bush prevailed far less often in 2007 than previously (New Majority Struggles 2008). His overall presidential support score in Congressional voting dropped 42 percent—from 80 percent in 2006 to 38 percent in 2007—exceeded only by Bill Clinton's decline in support in the new GOP Congress of 1995 (Benson 2008, 133). The unprecedented drops of Clinton and Bush reflected the strong polarization of Congress in recent decades, which Bush's partisan leadership had facilitated much of the time from 2001 through 2006. Rare indeed were bipartisan accomplishments like 2008's energy bill and federal surveillance law revamping. Bush faced constant conflict with the Democratic Congress over Iraq war funding and budget priorities. With his informal powers of political capital greatly diminished, he was only able to prevail by employing his formal veto power, bolstered by support from the diminished ranks of GOP lawmakers in the House and Senate. His fellow congressional partisans prevented several override attempts and forced Democratic leaders to cut deals with the president.

A second cost of partisan rule was the manipulation of chamber rules by both parties for partisan gain. This manipulation was most pointedly used by the majority House Republicans during final passage of the Medicare prescription drug bill in 2003. Normally, House floor votes take about fifteen minutes to complete. On November 23, 2003, the vote on final passage of the Medicare bill began at 3:00 A.M. and did not conclude until two hours and fifty-one minutes later. Why the delay? The Majority GOP leadership had to cajole dissident Republican members into supporting the bill, which ultimately passed 220 to 215. Democrats, understandably, were fuming. One anonymous House Republican who voted against the bill admitted that "It was an outrage. It was profoundly ugly and beneath the dignity of Congress"

(Mann and Ornstein 2006, 3). Senate rules gave minority Democrats more procedural clout than their House counterparts possessed. Minority Leader Harry Reid in 2005 effectively "shut down" the Senate for a day to score symbolic points with his partisan base about the Iraq war. Reid invoked a rarely employed rule to force the Senate into a closed session to pressure Senate Republicans to complete a long-delayed investigation of the administration's use of prewar Iraq intelligence. Reid's predecessor as minority leader, Tom Daschle (D-SD) had considered using this tactic but did not want to do so without warning the majority leader first. Reid, in contrast, sprang it on Majority Leader Bill Frist (R-TN) unawares. As the *Washington Post* noted at the time, the "notion of one party springing the rule on another party without warning was so alien that senators could not cite a previous example" (Brownstein 2007, 340).

Several other congressional procedures fell victim to partisan manipulation from 2001 to 2006. In the House, use of closed rules that prohibit floor amendments steadily increased over the time the GOP controlled Congress (Wolfensburger, 2005). The House Rules Committee, responsible for setting the floor schedule and terms of debate for bills, at times rushed major legislation to the floor for a very quick vote. It did this by waiving all points of order on conference committee reports, which are the statements of the agreement between House and Senate conferees on the language of a bill for final passage. This allowed votes on final passage in such haste that House members could not fully comprehend the contents of the conference reports. But then, conference committees usually involved bargaining between House and Senate Republicans, with Democrats left out of any meaningful participation in creation of the final compromise version of legislation (Mann and Ornstein 2006, 172).

Another cost of party rule was the great decline in congressional oversight of the administration. Though the Republican Congress had showered subpoenas upon present and former Clinton administration officials in the late 1990s, the Republican Congress issued no subpoenas compelling testimony by Bush administration officials from 2001 to 2006. The absence of aggressive oversight was most notable regarding the ongoing military occupation of Iraq. The Senate Intelligence Committee moved so slowly in examining the administration's use of prewar intelligence that its investigation was incomplete when the party lost control of the chamber in the 2006 elections. When the Abu Ghraib prisoner abuse scandal arose in 2004, the House Armed Services Committee held a single day of hearings in May. The counterpart Senate committee, chaired by John Warner (R-VA), held a longer series of hearings, but Pentagon resistance caused Warner to end the hearings in the summer.

Representative Chris Shays (R-CT) explained the partisan thinking behind the demise of oversight: "We confused wanting to get through a joint agenda [with the White House] with not doing the kind of oversight [we should have been doing] . . . The argument, subtly, without being spoken, is 'why do we want to embarrass the administration'" (Brownstein 2007, 277).

The abuse of long-standing procedures, demise of oversight, and deterioration of established norms all point to a decline in the deliberative capacity of Congress during the Bush presidency. The legislature sacrificed its internal decision making procedures in order to subordinate itself institutionally to the agenda of the Bush administration. This is not to say that the Bush administration could readily work its will on Capitol Hill. The narrow margins of GOP control meant that the agenda had to be carefully devised to include those items that would receive unified support from Hill Republicans. When the administration attempted proposals that violated this requirement, its agenda stalled. A pointed example involves its 2005 immigration reform proposal, which never received serious consideration in the House. Speaker Dennis Hastert (R-IL) shelved the initiative because it violated his rule that no bill would come to the floor unless it had the support of a "majority of the majority party." Perhaps reflecting the need to keep a limited agenda because of such constraints, the administration took fewer positions on legislation than did its predecessors (Poole 2006).

The strong executive style of George W. Bush sought dominance over Congress and, by carefully limiting its agenda, often achieved it. It has been many decades since Congress deferred so consistently to the White House in its internal operations and legislative output. Future administrations will probably try to emulate the administration's partisan "stake in the sand" strategy when possible. The rules of such a strategy are clear: "focus on a few big things, don't negotiate with yourself, House first and to the right and go public" (Sinclair 2007, 168). But the risks of this strategy became quite apparent in the last two years of the Bush presidency, as Democrats ramped up oversight, investigations, legislative challenges, and public arguments against the administration. Barbara Sinclair summarizes the downside of Bush's strategy: "a president who relies mostly on his base and pursues a partisan strategy almost exclusively finds that when adversity strikes, he has little good will beyond his base—in Congress or the country" (Sinclair 2007, 185).

Managing the Federal Courts

The Bush administration's task of appointing federal judges was of crucial importance to its ambition to create a lasting political regime. Given the lifetime appointments of federal judges and their power in shaping the meaning and enforcement of law, a president can influence legal affairs for many years beyond his time in office. The GOP had embraced a far-reaching agenda in which judicial interpretation would be essential to its achievement: "the devolution of power to state and local governments; economic individualism and privatization of responsibility for social welfare; the use of markets and market principles in lieu of administrative regulation of business, the economy and the environment; and religious or moral revivalism" (Clayton 2005, 8). The courts would play a key role in legitimizing this agenda. Courts often play this role in national politics. Robert Dahl argued that it is unreasonable to expect federal courts to challenge a dominant political regime. Federal judges receive appointment from national party leaders, who choose appointees based on their sympathy with the party's agenda. So presidents and senators overwhelmingly select federal judges from among their own party loyalists (Dahl 1957).

The Bush administration attached high priority to judicial appointments. Given the great regime stakes, the administration faced considerable endogenous pressures from within its coalition to appoint conservative jurists. The revolt of the GOP base over Bush's 2005 Supreme Court nomination of White House Counsel Harriet Miers, a person with no experience as a judge, illustrated the high priority the issue received in Republican circles. Bush also faced considerable exogenous resistance elsewhere in the political environment. Democrats in the Senate, where nominees are approved by majority vote, were aware of the stakes and engaged in unprecedented tactics to block a small number of controversial federal court nominees. To thwart the GOP majority in the chamber from 2001 to 2006, Democrats "challenged some highly experienced, qualified nominees strictly for ideological positions" and "employed the threat of a filibuster, which had seldom been used before then to challenge nominations of any kind" (Yalof 2007, 200). The heat surrounding judicial appointments produced remarkable battles over Senate rules, noted later in this chapter.

The Democrats' strong resistance to certain nominees reflected their distaste toward the Bush administration's partisan, hierarchical, and managerial approach to federal judicial appointments. The administration thoroughly investigated the backgrounds of possible court appointees to make certain they were compatible with the administration's conservative agenda. Support for a strong unitary executive ranked high on the list of issues about which to screen prospective appointees. The administration's two successful Supreme Court appointees, John Roberts and Samuel Alito, both were on record endorsing the unitary executive concept prior to their nominations

(Yalof 2007, 210). Expansion of formal executive power was a central theme in the Bush administration's approach to the judiciary, as it was in just about every other aspect of its approach to Washington governance. Conservative author Terry Eastland explained the strategic importance of executive power for the GOP regime's agenda: "if limited government is your goal, you need a strong presidency to effect that end. If you have a presidency that's simply passive, given the inertial tendencies of Washington, the central government will only grow" (Rosen 2006, 9).

In addition to deference to executive power, the Bush administration sought nominees who would sustain a "strict constructionist" approach to constitutional interpretation. In the administration's view, judges should be governed by the "original intent" of the founders who wrote the Constitution, an approach long advocated by Supreme Court Justice Antonin Scalia, a Reagan appointee. Not for Bush was the concept of a "living Constitution," requiring judges to find new meanings and rights in order to adapt the general wording of the Constitution to contemporary circumstances. For conservatives, this had produced what they saw as the abomination of a constitutional right to abortion in *Roe v. Wade* 410 U.S. 113 (1973), among other abuses of the more liberal courts of the 1960s and 1970s. Bush himself endorsed a conservative judicial philosophy in his first debate with Al Gore in 2000: "I believe that judges ought not to take the place of the legislative branch of government . . . I don't believe in liberal, activist judges. I believe in—I believe in strict constructionists. And those are the kind of judges I will appoint."

The new administration initiated several changes in the judicial appointment process that early on signaled its managerial, hierarchical, and partisan style. First, the White House removed the American Bar Association's (ABA's) Committee on Judicial Selection from its formal role in rating the qualifications of potential judicial candidates. This reflected conservatives' long-held suspicion that the ABA had become a liberal-dominated institution. The committee continued to rate nominees despite this, and those ratings continued to gain the attention of Senate Democrats. Second, the administration drew considerable legal talent from the Federalist Society, a group of lawyers and jurists dedicated to conservative constitutional interpretation. John Roberts and Samuel Alito came from these ranks, and continued to speak before the society once on the Supreme Court. Third, the Bush White House resurrected the Office of Legal Policy (OLP) in the Department of Justice, created by the Reagan administration but abolished during the Clinton presidency. Under Reagan, the office conducted "a rigorous judicial selection process" including daylong interviews by prospective nominees with OLP lawyers

(O'Brien 2004, 138). The Bush administration implemented a similarly rigorous process involving the OLP. OLP lawyers in early 2001 joined with members of the White House Counsel's Office to staff a Judicial Selection Committee, which met regularly to identify potential judicial nominees (Gorman 2004). Because of effective stalling tactics of the Republican Congress during the final years of the Clinton presidency, a large number of federal bench positions remained to be filled. The resurrection of the OLP sent the administration's partisan base a reassuring message about the priority placed on judicial nominations. So did its appointment of Ted Olson as the administration's first solicitor general, the lawyer who usually argues the administration's case before the Supreme Court. Olson had argued *Bush v. Gore* 531 U.S. 98 (2000) on Bush's behalf, had served in Reagan's OLP and was long associated with the Federalist Society. Vetting for conservative constitutional views even extended to the hiring for nonpolitical positions in the Justice Department, an apparent violation of federal civil service law.

A fourth change in the judicial nomination process roiled partisan waters in the Senate. Traditionally, the procedure for federal judicial appointments operated with a norm of deference toward Senators in whose states vacancies existed. The chair of the Senate Judiciary Committee would send a blue slip (named after the paper's color) asking home state Senators if they supported the nominee. If a Senator did not return the blue slip, the committee would not hold a hearing or vote on the nominee. The committee chair in 2001, Senator Orrin Hatch (R-UT), indicated that he would change this procedure to require both Senators to withhold blue slips before halting the progress of a nomination, but not in all cases. This produced a strongly negative reaction from committee Democrats, and Hatch's plans became moot when Democrats took over control of the Senate in early May of 2001. But when Hatch resumed the chair after the 2002 elections, he followed through with his initial blue slip policy.

This change, consistent with the administration's desire for hierarchical partisan management of the judicial nomination process, produced a series of procedural headaches for Senate Republicans. Democrats for the first time resorted to filibusters and filibuster threats to prevent controversial nominees, approved on party-line votes in the Judiciary Committee, from receiving a floor vote. The main battles concerned nominations to circuit courts of appeal, of particular importance because the small number of cases accepted by the Supreme Court on appeal from these courts meant their decisions were often final (Maveety Forthcoming, 12). Over a year after Bush put forth his initial eleven circuit court nominations, only three had received Senate confirmation (O'Brien 2004, 146). The battle really raged in 2003, when Senate Republicans repeatedly tried to end debate and vote on the nominations. Sixty votes are needed to end debate, but forty-five Democrats held firm in refusing to shut off debate. Bush resorted to recess appointments for two of his most controversial circuit court nominees, William Pryor and Charles Pickering, though those appointments lasted only until the end of the next congressional session.

After the 2004 election, in which the GOP gained four seats to increase its majority to fifty-five, Senate Majority Leader Bill Frist proposed a "nuclear option" to end the obstruction. This involved a change in Senate rules to prevent filibusters on judicial nominations, enforceable by a majority vote (Ornstein 2003). His ambitions were derailed by a bipartisan "Gang of Fourteen," led by Senators Ben Nelson (D-NE) and John McCain (R-AZ). Their May 2005 compromise allowed immediate cloture votes on three controversial nominees—William Pryor, Priscilla Owen, and Janice Rogers Brown—and a reservation of future filibusters only for "extraordinary circumstances." Pryor, Owen, and Brown received Senate confirmation. Procedurally, the compromise helped the GOP, because Democrats throughout the remainder of 2005 and 2006 could not amass forty-one votes to reemploy the filibuster weapon. As a result, John Roberts and Samuel Alito gained appointment to the Supreme Court without a threat of a filibuster.

Roberts' nomination, first as an associate justice and then as chief justice upon the death of Chief Justice William Rehnquist, sailed through the Senate because of his sterling legal credentials and sparse record of opinions from the D.C. Circuit Court of Appeals, where he had briefly served. According to an analysis by scholars Jeffrey Segal and Lee Epstein, Roberts placed among the top ten most qualified nominees since the 1930s (Epstein and Segal 2005). Alito's nomination drew more controversy for two reasons. First, as a conservative he was replacing a "moderate" justice, retiring Sandra Day O'Connor, which could tip the court's balance decisively toward judicial conservatism. Second, Alito had an extensive track record of opinions issued during several years as a member of the Court of Appeals for the Third Circuit, inviting much critical scrutiny. In carefully choreographed hearings before the Judiciary Committee, Alito avoided engaging in substantive discussions of controversial judicial issues. Hatch's successor as Judiciary Committee chair, Republican Arlen Specter of Pennsylvania, though one of the party's few moderates in the Senate, faithfully shepherded both Roberts and Alito through the confirmation process. Roberts won confirmation by 78–22; Alito by a narrower margin of 58–42.

Between the Roberts and Alito confirmations was the Bush administration's one major managerial misstep regarding judicial nominations. Shortly after O'Connor's retirement announcement, the president announced the nomination of Harriet Miers, White House counsel, to the Supreme Court.

Miers had never served on the bench and her credentials earned her a rating as one of the least qualified Supreme Court nominees since the New Deal; sixth from the bottom in Epstein and Segal's analysis, with three of the six ranked below her never gaining confirmation (Epstein and Segal 2005). Conservative critics, including George Will, Patrick Buchanan, and defeated Reagan Supreme Court nominee Robert Bork raised concerns about her lack of experience and fidelity to conservative constitutional interpretation. Her initial interviews with Judiciary Committee members did not go well, and when the Judiciary Committee demanded internal White House memos Miers had written on constitutional matters, the White House withdrew her nomination.

Why had this gone so badly for the administration? The president may have assumed that he had more political capital in late 2005 than he in fact had. Katrina mismanagement had hurt his public standing, as had the ongoing bad news from Iraq. The administration also probably miscalculated the importance of the appointment to the GOP base, who very much wanted a proven conservative figure added to the Supreme Court bench. This is another example of the narrow margin for error produced by Bush's partisan governing style. Without unified GOP support, he could not prevail on Supreme Court appointments. Endogenous coalition constraints forced him to an abrupt about-face.

The arrival of a Democratic Congress in 2006 greatly reduced administration success in pushing judicial nominations through the Senate. Incoming Judiciary Chair Patrick Leahy (D-VT) signaled a more defiant stance toward the administration, reinstating the traditional blue slip procedure, which enhanced the power of home state Senators over Bush's nominees. During 2007, only five appellate court nominees gained confirmation, compared to eight of Bill Clinton's nominees approved in 1999, the year of his impeachment and trial by a Republican Congress. Only four hearings on appellate nominees occurred in 2007, compared with ten for Clinton in 1999 (Whelan 2007). The slowdown continued in 2008.

Overall, Bush was able to leave a strong mark upon the federal judiciary through his appointments. The years 2001 to 2005 produced many judicial appointments for conservatives. As of late 2006, Bush had brought the federal judiciary up to 95 percent capacity, with his administration having appointed 46 judges to the US Circuit Court of Appeals and 203 to federal district courts. These totals compare favorably with the record of recent two-term presidents Reagan and Clinton (Yalof 2007, 201). Two relatively young and reliably conservative Supreme Court justices were now on the bench, bolstering the narrow conservative majority in that body. The Bush administration's ideological screening had produced clear success. Scholars Robert Carp, Keith Manning, and Ronald Stidham found that through 2004, Bush's appointees had produced a record of conservative interpretation in their decisions rivaled only by Ronald Reagan's appointees over the past fifty years (Carp, Manning and Stidham 2004, 20–28).

Though the costs of Bush's partisan, hierarchical, and managerial approach to judicial appointments became clear once Democrats assumed control of Congress, for much of Bush's presidency this approach ably achieved the administration's goals. Judicial scholar Nancy Maveety summarizes his legacy: "George W. Bush unquestionably leaves a personal policy legacy and an enviable record of presidential managerial success with respect to judicial staffing" (Maveety forthcoming, 27).

Supreme Court Challenges to Executive Power

The Bush administration's embrace of unitary executive theory included pressing expansive claims of executive power in the federal courts. The White House emphasized support for enhanced executive power as an agenda imperative for its judicial nominees and argued for broad executive power in a series of important cases before the Supreme Court. These cases concerned the status and rights of "unlawful combatants" captured during the administration's campaign against global terrorism. The treatment of such individuals became a matter of great controversy for the administration, as abuses at Abu Ghraib and criticisms of prisoner treatment at the Guantánamo detention facility led to charges that the administration was engaging in torture.

In the wake of the attack on the World Trade Center, the administration in November 2001 issued a military order authorizing the detention of terrorism suspects and their subsequent trial by US military commissions, which are subject to less stringent standards than in US criminal courts. In January 2002, the first terrorism suspects arrived at the Guantánamo Bay detention facility. Under the guidance of White House Counsel Alberto Gonzales, the White House developed a series of controversial guidelines for the handling of detainees. The White House counsel's office wrote a legal memo in January 2002 arguing that the Geneva Conventions on prisoner treatment were inapplicable to detainees. It also approved a July 2002 memo from the Office of Legal Council of the Department of Justice holding that the international Torture Conventions of 1994 prohibit only the most heinous and extreme acts inflicted with an "intensity akin to that which accompanies serious physical injury such as death or organ failure" (Greenberg and Dratel 2005, 215). This became known as "the torture memo." In the spring of 2004, controversy over prisoner treatment reached new levels of intensity with the disclosure of prisoner abuse at the Abu Ghraib detention facility in Iraq.

Was the president constitutionally empowered to so treat prisoners without court review? Due process questions about prisoner treatment soon made their way to the Supreme Court. In June 2004, the Court handed down *Hamdi v. Rumsfeld* 542 U.S. 507 (2004) concerning whether Yaser Esam Hamdi, an "illegal enemy combatant" who was an American citizen, could be detained indefinitely without receiving the habeas corpus right to know the changes against him. The White House argued that given Hamdi's status as an enemy combatant, the executive had legal power to detain him indefinitely without charges. Eight of nine Supreme Court justices disagreed. As an American citizen, Hamdi was entitled to challenge his imprisonment before an impartial judge. The executive branch, the court held, does not have the power to hold a US citizen indefinitely without basic due process protections enforceable through judicial review. Justice O'Connor, writing for the court, argued that while the administration had the right to detain Hamdi: "Threats to military operations posed by a basic system of independent review are not so weighty as to trump a citizen's core rights to challenge meaningfully the government's case and be heard by an impartial adjudicator" (*Hamdi v. Rumsfeld* 542 U.S. 507 2004, 28–29).

A similar controversy reached the Supreme Court in 2006. Salim Ahmed Hamdan was a Yemeni citizen captured by the United States, charged with conspiracy to commit terrorism, and placed in Guantánamo Bay. Once there, he submitted a petition for habeas corpus, challenging the legality of a military commission by which he was about to be tried. The Supreme Court ruled on Hamdi's petition in June 2004. The Bush administration again had claimed that the president, in his capacity of commander in chief, had the power to set up the commissions and operate them. The Supreme Court disagreed, arguing that the commissions were illegal according to both military justice law and the international Geneva Conventions. Justice John Paul Stevens— writing an opinion for a 5–3 majority of a court that was divided over several of the matters at issue (Justice Roberts recused himself, having heard the case prior to his arrival at the Supreme Court)—clearly rejected the administration's arguments: "the executive is bound to comply with the rule of law that prevails in this jurisdiction." Exigency in wartime, he asserted does "not further justify the wholesale jettisoning of procedural protections" (*Hamdan v. Rumsfeld,* 126 S. Ct. 2749 2006, 61). The remedy for this situation, the court held, was a new congressional law creating military commissions with the necessary procedural protections to preserve due process of law.

The Bush administration and Republican Congress responded to the *Hamdan* case by passing into law the Military Commissions Act of 2006, which overrode important aspects of the Supreme Court decision. The law, passed by a largely party-line vote, contradicted the *Hamdan* ruling on several central matters. The law changed previously existing statutes to explicitly forbid the invocation of the Geneva Conventions when executing a writ of habeas corpus, as *Hamdan* had done in bringing his case to court. The law further prevented the use of the Geneva Conventions in any civil actions before federal courts. Any alien determined to be an "enemy combatant" or awaiting determination regarding that status no longer would have access to the courts, which allowed the government to detain such aliens indefinitely. Regarding torture, the law gave the president the power to interpret the meaning and applications of the Geneva Conventions and to set standards for violations or for prisoner treatment that are not grave violations of the Geneva Conventions. Opponents of the law, such as ranking Senate Judiciary Committee member Patrick Leahy, called the act "truly dangerous" and a threat to civil liberties, while Senate Majority Leader Bill Frist spoke for the law's supporters in terming it "another offensive strike against terrorism" (Rowley 2006). In defiance of *Hamdan,* the law placed "a large seal of approval on many initiatives taken by the Bush administration in the war on terror" (Addicot 2006).

The new law did not end the controversy over interrogation techniques and the detention facilities at Guantánamo Bay. Human rights activists continued to denounce US interrogation techniques and the treatment of detainees at Guantánamo. In 2007, Bush's former Secretary of State, Colin Powell, publicly urged the closing of the Guantánamo facility, arguing that its continued existence was embarrassing to the United States in the world community (Reuters 2007). Bush remained resolute in his defense of prisoner treatment practices throughout the remainder of his presidency, arguing that national security required them, and that torture was never permitted. Acknowledging that interrogation techniques "were tough, and they were safe and lawful and necessary," Bush in 2006 claimed "these are dangerous men with unparalleled knowledge about terrorist networks and their plans of new attacks. The security of our nation and the lives of our citizens depend on our ability to learn what these terrorists know."

The Supreme Court again challenged Bush's approach in their decision, *Boumediene v. Bush,* 553 U.S. (2008), concerning the habeas corpus rights of Guantanamo detainees. The court declared unconstitutional a provision of the 2006 Military Commissions Act that "stripped federal courts of jurisdiction to hear habeas corpus petitions from detainees seeking to challenge their status as enemy combatants" (Greenhouse 2008, A1). Writing for a 5–4 majority, Justice Anthony Kennedy asserted that "petitioners may invoke the fundamental procedural protections of habeas corpus. The laws and Constitution are designed to survive, and remain in force, in extraordinary times" (Kennedy 2008, A20). In dissent, Chief Justice John Roberts claimed the decision made losers of the American people, "who today lose a bit more control over the conduct of this nation's foreign policy to unelected, politically unaccountable judges" (John Roberts 2008, A20). The decision promised a surge of lawsuits from Guantanamo detainees. President Bush, though disapproving of the opinion, stated that he intended to uphold and enforce it.

Despite the important setback of the *Boumediene* decision, the Bush administration enjoyed much success in achieving its goals with the federal judiciary. In this area perhaps more than any other, George W. Bush satisfied the agenda of his conservative GOP regime. Through the first six years of his presidency, Bush appointed a large number of uniformly conservative federal judges, as well as two Supreme Court justices sharing the president's preference for strict construction and a permissive constitutional interpretation of executive power. Much of this progress ground to a halt during the last two years of the Bush presidency, as Senate Democrats effectively slowed the stream of federal court appointments, much as GOP Senators had done in the waning years of the Clinton presidency. Bush, however, was able to count on a supportive Republican Congress to overturn many key elements of his most notable court reversal in *Hamdan*. In this case, the court found it difficult to prevail in a case that limited executive power over detained prisoners during a period of military conflict. The war on terror served to increase executive power, an outcome much prized by the Bush administration. Once the GOP lost control of Congress, however, Bush could not successfully reverse another adverse Supreme Court decision regarding detainees, the *Boumediene* decision of 2008.

Conclusion

Two "headline" events—the Iraq occupation and the Hurricane Katrina cleanup—helped to create an impression of administrative incompetence plaguing the George W. Bush presidency. In the wake of them, Bush's professional reputation, an important component of his informal powers of political capital, declined. These were major events in the life of that presidency and much of the criticism of the administration regarding its handling of these troublesome matters is deserved. But it is wrong to assess the governance record of the Bush administration simply on these two cases, as important as they may be. We must also ask if, in the daily operations of national government, the Bush administration was effective in achieving its goals. And below the headlines, the answer to that question is "yes."

The Bush White House set ambitious management goals for the executive branch, seeking to reduce federal regulation and to restructure federal employment through increased outside contracting. By its own standards, the administration made much progress on each of these goals, as it did with judicial appointments. The Bush administration sought congressional compliance for its major initiatives and for several years—from 2001 to 2005—received it. When the president himself overreached in 2005 by proposing a politically precarious restructuring of Social Security and an immigration reform that split his partisan coalition, he helped to precipitate a lasting drop in his political capital and agenda dominance. The "headline" miscues regarding Iraq and Katrina also facilitated that slump. The steep decline in Bush's informal powers increased endogenous constraints from his more restive GOP coalition and imposed exogenous constraints from a hostile political environment riven with partisanship.

The George W. Bush presidency, nevertheless, contains valuable lessons in effective governance for future chief executives. In managing the executive branch, it is important to monitor ongoing performance, as did Bush's OMB. When restructuring, try not to involve Congress and its parochial agendas so often at variance with a president's wishes. The Bush White House did this by increasing federal contracting through executive order, not legislative proposals. It's also important to identify key organizations central to a president's agenda and staff them with the right appointees, as the Bush administration did with OMB's Office of Information and Regulatory Affairs.

Legislatively, a president really must strike when the iron is hot. The GOP's narrow but ideologically homogeneous majorities in the House and Senate, combined with the first GOP control of the legislature and executive in fifty years, provided considerable possibilities for the Bush administration. From 2001 to 2005, the White House made much of those possibilities by careful agenda control, focusing on a limited number of important measures on which partisan GOP support was achievable. For lasting impact, a president must devote high priority to judicial appointments, as Bush did. The courts, as a top regime priority for the Bush administration, yielded much success for them. After six years, the federal judiciary was stocked with approximately 250 newly-appointed conservative judges and a conservative majority on the Supreme Court was more secure. The Bush administration was able to lengthen the impact of its unitary executive assertion of presidential power by making agreement with that view mandatory in federal court nominations. The challenge to executive power presented by the Supreme Court's *Hamdan* ruling was overcome with congressional support in 2006, though a similar challenge from the 2008 *Boumediene* decision prevailed against Bush's wishes. Thus was the Bush administration able to expand presidential power in the national political system as circumstances permitted. Perhaps the central enabling condition for this expansion came from the 9/11 attacks, but a supportive Congress helped quite a bit as well. But these advantages proved fleeting, as the problematic Iraq occupation dragged on, helping Democrats to retake the Congress in 2006.

Future chief executives can also learn from the shortcomings evident in the Bush administration's approach to Washington governance. Governing with Congress in an executive-dominant, partisan fashion is not a strategy for all seasons. The legislature is only situationally subservient, as George W. Bush found out in 2005 and later. Nor is it likely that all major items on a president's agenda will be passable with a strictly partisan coalition. Bush's failures on Social Security and immigration reform attest to that. National and international events regularly add to and subtract from a president's informal powers and the political authority of his partisan regime, as does the skill with which he reacts to those events. 9/11 handed George W. Bush an important opportunity. He pursued it forcefully, and at times skillfully, expanding the formal powers of the presidency and his authority within a ruling conservative political regime.

Opportunities of this sort don't often last long in national politics, and so it proved in Bush's case. As adverse events mounted and partisan opposition among Democrats hardened, Bush found himself the victim of negative consequences of his own governing strategy. A partisan governing style can permit big achievements, but such success is fragile. It engenders strong partisan hostility, enduring political controversy, and little in the way of a safety net to break a political fall. Combine it with an audacious unitary executive approach to expanding presidential power whenever possible, and a president has a recipe for mounting conflict with rival partisans and institutions throughout Washington that over time will weaken his professional reputation. Bush's conduct of the presidency did increase formal presidential powers in several ways. But his governing approach ultimately helped to drain him and his governing coalition of authority over the direction of national politics. Substantial success amidst growing conflict and rancor constitutes the George W. Bush legacy in Washington governance.

4 DOMESTIC POLICY

George W. Bush sought to use presidential power to expand the authority of his GOP regime to reshape government—but to what ends? Journalists and commentators have suggested various labels for Bush's approach to domestic government, but no brief description suits his large ambitions. His administration cut the fiscal resources of government while increasing spending in a few selected domestic areas and piling on large increases in defense dollars. One result was a sharp shift from national budget surpluses to deficits. Bush's approach to domestic government, however, was not scattershot or haphazard. He came into office with a clearly articulated set of priorities, encapsulated in his espousal of "compassionate conservatism" and an "ownership society," and had considerable success in winning passage of several of the initiatives into law, most notably large federal tax cuts in 2001 and 2003. But Bush fell short of his largest ambitions, failing to secure personal accounts in Social Security or to create a permanent federal system for aiding the needy through faith-based programs.

This chapter argues that events over the course of George W. Bush's presidency raised the skill level needed by his administration to achieve his large domestic policy initiatives. Once Bush's political capital declined after 2003, the administration failed to win passage of the president's big plans. The reversals of the Iraq occupation and the Katrina response in 2005 damaged Bush's professional reputation and confirmed that the administration's available skills—coalitional, managerial, bargaining, rhetorical, and heresthetic—could not sustain his ambitions. The rising endogenous costs of maintaining his partisan coalition and exogenous costs of an increasingly polarized and hostile political environment impeded Bush's domestic plans in the later years of his presidency. During his first term, however, Bush sought a presidency of achievement in domestic policy, and was able to be an event-making president—not just responding to occurrences elsewhere but making his own news with policy initiatives that became law.

From 2001 through 2004, Bush seemed to take Stephen Skowronek's description of the presidency as a "disruptive" institution very much to heart (Skowronek 1997, 6). Disruption lay at the center of Bush's domestic agenda. His tax cuts shrank the fiscal revenue of the national government, ending a multiyear period of budget surpluses. Bush's education reform challenged traditional elementary and secondary education schools throughout the country. Proposals for faith-based social programs threatened established boundaries between church and state and long-established welfare bureaucracies. Social Security reform aimed to restructure fundamentally the most costly program in the national government, accounting for 21 percent of federal spending. Of these initiatives, a particularly sweeping change involved reducing federal taxes, for on that revenue stream most of national government depends. Reducing that cash flow is a large and potentially disruptive alteration of how government works. Why was this a central initiative of the Bush presidency, and how did Bush succeed in achieving it?

Tax Cuts: Closing the Government Spigot

George W. Bush's embrace of tax cuts reflected the consensus within his party about their importance. Jacob Hacker and Paul Pierson argue that "it is not too much of an exaggeration to say that taxation has become the essential policy glue that holds together the contemporary Republican party" (Hacker and Pierson 2007, 260). For Republicans, tax cuts are good policy for several reasons. They stimulate the economy by providing more money for private consumption and investment, this latter effect serving as a "supply side" stimulus extolled by many conservative economists. Tax cuts also serve to "starve the beast" by depriving the government of funds, thus making smaller government, a long time goal of many Republicans, more attainable. Tax cuts further supply benefits to taxpayers in lieu of the rewards that might come to them through increased government spending. Finally, tax cuts are good strategy because they appeal broadly to Republicans and to other voters leery of governmental intervention. Grover Norquist, head of Citizens for Tax Reform, a prominent antitax organization, argues that opposition to taxation has created a broad, durable coalition: "It holds together because while members vote on different issues, and hold often wildly conflicting views on secondary issues, they are not in conflict on their primary, vote-moving issues. They vote for candidates and parties that work to limit the size, scope and cost of government to where the state protects the lives and liberties of its citizens and calls it a day" (Norquist 2008, 33).

George W. Bush reflected these views in advocating a large round of tax cuts upon taking office in 2001: "Investors and consumers have too little money, and the government is holding too much. The federal government is simply pulling too much money out of the private economy, and this is a drag on our growth. Over the past six years, the federal share of our GDP (Gross Domestic Product) has risen from 18 percent to 21 percent—about as much as our government took in during World War II." For Bush, tax cuts, smaller government, economic growth, and prosperity went hand-in-hand. And tax cuts satisfied and unified his political coalition. Small wonder they were at the top of his domestic policy agenda in 2001.

2001 was a time of budget surpluses. It was the fourth consecutive year of budgets in the black, resulting from a growing economy and fiscal cooperation between a GOP Congress and Bush's predecessor, Bill Clinton. The budget surplus in 2000 was $236.4 billion; in 2001, $127.4 billion as the economy slowed. Republicans and some Democrats in Congress thought the economic stimulus of tax cuts, coupled with existing budget surpluses, made tax cuts very much in order. In this environment, Bush was able to win passage of tax cuts totaling $2.1 billion over ten years (Orszag 2001). In the wake of 9/11, the already slowing economy slumped further, spiking the federal deficit and prompting Bush to ask for another round of tax cuts in 2003 to stimulate the economy. These cuts passed on a more party-line vote and totaled an additional $1 trillion dollars over ten years. The administration also secured a smaller cut in taxes on business in 2002. All of the cuts passed with overwhelming GOP support, demonstrating the centrality of tax cuts for Republicans and the Bush administration's coalitional skills in prevailing in usually narrow, party-line victories.

The 2001 to 2003 tax cuts combined were greater than either of the two other major tax cuts of recent decades, those proposed by John Kennedy (enacted in 1964) and Ronald Reagan (enacted in 1981), as a share of net national income (Ahern 2004). Kennedy's cuts passed when the budget was in deficit equaling one percent of national income and Reagan's when the deficit was a larger 2.8 percent of national income. Bush's 2001 cuts began when the national budget surplus equaled 1.5 percent of national income (Ahern, 2004). But a recession following 9/11, combined with the tax cuts and large increases in defense spending to prosecute the war on terror, moved the budget into a deficit equaling 4.5 percent of national income, or $674 billion dollars, by 2004 (Economic Report 2008, 377–78). Coupled with an easing of the money supply to spur lending and spending, effected by the Federal Reserve Board led by Alan Greenspan, the economy received a large fiscal and monetary stimulus beginning in 2002.

What were the short-term economic effects of the tax cuts? Liberal and conservative analysts differ greatly over the details, but agree that some immediate economic stimulus resulted from the cuts, helping to end the recession of 2001 to 2002. Economist Mark Zandi argued in 2004 that "nearly all of the economic growth experienced since the president took office is due to the aggressive easing in monetary policy and greater federal government largesse" through deficit spending and tax cuts, adding an estimated 2.5 percent to real GDP growth by 2004 (Zandi 2004). These results did not eliminate controversy about the tax cuts, however—particularly concerning the distribution of tax cuts across income groups and long-term effects of the cuts.

Liberal and conservative analysts engaged in strong arguments about the fairness of the Bush tax cuts. The Bush cuts reduced tax rates across all income categories. Liberal groups, such as the Center for Budget and Policy Priorities, note that in dollar terms, the greatest beneficiaries of the Bush tax cuts were those in the highest income bracket, with the top one percent in 2004 getting 24.2 percent of the tax cut dollars while the middle 20 percent gained only 8.9 percent of those dollars (Center on Budget and Policy Priorities 2004, 8). The conservative Heritage Foundation, in contrast, emphasized that the highest income earners paid a larger percentage of income taxes—a figure that rose from 81 to 85 percent from 2001 to 2004—while the bottom 40 percent of earners by 2004 received net subsidies from the Internal Revenue Service equal to four percent of the total tax bill (Riedl 2007, 9). Both patterns are true. The Congressional Budget Office found that the Bush tax cuts made the overall income tax structure slightly more progressive, meaning that high income earners paid a slightly larger share than previously, but that the overall tax bill was lower, producing large tax cut gains for those of high income (Congressional Budget Office 2004). Wealthier Americans shouldered more of the overall burden as a result of the Bush tax cuts, but that burden was smaller.

The Bush tax cuts also stirred controversy over their long-term effects. Liberal economists at the Urban Institute and Brookings Institution argued that the tax cuts spurred deficits that were a greater economic threat than the deficits of previous decades. This was because the retirement of baby boomers was much closer, meaning that big spending pressures were not far away while the budget remained in deficit. Further, in the 1980s, private saving was much higher, public debt was a smaller share of GDP and America's international trade balance was much more favorable (Tax Policy Center 2008). The Heritage Foundation noted, however, that by 2006, nearly all of the federal deficits could be accounted for by increased spending, not tax cuts. Repealing the tax cuts would have only a slight effect on the coming spending crunch from entitlement spending on elder baby boomers. The projected gap in revenues and spending in 2050, according to Heritage, is about 15 percent of GDP, a mammoth imbalance indeed (Riedl 2007, 5).

Both liberal and conservative economists agree that a large imbalance in entitlement obligations for retirees and available tax revenue looms over the coming decades. Though the Bush tax cuts do not hugely contribute to the problem, they do little to solve it, unless the long-term growth effect of the tax cuts provides more tax revenues than are presently projected. In the short term, the Bush administration gained much from the tax cuts. The GOP coalition responded favorably to their passage. The cuts stimulated the economy and helped to end the recession. The taxing capacity of the federal government was considerably reduced. "If the 2001 to 2003 tax cuts were extended as advocates desired (they currently expire in 2010), they would cost more than $4 trillion through 2013. In that year, the revenue loss would total 2.4 percent of GDP" (Hacker and Pierson 2007, 257). That is indeed "starving the beast" in the service of Bush's conservative political coalition.

Large deficits and the economic stimulus they provided to the economy's aggregate consumption were immediate effects of both Ronald Reagan's and George W. Bush's tax cuts. During Reagan's eight years in office, the deficit averaged 4.25 percent of Gross Domestic Product. This is a substantially larger percentage than the 2.38 percent of GDP averaged during the four large deficit years of the second Bush presidency, from 2002 to 2005 (Economic Report 2008, 377). The economic stimulus of the cuts helped Reagan enjoy a booming economy that facilitated his landslide reelection victory in 1984. Economic recovery in 2004 had proceeded just enough to permit Bush's narrow reelection victory. The longer term implications of such deficits, as noted above, are more ominous in the Bush case. Unlike Reagan's successors, the presidents following Bush will have to deal with an explosion in Social Security and Medicare spending resulting from the retirement of the baby boomers that will soon dramatically worsen the budget deficit trend established by the Bush presidency.

Beyond reelection, the economic recovery following 2001 to 2002 did not produce great political benefits for George W. Bush. Between the end of the recession in 2002 and the onset of another economic slowdown in 2008, the economy grew at a moderately healthy clip, inflation remained low, and unemployment slowly declined. This combination of circumstances usually produces public support for the economic policies of the president. Bush, however, failed to benefit in this usual way. His poll ratings on the economy followed a bizarre and counterintuitive pattern. His highest ratings occurred during a recession in 2001 to 2002, when presidential ratings are usually in the toilet. This probably reflects a "rally around the flag" effect in the year after 9/11, when Bush's overall job ratings were quite high. As the economy improved, his economic approval ratings steadily declined. Again, the explanation of this probably lies beyond the economy. Bush's overall job approval steadily slumped as the Iraq occupation worsened and Democrats and many independents developed strong disapproval of all policies regarding George Bush, regardless of their outcomes (Jacobson 2007B).

Public approval began to finally square with economic events in the last year of the Bush presidency. Despite the administration's quick action to address a sputtering economy, Bush's poll approval on economic matters slumped because of economic difficulties (Saad 2008). The economy steadily slowed in late 2007 and 2008, due to declines in consumer spending brought on by a depressed housing market and rising gasoline and commodity prices. A speculative bubble in real estate collapsed, leading to panic in the stock markets, already slumping in anticipation of a recession. Economic growth creaked to a near stop in 2008 and inflation began to creep up. Commentators began employing the term "stagflation" for the first time since the late 1970s.

The administration in January 2008 speedily came to agreement with the Democratic Congress on a stimulus plan totaling $163 billion in immediate tax rebates for individuals and cuts in business taxes (Meece 2008). The quick consensus on short-term stimulus continued the well-established tendency of Washington politicians to use fiscal policy to manage economic fluctuations (Schier 1992). Two months later, Treasury Secretary Henry Paulson responded to credit market problems with proposed legislation to "consolidate federal agencies that regulate the nation's securities and commodities futures markets" and create a commission to set minimum standards for issuing mortgages (Labaton 2008). The plan received a cool reception from the Democratic Congress.

Growth in federal spending under Bush engendered much controversy, drawing strong criticism from conservatives (Bartlett 2006; Tanner 2007; Viguerie 2006). Discretionary spending, which is subject to annual spending decisions by the President and Congress, did increase considerably. According to the Heritage Foundation's Brian Riedl, from 2001 to 2008, defense and homeland security discretionary spending rose 102 percent—67 percent after inflation—and domestic discretionary spending leapt upward by 49 percent—23 percent after inflation (Riedl 2008, 6). Liberal analyst Richard Korgan of the Center for Budget and Policy Priorities, however, estimates that the annual rate of growth in domestic discretionary spending averaged only 1.3 percent annually after inflation (Kogan 2008, 6). A broader perspective on such increases, however, results from examining their role in the overall growth in government size during the Bush presidency. Conservative grievances result from the overall increase in government as a percentage of

America's Gross Domestic Product from 18.5 percent in 2001 to 21 percent in 2007. But the large majority of those increases came from increases in three budget areas: defense, up from three to four percent of GDP, and Medicare and Medicaid, programs providing health care for retirees and the poor, up from 3.4 to 4.6 percent of GDP (Krugman 2008).

These patterns created considerable angst among fiscal conservatives, leading to increasing public criticisms of the administration's lack of spending restraint as Bush's second term proceeded. David Keating, executive director of the Club for Growth, a prominent anti-spending organization, termed Bush "a big spender;" Steven Slivinski of the libertarian Cato Institute called him "a big government guy" (Lightman 2007). Conservative journalist Fred Barnes summarized Bush's approach to spending: "Bush has never proclaimed himself a small-government conservative . . . He has explained his policy as favoring all the government that's required and no more. That leaves a lot to Bush's discretion. He prides himself on using his political capital rather than conserving it. . . . But he hasn't spent that capital on terminating any federal agencies or programs" (Barnes 2006, 167–68). Some of the increased spending under Bush resulted from funding for two of his major domestic policy initiatives: pursuing "compassionate conservatism" and the creation of an "ownership society."

Compassionate Conservatism

As George W. Bush contemplated a presidential candidacy as governor of Texas, he sought a domestic agenda consistent with his distrust of liberal domestic programs and his evangelical faith, which counseled compassion for the poor. His political advisor, Karl Rove, introduced him to books by two authors, Marvin Olasky and Myron Magnet, which criticized traditional liberal approaches to poverty and advocated conservative alternatives (Olasky 1997; Magnet 1993). Bush as governor met with both Olasky and Magnet in the process of creating his approach of "compassionate conservatism," which he touted throughout the 2000 campaign.

Bush administration advisor and former Indianapolis Mayor Stephen Goldsmith listed the core tenets of compassionate conservatism in 2000: first, "it is optimistic and confident about how all individuals can do better," second, it holds that "the best way to help people is through the marketplace," and third, "prosperity must have a purpose—that is, more than just the marketplace is necessary for America to be a successful country." In contrast, Goldsmith argued, traditional liberalism is "fundamentally pessimistic" about whether people can ever overcome their problems and so "promotes redistribution of income rather than the creation of new wealth and new opportunities for investment." This creates a culture of dependency among the poor who then depend "for their survival on the largesse of the state and the distant decisions of bureaucrats" (Goldsmith 2000, 2). Compassionate conservatism, in contrast, would focus on giving people the tools and skills they need to end their dependency and enter the "economic mainstream" (2000, 2).

Characteristic of George W. Bush, this seems a very ambitious policy undertaking, at least in the abstract. What policies would constitute a compassionate conservative agenda? Several of them, announced at the outset of the Bush presidency, were included in a comprehensive Bush speech on compassionate conservatism in 2002: reforming foreign and development aid, maintaining the welfare reform of 1995 that included work requirements, and passing two major administration initiatives, the No Child Left Behind education reform and a faith-based initiative to involve religious institutions in addressing problems of poverty. Bush described the overall approach behind these programs: "It is compassionate to actively help our fellow citizens in need. It is conservative to insist on responsibility and results."

Education Reform: No Child Left Behind

The No Child Left Behind education reform and the faith-based initiative were the two major legislative initiatives comprising Bush's compassionate conservative agenda in 2001. Bush had long been interested in elementary and secondary education reform during his time as Governor of Texas. He became convinced that public schools underserved certain groups, particularly African American, Latino, and low income students, subjecting them to, in his words, "the soft bigotry of low expectations." At Bush's behest, the state's curriculum requirements were rewritten and streamlined, charter schools established, mandatory skills testing implemented in the third, fifth, and eighth grades that determined progress to the next grade, and funding increased for early intervention and teacher training programs (Bush 1999, 218–20). The national legislation proposed by the new administration had similar features, and ranked near the top of the administration's short list of legislative priorities for 2001.

Bush's Texas reforms had gained bipartisan support, and the new president engaged two liberal congressional Democrats long at the center of education policy—Senator Edward Kennedy of Massachusetts and Representative George Miller of California—in extensive negotiations prior to the introduction of new legislation. Both were interested in increased funding for education and Miller in particular sought to improve teacher performance by setting new standards for student performance. Together with the GOP chair of the House Education Committee, Representative John Boehner of Ohio, and Republican Senator Judd Gregg of New Hampshire of the Senate Education Committee, this bipartisan group, along with President Bush, constituted the "big five" who provided the energy, negotiation skills, and policy knowledge to shepherd the initiative through the legislative process (Mycoff and Pika 2008, 61).

The original Bush proposal reflected many goals of the Clinton administration on education reform that attracted Miller and Kennedy to the possibility of a compromise. Bush proposed a boost in federal aid to state and local education, reduction of fifty education programs into five block grants to states, annual testing in grades three through eight in reading and math, testing for teacher competence, school report cards on how students performed on tests, state-level assessment tests for fourth and eighth graders, student progress disaggregated by targeted group such as African Americans and Latinos, and a modest voucher proposal, under which students in poorly performing public schools could fund their switch to private schools (Mycoff and Pika 2008, 41). With the exception of vouchers and block grants, all of the above features of the reform became law. This, however, was compromise legislation that not all conservatives or liberals would love. The proposal "violated two conservative principles, local control of schools and minimal federal intrusion, at the same time that it promoted two others, high standards and accountability" (Barnes 2006, 165).

Bush, for his part, devoted much time and energy to moving the reform through Congress, effectively displaying coalitional and bargaining skills, keeping GOP lawmakers behind him while attracting Democratic support. He proved flexible in dropping the voucher proposal when it encountered objections from Senator Kennedy and failed to pass the House Education Committee. He agreed to increase funding levels that drew objections from some fiscally conservative Republicans. Many GOP lawmakers were skeptical of increased federal regulatory control of elementary and secondary education. Thirty-four GOP House members and six GOP Senators voted against initial passage of their chamber's version of the legislation. Despite their opposition, large bipartisan majorities supporting the legislation formed in both House and Senate. A lengthy conference committee over the rival chamber versions led to hard-fought compromises over social issues, funding and the testing features of the reform. The final bill increased federal spending on education from $18.6 billion in 2001 to $23.6 billion in 2002; the total number of education programs was reduced from fifty-five to forty-five.

Compliance time for failing schools was extended from ten years to twelve years to satisfy Senate conferees. Compromise language on school prayer and other social controversies was found. Bush was centrally involved in this final stage, facilitating agreement on the major provisions of the law.

Congressional approval of Public Law 107–10, according to Jason Mycoff and Joseph Pika, was "nothing short of miraculous" given the difficult environment in which the law was formulated and approved (Mycoff and Pika 2008, 34). Republicans had lost control of the Senate in May 2001 when GOP Senator James Jeffords became an independent and started caucusing with Democrats. Jeffords at the time of his defection chaired the Senate Education Committee. During conference committee negotiations, the 9/11 attacks occurred, shifting national and congressional attention away from education reform and slowing progress on the issue. In the ensuing weeks, discovery of anthrax spores in several Senate offices led to frequent, extended disruptions of congressional business. Bush nevertheless signed the bill into law on January 8, 2002.

Final passage of the law hardly ended the controversy over its contents. It created new federal regulatory pressures on school districts throughout the nation. The three most important were state testing, specification of students' "adequate yearly progress," and teacher quality. Proponents of the law argue that it has improved test scores, education standards, accountability of schools, attention to minority populations and flexibility in school funding. Opponents hold that it has limited local control of education, narrowed curriculums to focus on testing subjects, actually hindered low-income students by imposing penalties on poorly performing public schools, created incentives to overlook highly achieving students, and created an unattainable 100 percent compliance goal with the new educational requirements by 2014 (Ryan 2004; Holland 2004).

Bush's coalition of GOP congressional supporters began to fray as the law took effect. Discontent with the law's "big government conservatism" became increasingly evident in GOP ranks as complaints arose over the law's implementation and as Bush's political capital fell during his second term. In 2007, more than fifty GOP House members cosponsored a bill allowing states to opt out of the reform entirely. Senator Jim DeMint of South Carolina, who voted against the legislation as a House member in 2001, argued that "So many people are frustrated with the shackles of No Child Left Behind," claiming the law promotes "testing, testing, testing and reshaping the curriculum so we look good" (Weisman and Paley 2007). Debate over these issues continued as the administration sought reauthorization of the law in 2008.

What effect has the No Child Left Behind law had on American education? A blizzard of studies has produced varying results on the many aspects of this complex reform. A comprehensive study by the RAND Corporation, a leading policy analysis organization, gave No Child Left Behind "mixed grades" in its operation since 2001. RAND found that all states have complied with the law's testing requirements in reading and math. Student "proficiency," RAND discovered, varied widely in its definition across states, as did the criteria for determining failing schools that are subject to sanctions. The large majority of teachers satisfied the law's requirement that they be "highly qualified," but those requirements also varied considerably from state to state. The few students who transferred to higher-achieving schools saw no improvement in their academic performance, but students from low-scoring schools who enrolled in "tutoring or other supplemental services" did improve their scores on reading and math tests (Hamilton et. al. 2007, 1–2).

Bush's emphasis on elementary and secondary education reform produced the biggest change in federal policy in this area since the passage of the landmark Elementary and Secondary Education Act of 1965, which first established the current system of federal aid to state and local education. With this initiative, Bush departed from a traditional GOP aversion toward activism in federal education policy. Ronald Reagan, for example, had called for the abolition of the Department of Education, and the new GOP Congress in 1995 had further pursued that objective. No Child Left Behind, in contrast, increased federal regulation and spending in elementary and secondary education. It is not surprising that Bush's education reforms became controversial within GOP ranks, or that the scale of the changes has produced widely varying evaluations of the policy among teachers, administrators, students, and parents. In terms of its scope alone, No Child Left Behind ranks as one of the most consequential domestic policies of the Bush presidency, a classic presidential "disruption" of long-established governmental routines.

The Faith Based Initiative

Alongside education reform, Bush's push to increase the role of religious institutions in providing social services lay at the center of his compassionate conservatism agenda. The faith-based initiative, however, would encounter several insuperable congressional obstacles, resulting in legislative policy changes that fell far short of the president's original ambitions. This led Bush to pursue an executive branch strategy that implemented a reduced version of the reform.

Bush consistently voiced a strong desire to increase the role of faith-based institutions in the delivery of social programs. In a 2002 speech, he claimed: "Faith-based charities work daily miracles because they have idealistic volunteers. . . . They know the problems of their own communities and, above all, they recognize the dignity of every person and the possibilities of every life. . . . Yet many lack the resources they need to meet the needs around them. . . . They deserve, when appropriate, the support of the federal government." Support for this policy came at the very outset of the Bush administration. On January 29, 2001, Bush announced executive orders establishing the White House Office of Community and Faith-Based Organizations and similar centers in five cabinet departments—Labor, Health and Human Services, Justice, Education, and Housing and Urban Development (eventually, five more such agencies were established in the executive branch). The head of the White House office was John Dilulio, a prominent political scientist and Democrat who was attracted to the administration by the faith-based agenda. Dilulio's task was to facilitate the direction of more federal grant monies to faith-based organizations and to promote legislation in Congress that would boost giving to such organizations.

Dilulio's ambitions immediately ran into obstacles within the administration and Congress. He found that other White House staff people were not interested in a bipartisan bill, but rather in steering legislative proposals "as far right as possible" (Dilulio 2002, 4). In addition, the GOP congressional leadership had very little interest in the legislation. Michael Gerson, chief White House speechwriter and an advocate of faith-based reform, described the objections: "Some . . . didn't want to spend any money on the effort. Others, such as Congressman Dick Armey, thought it sounded like a Democratic idea. After grudgingly accepting the new spending on No Child Left Behind, conservatives on the Hill had little appetite for more spending on the poor" (Gerson 2008, 169–70). Conservative House Republicans drafted a version that had no chance of bipartisan support, and from that unpromising beginning, legislation went nowhere in 2001 and 2002 (Dilulio 2002, 4). White House staff did little to press the issue, according to one frustrated administration advocate of the initiative: "Very few people in the White House made it a priority. They wanted to use the failure to pass faith-based legislation as a club to beat up Democrats" (Black, Koopman, and Ryden 2004, 111).

Eventually, the administration prevailed upon Congress to pass modest laws encouraging food-bank donations and the rollover of IRAs for charitable purposes. The major strides in pursuing the faith-based initiative came from the executive branch, led by the president's focus upon the issue. In late

2002, Bush announced an executive order implementing religious protection provisions included in the failed congressional legislation. These provisions allowed religious organizations to maintain their doctrinal commitments on controversial topics, such as homosexuality, while still receiving federal funds (Black, Koopman, and Ryden 2004, 183). While a largely fruitless battle had raged on Capitol Hill in 2001 and 2002, the faith-based centers in the executive branch "were quietly beginning to change regulations, earmark money for faith-based organizations, and generally transform the relationship between the executive branch and religious groups. . . . The story of administrative reform . . . appears to be a qualified success" (2004, 222). By 2002, a survey of new publicly funded faith-based programs in fifteen states showed a substantial increase in the number of such programs operating with government funds, some seven hundred federal contracts totaling $125 million (Sherman 2002).

The Bush administration did create changes in federal policy toward faith-based organizations, but these changes were much more modest than those of No Child Left Behind. The major difference in these outcomes lay in the involvement of Congress in the reforms. No Child Left Behind was a sweeping change in national education policy, made possible by congressional consensus and made real by energetic presidential efforts. This allowed Bush to overcome objections within his own party about the basic direction of his reform. The faith based initiative, however, suffered from a lack of enthusiasm in either congressional party for the president's ideas. Neither partisan coalition building nor bargaining with Democrats would move the legislation. Perhaps an exuberant effort by the president might have created more substantial legislation funding social services by faith-based organizations, but from the outset those prospects were dim. This led Bush to an executive strategy, which produced some results but was guaranteed to last only as long as his presidency, since his executive orders can be quickly revoked by a White House successor.

Combating AIDS

The administration's compassionate conservative agenda also extended to foreign affairs. Bush secured passage in 2003 of a $15 billion, five-year effort to combat AIDS in Africa. The program dramatically reduced the number of AIDS-related deaths and illnesses. As the *Washington Post* reported in 2008, the program "has extended the lives of hundreds of thousands of people and eased the sense of certain doom once experienced by millions of others" (Timberg 2008, A9). This initiative earned him international praise and public adulation during a 2008 tour of Africa. In addition, Millennium Challenge Accounts reshaped foreign aid by linking American assistance to respect for human rights and the rule of law in recipient nations. Created in 2004 and administered by a newly created federal Millennium Development Corporation, the program received limited funding from Congress of less than $2 billion per year since its inception. A 2006 study from the Kennedy School of Government found "substantial evidence that countries respond to MCA incentives by improving their indicators" regarding proper behavior toward their citizens (Johnson and Zajonc 2006).

Toward the Ownership Society

Though compassionate conservatism became a prominent label of the Bush presidency, even greater White House ambitions were vested in the development of an "ownership society," described by Bush in his 2004 acceptance speech at the Republican National Convention: "In an ownership society, more people will own their own health plans and have the confidence of owning a piece of their retirement." By the time of his speech, the administration had already won passage of two such reforms. Individual Health Savings Accounts, established in 2003, were tax-free and paid for health expenses. The Medicare prescription drug benefit, also passed into law in 2003, allowed private health plans to compete for individual senior's federally subsidized prescription drug coverage. In his second term, Bush would press for the greatest ownership society reform of them all. Personal Social Security accounts, modeled on private, defined contribution pension plans, would provide greater control and greater risk for individual retirement benefits.

Though the ownership society was a new rhetorical label employed by Bush, a sort of ownership society has been gradually evolving in America in the later decades of the twentieth century. Defined benefit pension plans, in which an employer guarantees retired workers a given payment through their retirement as long as they retire from the company at the end of their careers, gradually disappeared in favor of defined contribution plans. In these plans, employers grant to employees a share of profits or a defined monthly payment over which the employee has some investment control. Upon leaving the company, these benefits travel with the employee. Changes in federal law in the 1970s permitted tax-exempt defined contribution plans, and they gradually grew in popularity in the following decades. Unionized sectors of the economy declined, and unions had long preferred the defined benefit pension. Increased employee mobility and the growth of lightly unionized service and high tech industries made defined contribution plans, with the easy portability, increasingly popular (Zelinsky 2007, 34). By 2006, twenty million American workers had defined benefit pensions, but fifty million had portable defined contribution pensions (Investment Company Institute 2006).

The concept of an ownership society had great appeal to Bush and his GOP coalition. Economically, it sought market-based solutions to major domestic policy problems such as health care and retirement pensions. Politically, defined contribution pensions increase the number of people operating as investors of their own capital. Polls have shown that increasing share ownership correlates with an increased propensity to vote Republican (Rasmussen 1997). The political attractiveness of these ideas for Republicans was not lost on Democrats, who saw great risks for vulnerable citizens in such initiatives. These concerns, combined with a strong distrust of the Bush White House among congressional Democrats and the president's declining political capital, forestalled establishment of Bush's ownership society during his second term. The major ownership society successes came in 2003, with the passage of the Medicare prescription drug benefit program and Health Savings Accounts.

The prescription drug program constituted the first major expansion of Medicare, the national health care program for retirees, since its creation in 1965. The Bush administration saw the reform as an opportunity to address a problem in coverage for seniors faced with increasingly expensive prescription drugs, while taking an issue away from the Democrats, who had long been favored in public opinion on health care issues. It could forestall momentum for more comprehensive national health insurance programs by allowing seniors to pick insurance coverage from competitive private insurers, an outcome consistent with the administration's emphasis on an ownership society. The new law provided a subsidy to large private employers to discourage them from dropping prescription drug coverage. It prohibited the federal government from negotiating discounts with drug companies, reflecting the administration's faith in private markets to create fair prices. The program covered the large majority of prescription costs up to $2,400 annually. Program participants then paid all costs from $2,401 to $3,850 annually (known as the "donut hole" in the coverage), with recipients limited to paying 5 percent of costs over $3,850 (Centers for Medicare and Medicaid Services 2008).

Also included in the Medicare legislation were provisions establishing Health Savings Accounts (HSAs). These tax-free accounts allowed individuals to make tax-deductible contributions to an account used to pay costs not covered by a high deductible health insurance plan. The annual deductible had to be at least $1,000 for individuals and $2,000 for families. Health Savings Accounts were portable, like an individual retirement account (IRA), and owned by the individual (White House 2003). The accounts furthered the administration's ownership society goal of placing individuals in greater charge of their own health coverage. HSAs did this by diminishing the third party payment features of much health coverage, features that gave individuals inadequate incentive to economize on care.

Passage of these reforms was a lengthy, difficult process. Administration efforts were bolstered by the support of the American Association of Retired Persons (AARP), one of the nation's largest membership interest groups, for a prescription drug program. The administration pursued a bipartisan bargaining strategy in the Senate but had to resort to a partisan coalition building approach in the House. Though a large, supportive, bipartisan majority formed in the Senate, the House presented a formidable obstacle for the administration. House Democrats voiced party-line opposition because many of them desired more extensive medical coverage and also sought to deny the administration a major victory. House Republicans included several dozen strong conservatives who opposed such a large expansion of federal entitlement programs, preferring instead private market solutions to the problem. After much bargaining between the administration and House GOP leaders, Speaker Dennis Hastert introduced the agreed-upon bill on June 25, 2003. After two days of debate, a floor vote produced an initial count of 214–218 against the Hastert bill. Three GOP Representatives then changed their votes to produce a 216–215 victory. Once the Senate version passed by a 76–21 vote, the conference committee product ran into problems again on the House floor. With former House Majority Leader Dick Armey (R-TX) leading the GOP opponents, the bill was losing 219–215 at 3:00 A.M. on November 22, 2003. The GOP House leadership then held the vote open for three hours while they sought additional support—a highly unusual move, since such votes are usually only held open for fifteen minutes or so to let absent members get to the chamber to vote. Majority Leader Tom DeLay (R-TX) used all manner of persuasive tactics and convinced three GOPers to switch their votes, leading ultimately to a 220–215 victory.

This blatant manipulation of House rules produced considerable complaint from editorial boards and some congressional scholars (Mann and Ornstein 2006, 1–6). A related controversy arose when it was disclosed after the vote that Medicare administrator Thomas A. Scully had ordered his actuary, Richard Foster, to withhold information indicating that the bill would cost $139 billion more than the White House was claiming at the time of the House vote—$534 billion versus $395 billion from 2004 through 2013 (Heil 2004, 1). In fact, the cost of the program in its initial years came in well below either of these estimates. Due to lower drug costs, increasing use of generic drugs and higher rebates by drug manufacturers, the cost of the program in 2008 was estimated to be 38.5 percent lower than originally predicted and enrollees in the plan have reported high satisfaction (Centers for Medicare and Medicaid Services 2008). Evaluations of Health Savings Accounts have produced mixed results, with some studies reporting high user approval and others considerable disapproval (Government Accountability Office 2006; Towers Perrin 2007).

Social Security Reform

The Medicare prescription drug program remained controversial within conservative circles because of its status as an expanded government entitlement. Though the program supported ownership society principles by allowing beneficiaries a choice of private market plans, it also cost hundreds of billions of federal dollars in expanded health insurance benefits. The expanded benefits explain why the American Association of Retired Persons, hardly a component of the conservative regime, had lobbied hard for the prescription drug benefit. President Bush's 2005 campaign for private Social Security accounts was better received by many conservatives, but ultimately went nowhere. Every administration skill deployed regarding this issue—rhetorical, heresthetic, coalitional, and bargaining—failed. Bush's failure illustrates the political limits of the ownership society agenda and the questionable effectiveness of presidents "going public" to achieve major domestic policy changes.

Liberals and Democrats have long viewed Social Security, the government's system of public pensions for retirees, as the cornerstone of the American welfare state. Created in 1935 at the behest of Franklin D. Roosevelt, by 2005 the program was mammoth in size, constituting more than one in five dollars (21.1 percent) spent annually by the Federal government. But the long-term financing of Social Security faced great problems. Each year since 1983, payroll tax receipts and other income had exceeded benefit payments and other expenditures, an annual surplus that in 2005 alone equaled $170 billion dollars. At the end of 2005, the Social Security Trust Funds stood in surplus by $1.85 trillion dollars. But the government had used all of those funds for other spending purposes, leaving the equivalent of governmental IOUs in the trust funds in the form of treasury notes. Estimates in 2005 indicated that the government would need to draw on these surplus funds in the early 2020s as baby boomers retired, and the trust funds themselves would be depleted by 2042 or 2052, assuming proper repayment of treasury notes to the funds. This all added up to a gradually growing funding burden for Social Security as it was presently constituted.

This future funding problem was not the central focus of Bush's Social Security reform proposals in 2005. During his first term, Bush had appointed a bipartisan commission, headed by former Senator Daniel Patrick Moynihan (D-NY) to examine Social Security's difficulties, with specific instructions to consider how to incorporate "individually controlled, voluntary personal retirement accounts" into Social Security. The commission proposed three plans, one of which became the basis for Bush's 2005 reform proposal. In January 2005 he declared in his weekly radio address that Social Security "is on the road to bankruptcy," but in his State of the Union Address later that month, he called for voluntary personal accounts and offered no proposal to solve the program's long term financing. Bush's plan, he claimed, would have a "net neutral effect" and he would discuss with Congress how to address Social Security's projected shortfall (Lochhead 2005).

Bush specifically proposed that individuals be allowed to divert up to four percent of taxable wages from their Social Security accounts into private investment accounts. Beyond that, Bush promised a dialogue with Congress that he hoped would gain momentum as he pursued an aggressive heresthetic and rhetorical campaign of public persuasion, spending his political capital in pursuit of a keystone ownership society reform. In the following months, the White House "launched the most extensive public relations campaign in the history of the presidency in an effort to reform Social Security" (Edwards 2008, 40). The president first talked up reform in "60 stops in 60 days." Although his appearances were called "Town Hall meetings," the participants were actually limited to supporters of the president and the events were arranged so that the president could advocate reform, not encounter a wide variety of public views on Social Security (Mycoff and Pika 2008, 221). The national Republican party and sympathetic interest groups, such as the Club for Growth, spent millions on radio and television ads in support of the president's reforms.

All this produced little shift in public opinion, as noted in chapter two, or in congressional responsiveness toward Bush's proposals. Democrats remained united against personal accounts, sensing the initiative as an attempt to reduce benefits and the scope of Social Security. AARP vociferously opposed Bush's plan, arguing that it saddled retirees with too much risk and uncertainty. Bush had proposed no plan to cover the very expensive "transition period" when retirees would greatly depend on Social Security while younger workers reduced funding for Social Security by diverting money into personal accounts. House Ways and Means Committee chair Bill Thomas

(R-CA) wanted a broader approach to retirement reform, but his hearings on the matter led to no legislation and ended by the summer of 2005. Senate Finance Committee chair Charles Grassley (R-IA) encountered hostility to Bush's reform among moderate Republicans and blanket opposition among Democrats. Majorities were not to be had in either chamber.

Bush attempted to meet some Democratic objections in April 2005 by endorsing the concept of "progressive indexing" that reduced benefit increases for higher-income beneficiaries, in effect adding an element of "means-testing" to Social Security benefits. Conservatives objected to the progressive benefit structure, effectively splitting the GOP coalition, and the idea made Democrats no more willing to bargain. By the end of the summer, the proposal was stillborn, and Washington's attention focused on the disaster of Hurricane Katrina and the continued bad news from Iraq.

Restructuring the largest federal entitlement program via personal accounts—a large step toward the entrenchment of an ownership society—is a daunting task in any political season. Bush picked an inauspicious time to pursue it. As problems in Iraq festered, and partisan hard feelings from the 2004 election lingered in Washington, the president's own popularity gradually ebbed as he pressed this audacious reform. Presidential scholar George Edwards argues that Bush greatly overestimated his political capital in this case—a judgment that is hard to dispute (Edwards 2007). By swinging for the fences, he struck out on the most ambitious domestic policy proposal of his presidency and in the process diminished his popular approval and professional reputation.

Immigration Frustration

Another ambitious initiative of the Bush presidency that came up short was a reform of the nation's immigration laws. The number of undocumented immigrants in 2006 was estimated by the Pew Hispanic Center at between 11.5 and 12 million, with approximately 57 percent of that number of Mexican origin and another 24 percent from Central and South America (Passel 2006). What should be the federal response? Illegal immigrants place stress on America's job markets, schools, law enforcement, and health care systems. Yet they take work American citizens often won't, and are desired by many employers for that reason.

On this issue, Bush stood contrary to many in the ideological base of his party. No administration efforts to unify their partisan coalition on this issue would bear fruit. GOP conservatives had long argued that the problem of illegal immigration from Mexico should be addressed through increased border security and strong sanctions against employers of illegal immigrants. An outspoken leader of this approach, Representative Tom Tancredo (R-CO), launched a presidential campaign in 2008 based on the argument that illegal immigration was a central national security issue. George W. Bush, since his time as governor of Texas, had rejected an enforcement-only policy. In his campaign biography, he urged strong border security, but recalled: "I also said in Texas that we should educate children, all the children who live in my state . . . regardless of the status of their parents" (Bush 1999, 236–37). During his presidency, Bush waded into the middle of an "intraparty dispute pitting champions of border security and opponents of 'amnesty' for illegal immigrants against a business community hungry for a reliable supply of low-cost labor through some kind of temporary worker regime" (Foreman 2007, 279). The Bush administration tried to accommodate both sides of the debate with its immigration proposals, but could never heal the rift. It was an issue that would greatly challenge any occupant of the White House.

In 2004, 2006, and 2007, the Bush administration sought a comprehensive immigration reform bill, to no avail. White House political strategists viewed increasing Latino support through an immigration reform law as essential for the long-term electoral health of the GOP. The administration supported a temporary worker program, but not "amnesty because rewarding those who break the law would encourage more illegal entrants and increase pressure on the border" (White House 2005). The program would allow workers to reapply for temporary worker status after having returned to their home country, an option GOP opponents of the Bush approach termed a "path to citizenship" for illegal immigrants. Accompanying this was a White House emphasis on increased border enforcement by increasing the Border Patrol and, in 2006, by supporting a House GOP plan to build a border fence. Many Democrats found the administration and GOP proposals too punitive and questioned the effectiveness of a border fence.

The administration placed increased emphasis on securing an immigration proposal in 2006 and 2007. Each year, the administration's bargaining with Democrats and coalitional leadership among Republicans failed to win its passage. In April 2006, the Senate passed a bipartisan immigration reform plan containing many features desired by the administration. The bill created multiple "tiers" toward citizenship of increasing difficulty for more recent illegal immigrants, along with "increased border security, restricting felons' ability to get work permits and restricting the right to petition for citizenship" (Weisman 2006). House Republicans would have none of it, refusing to act on a companion bill and beginning a series of field hearings emphasizing border enforcement (Hulse 2006). In 2007, Bush strongly supported another bipartisan compromise reform that also had the backing of Senate Majority Leader Harry Reid (D-NV) and Edward Kennedy (D-MA). In addition to increasing border patrol and providing for more border fencing, the bill created a new "Z visa" that would be given to all illegal US residents. This visa would give illegal residents access to a Social Security number and the right to reside in the United States for life. Z visa recipients could then, by paying a $2,000 fine, receive a green card which in five years made them eligible to apply for US citizenship.

This final attempt at bipartisan reform went down to defeat in a series of Senate votes in late June 2007. So many opponents contacted senators that the Senate Internet server and phone system crashed for a time; intense support, in contrast failed to materialize (Dinan 2007). Liberals and labor unions criticized the guest worker program, arguing that it created an underclass of workers. Conservatives, spurred on by talk radio hosts, rejected the "amnesty" for illegal immigrants contained in the bill.

Immigration and private Social Security accounts appeared on the national agenda as Bush's political capital was declining, and the ensuing battles over them probably further contributed to that slump. Predictably, endogenous coalition maintenance had become more difficult for Bush by this time. Social Security failed because congressional Republicans did not want to reshape a large, popular program in the face of stout Democratic opposition. Immigration reform split the GOP congressional coalition apart. In neither case was Bush able to facilitate passage through bargaining with Democrats, partisan coalition leadership, or heresthetic and rhetorical efforts with the public. The immigration failure may be particularly telling in future decades, as Latinos, who found little to applaud in the GOP response to an issue of central importance to them, become a steadily larger part of the American electorate.

Controversies over Environment and Energy

Environmental and energy policy is a domain of complex political visions and motives and a source of unending conflict. George W. Bush's initial agenda had support from most in his GOP coalition, except for a small and crucial group of Senate moderates, and encountered much opposition from Hill Democrats. It's not surprising that Bush, with his pro-market policies, would also encounter enduring hostility from environmentalists that produced the political equivalent of low-intensity warfare in this policy area. Michael Kraft describes environmental and energy policy as an arena of chronic policy gridlock. The reasons for this are several. The two national parties diverge in their policy views, with pro-business Republicans battling environmentalist

Democrats. Environmental and energy problems are technical and complex, often involving considerable scientific uncertainty and making consensus hard to achieve. The public pays little attention to environmental and energy issues, thus presenting no consensus for leaders to follow when making policy. Interest groups dominate the environmental and energy policy landscape, leading to pitched conflict between business and environmental interests (Kraft 2006, 129–31). Presidents can expect political costs and limited public credit when they involve themselves in environmental and energy policy.

This may explain why presidents often resort to administrative tools under their direct control to reshape environmental and energy policy. The many instruments at their disposal include presidential signing statements, executive orders, budget allocations, supervision of regulations through the Office of Management and Budget, and appointments to federal agencies and federal courts (Bosso and Gruber 2006, 93). George W. Bush employed all of these tools in policymaking regarding energy and the environment. Bush's approach to these issues did evolve during the course of his presidency. His initial actions in office—suspending pending environmental regulations from the Clinton presidency, withdrawing from the international Kyoto Protocol agreement requiring mandatory reductions in carbon emissions, and creating a secret task force on energy policy headed by Vice President Cheney, himself a former oilman—earned him the outspoken enmity of environmentalists. By 2007, however, Bush actively sought a response to climate change and signed a bipartisan bill to curb energy use that included increases in mandatory automobile fuel efficiency standards (Baker 2007A).

Bush's initial use of his formal executive powers aimed to revise certain long-standing environmental policies. His first five budgets called for cuts in funding for the Environmental Protection Agency (EPA). His appointments to subcabinet positions with environmental responsibilities were described in the *New York Times* as "pro-business advocates who had worked on behalf of various industries in battles with the federal government, largely during the Clinton years" (Seelye 2001). Christine Todd Whitman, the former New Jersey Governor appointed to head the EPA, found herself publicly contradicted by President Bush in March 2001 when, in response to complaints from industry groups, he reversed his campaign promise to regulate power plants' emission of carbon dioxide (Jehl and Revkin 2001). She resigned in early 2003. Bush entrusted energy policy development to a secret task force dominated by energy producers. Throughout the Bush presidency, the Office of Management and Budget's Office of Information and Regulatory Affairs (OIRA) stressed the need to "monetize costs and benefits and to demonstrate the 'net benefits' of environmental, health and safety regulations"

(Vig 2006, 114). This led to criticisms from scientists and environmentalists that the Bush administration was excluding inconvenient evidence and thus "politicizing science."

The administration's initial environmental and energy agenda in Congress moved slowly. Congress refused to approve the administration's Clear Skies Initiative, a "cap and trade" approach that would allow polluting industries to buy and sell emissions credits. Opponents argued that the proposal allowed for a substantial increase in air pollution. The White House's initial energy policy proposal, announced in 2001, finally became law in a modified form in 2005. The legislation had been stalled by Senate refusal to approve drilling in the Arctic National Wildlife Refuge, in which opposition from a handful of moderate GOP Senators proved decisive. After that contentious issue was set aside, the Energy Policy Act of 2005 became law, providing about $85 billion in tax incentives and subsidies for energy producers and provisions to stimulate research in energy conservation (White House 2005). One relatively speedy success for the administration was passage of the Healthy Forests Initiative, which promoted forest thinning in "wildland-urban interface areas" subject to risk from wildfires. But this also engendered controversy. Environmentalists charged that the law benefited timber companies under the guise of property protection, and battled implementation of the law (National Resources Defense Council 2006).

Fights over the Bush administration's approach to environmental regulation led in 2007 to the Supreme Court's first decision about global warming. In 1999, several environmental groups petitioned the Environmental Protection Agency to set standards for greenhouse gas emissions for new vehicles. In 2003, Bush's EPA declined to do so, arguing that it had no authority to regulate emissions and that even if it did, it might not because of "numerous areas of scientific uncertainty" about global warming's causes and effects (Barnes and Eilperin 2007, A1). The court, however, in a 5–4 decision ruled that the EPA indeed had such authority and that its reasons for not regulating had no basis in law. Further, the agency could not sidestep its authority to regulate greenhouse gases "unless it could provide a scientific basis for doing so" (Barringer and Yardley 2007). Despite this, the administration decided to postpone any new EPA steps to regulate greenhouse emissions until after Bush's final term of office. By 2008, Bush's EPA was a weakened force, due to budget cuts and its frequent subordination to the White House regarding policy (Kriz 2008).

Accumulating evidence regarding climate change did lead to some rethinking by Bush later in his second term. After a series of secret briefings on the subject during the summer of 2006, he came to believe that more needed to be done. In early 2007, he mentioned climate change for the first time in a State of the Union address and accompanied that with a plan to "cut gasoline consumption and, by extension, greenhouse gases, and [convene] a conference of major world polluters to start work on an international accord to follow the Kyoto Protocol" (Baker 2007B, A1). The international talks produced little immediate result, in part because the administration continued to oppose mandatory carbon emission limits for polluting nations. Bush, however, did devote more attention to bargaining with congressional Democrats, and this produced results. Working with a Democratic Congress, Bush was able to sign the second energy bill of his presidency with priorities different from those of the 2005 energy law. The 2005 energy law emphasized research and development and minimal regulation, but the 2007 bill created a variety of regulations to reduce carbon emissions. Auto fuel efficiency standards required producers' fleets to average 35 miles per gallon by 2025, up from the previous 25 mpg requirement. Incandescent light bulbs were banned by 2013, and greater energy efficiency standards for buildings became law. The law also required fuel producers to use at least 36 billion gallons of ethanol and other biofuels by 2022, a fivefold increase over preexisting standards (Baker 2007A, A18).

Throughout most of his presidency, Bush could not develop support beyond his partisan base for his pro-business orientation toward environmental and energy policy. That produced limited legislation until his second term, when the administration became more flexible in its approach. The arrival of a Democratic Congress, accompanied by a change in the president's views, led to productive bargaining and a bipartisan 2007 energy law. Internationally, throughout its two terms the Bush administration reacted defensively to more aggressive emissions control plans proposed by European nations, and its efforts to interest other nations in less restrictive approaches achieved little progress. Domestically, the entrenched and warring interests over environmental and energy policy ensured that Bush would receive little political credit in this area. As Christopher Foreman put it: "the ever-treacherous politics of environmental policy makes it difficult for a business-oriented president to claim credit among environmentalists for decisions that he believes are both business friendly and environmentally sensitive" (Foreman 2007, 277).

The Domestic War on Terror

After 9/11, the war on terror became a guiding focus for the Bush administration throughout its time in office. This emphasis led to two major legislative initiatives: the Patriot Act of 2001 providing for domestic surveillance of

American citizens and the 2002 creation of a new cabinet-level Department of Homeland Security. The first became a source of political controversy and the second was the largest federal governmental reorganization of recent decades. The Patriot Act, recommended in the immediate wake of 9/11 by Attorney General John Ashcroft, rushed through Congress and received the president's signature in late October 2001. In contrast, the idea for a Department of Homeland Security originally arose in Congress, with the administration only gradually warming to the idea. Strong administration support for the department, however, made it a major issue in the 2002 congressional elections.

The Patriot Act was complex antiterrorism legislation that passed the Senate 96–1 and the House 337–79 "in an atmosphere of edgy alarm, as federal law enforcement officials warned that another attack could be imminent" (Toner and Lewis 2001). Reflecting this mood, bill supporter F. James Sensenbrenner (R-WI), chair of the House Judiciary Committee, declared that "time is of the essence in light of the increased threat the FBI has announced against the United States and its citizens" (Toner and Lewis 2001). Bush's great political capital allowed the administration to use a directive approach toward a compliant Congress. Only in the House did some vocal opposition appear. Carolyn Kilpatrick (D-MI), for example, argued that "we are now poised to consider a measure that grants our federal government broad sweeping powers to investigate not only terrorism, but all crimes. We are poised to consider legislation that may jeopardize the civil liberties that we hold dear" (Congressional Record 2001, H6771).

Signed by the president on October 26, 2001, the law increased penalties for supporters of terrorist groups and encouraged better sharing of information among intelligence and law enforcement agencies, including information gained by grand juries. It gave the government powers to monitor email among terrorism suspects and with a single warrant wiretap any phones a suspect might use. Its provisions were to be in force for two years, at which time the president could extend those provisions (as Bush did) for two more years. It was subject to reauthorization in 2005.

The sweeping law was bound to create controversies over its years of enforcement, and civil liberties groups challenged many of its provisions in court and public debate. Particularly controversial aspects of the law were the National Security Letter (NSL) provisions that allowed the FBI to search telephone, email, and financial records of suspects without a court order. In November 2005 it was disclosed that the FBI had issued tens of thousands of NSLs and had obtained one million records from the customers of targeted Las Vegas businesses (Dunham 2005). The American Civil Liberties

Union (ACLU) challenged NSLs in federal court, arguing that the lack of legal recourse for a company facing an NSL subpoena made the process unconstitutional. A federal district court agreed that the procedure was unconstitutional (*John Doe and ACLU v. Ashcroft* 2004 WL 2185571 S.D.N.Y).

Another controversial provision of the law allowed for indefinite detention of any alien whom the attorney general thinks may cause a terrorist act. Senator Russell Feingold (D-WI) claimed this provision "falls short of meeting even basic standards of due process and fairness as it continues to allow the Attorney General to detain persons based on mere suspicion" (Feingold 2001). The law's expansion of court jurisdiction allowing for nationwide service of search warrants also alarmed civil libertarians. Critics argued that agencies could shop for permissive judges, thus unduly expanding the use of search warrants (Electronic Frontier Foundation 2008). Opponents of the law went to federal court to overturn its provision permitting "sneak and peak" searches, which involve temporarily delaying notification of a search order in order to secretly examine a suspect's home or possessions. In late 2007, federal district court struck down this procedure, holding the searches violate the prohibition on unreasonable searches in the Fourth Amendment. This prompted the Justice Department to appeal the decision to a higher court (Singel 2007).

Despite legal controversies, overall enforcement of the law received a positive response from Congress during deliberations over reauthorization in 2005. Most lawmakers believed the executive branch had operated within the letter of the law in enforcing it. Senator Diane Feinstein (D-CA) of the Senate Judiciary Committee, stated in 2005 that "we were not able to come up with anything that really indicated an abuse of the Patriot Act . . . we should reauthorize the Patriot Act" (Cable News Network 2005, 5). That did not mean that reauthorization would proceed smoothly. Though the House passed a reauthorization in 2005 that kept much of the act's original language, the Senate approved a version with changes to several important provisions of the act. The Senate action, fueled by the civil liberties concerns of Democrats and moderate Republicans, led to a lengthy conference committee session in early 2006. Congress and Bush agreed to a temporary extension of the act during the negotiations. The final version removed most of the changes of the Senate version, and President Bush signed the renewed Patriot Act on March 9, 2006. The administration's coalitional skills with its GOP supporters prevailed over Democratic objections. Three provisions of the act were renewed for four years; the remaining provisions were renewed permanently, with few substantive changes in the Patriot Act resulting from the months of legislative controversy.

Despite the arrival of a Democratic Congress in 2007, Bush was able to hammer out bipartisan agreement on a major expansion of governmental surveillance powers. The House and Senate passed the amendments to the Foreign Surveillance Intelligence Act (FISA) by lopsided bipartisan margins in the summer of 2008. The amendments provided greater latitude for the executive branch's use of technology to track foreign terrorism suspects overseas. They expanded the federal government's power to invoke emergency wiretaps and, in an important victory for Bush, granted legal immunity for phone companies that cooperated in the controversial National Security Agency wiretapping program instigated by the White House after 9/11. Democrats, however, won a provision in the bill requiring that all future wiretaps occur only under FISA procedures, effectively ensuring federal court scrutiny of wiretaps (Lichtblau 2008, A1).

In contrast to its strong initiative in pressing for passage of the Patriot Act and FISA amendments, the Bush White House lagged behind Congress during efforts to create a cabinet-level Department of Homeland Security. In a speech to Congress nine days after 9/11, Bush announced that he had created by executive order a new Office of Homeland Security that would oversee the nation's security from terrorism. The administration modeled the new office on the National Security Council, which synthesizes information and advises the president on the international aspects of America's security. Bush appointed former Republican Governor of Pennsylvania Tom Ridge to the position. Ridge's task was overwhelming. At least forty federal agencies were involved in efforts to counter terrorist attacks, but none of them claimed antiterrorism as their primary mission. Many had "overlapping jurisdictions, long-time rivalries and histories of a lack of cooperation" (Mucciaroni and Quirk 2004, 177). In confronting this, Ridge had very sparse resources—limited legal powers, no budgetary authority, and a small staff for inducing compliance with his decisions (Becker and Scolino 2001). Ridge was reduced to responding to immediate crises, while suffering repeated bureaucratic reverses as "various cabinet departments openly flouted his advice and failed to address security problems identified by their own inspectors general" (Becker 2001).

Bush's assertions of executive prerogative concerning the homeland security office led to a series of clashes with Congress. In the spring of 2002, the administration refused to allow Ridge to testify before a committee of the Senate, then under Democratic majority control, about homeland security matters. The president argued that "Ridge was a political advisor serving in a position created by executive order, not congressional statute" and thus not required to testify (Mycoff and Pika 2008, 147). Later that spring, a bipartisan group of lawmakers introduced a bill to make the Office of Homeland Security a cabinet department. Ridge argued that cabinet status was not necessary for his effectiveness, but in fact he had lost a series of battles with cabinet secretaries, other administration officials, and state and local agencies (Bettelheim 2002; Parks and Dalrymple 2002). The Senate continued to press for Ridge to testify.

In early summer, Bush did an about face and presented his own proposal for a Department of Homeland Security. The main features of his proposal quickly satisfied Congress because many elements of earlier legislative plans were included in it and cabinet status permitted enhanced congressional oversight in the future. The task of the proposed department, however, would be no less complex than it had been for the Office of Homeland Security. An administration analysis indicated that eighty-eight congressional committees and subcommittees had some authority over the agencies Bush wished to move to the new department. Conflict soon arose between the administration and the Democratic Senate that had considerable impact on the 2002 elections. The administration's desire to create a "flexible personnel system" for department employees encountered objections from labor unions. Bush wanted broad discretion to set pay and qualifications for hiring, promotion, and firing of these employees, but Senate Democrats disagreed. The stand-off persisted through the election campaign. Bush frequently mentioned the Senate obstruction over this issue on the stump, arguing that "special interests" were impeding homeland security. This rhetorical attack may well have helped the GOP prevail in a number of close Senate races. It created a heresthetic framework equating support for a popular administration with national security itself. After the election, in which the GOP took Senate control by a 51–49 margin, the lame duck Senate quickly passed a bill with labor provisions that satisfied the president. Bush's success flowed from his ample post election political capital.

The creation of the Department of Homeland Security (DHS) was the largest governmental reorganization since the creation of the Department of Defense shortly after World War II. Given the massive scale of organizational change and the intricate bureaucratic politics attending such a transformation, in its initial years the department encountered several organizational difficulties. DHS began operation on January 24, 2003 under its secretary, Tom Ridge. Its duties involved coordinating twenty-two diverse agencies— including the Federal Emergency Management Agency (FEMA), Transportation Security Administration, US Customs Service, Strategic National Stockpile and National Disaster Medical System, and Federal Law Enforcement Training Center—that had previously long been located elsewhere in the federal bureaucracy. Pleading exhaustion with the complexity of managing the department, Ridge stepped down in December 2004 and was replaced by Michael Chertoff. The department continued to suffer from fragmented congressional oversight, lack of a central office location (its sixty offices were scattered throughout the Washington D.C. area), and low employee morale. The slow response of FEMA to Hurricane Katrina produced widespread criticism of the department. A Government Accountability Office investigation indicated $2 billion in waste and fraud by DHS employees (Jakes Jordon 2006; Lipton 2006). In a survey of thirty-six federal agencies in 2006, DHS employees ranked dead last in job satisfaction and in results-oriented culture (Homeland Security Employees 2008). Though no major attacks on the homeland occurred after 2001, bureaucratic management of the task remained far from perfect. The new department's difficulties help to explain why the Bush administration initially sought to centralize the response to terrorism as much as possible in the White House itself.

Conclusion

The Bush presidency's record in domestic policy consists of some major disruptions of established policy routines, coupled with a steady stream of incremental changes to established policies over time. David Mayhew's tabulation of major laws passed during Bush's presidency reveals the specific characteristics of this pattern (Mayhew 2008). All of the major shifts in domestic policy occurred when his political capital was relatively high—in the opening months of his presidency and in the wake of the terrorist attacks of 9/11. During this time, Bush achieved several of his event-making ambitions in domestic policy. The 2001 to 2003 tax cuts, No Child Left Behind education reform, the Patriot Act and Department of Homeland Security, and Medicare prescription drug-Health Savings Account legislation all issue from that 2001 to 2003 period. Eight of the thirty-one major domestic policy achievements with Congress, from 2001 to 2006, concerned the response to terrorism, and six of those eight came during Bush's time of great informal powers, when he had high political capital, enjoying strong public approval and a positive professional reputation.

As Bush's political capital shrank, so did the magnitude of his domestic policy achievements with Congress. After 2003, endogenous constraints within the administration's partisan coalition and exogenous barriers in the broader political environment became more imposing. The administration's deployment of coalitional, bargaining, rhetorical, and heresthetic skills proved steadily less effective with lawmakers and the public. Social Security reform went nowhere, immigration legislation stalled, and faith-based legislation resulted in very limited changes in law. Over two dozen more modest initiatives—concerning such matters as election administration, campaign finance reform, transportation legislation, bankruptcy and corporate regulation, postal service restructuring, and disaster relief—did pass during the 2001 to 2006 period, facilitated by GOP control of the legislature and executive branches. Though the arrival of a Democratic Congress reduced the number of even these modest measures, Bush was able to sign an energy bill in late 2007 and an economic stimulus plan and intelligence surveillance reform in 2008, all with bipartisan support.

Bush relied ever more on his formal powers as his informal powers withered during his second term. Throughout his presidency, his administration aggressively asserted executive prerogative under its guiding rubric of unitary executive theory, as noted in chapter three. The Bush White House and its Office of Management and Budget exerted domestic policy control via executive orders, signing statements, appointments, and executive branch management. Bush's extensive implementation of his faith-based initiative via executive branch actions exemplifies this. Such expanded use of formal powers may provide future presidents with important resources for directing domestic policy. The major disruptions in domestic policy that many presidents seek, however, will continue to be elusive and situational, dependent upon the presence of the informal powers of political capital—an evanescent yet vital presidential resource.

5 FOREIGN POLICY

The course of the George W. Bush presidency turned on its foreign policy decisions, particularly those concerning Iraq. The choice for war in Iraq came in a context of perceived threats in the wake of 9/11, confidence born of initial military success in Afghanistan, and Washington consensus on Iraq's danger as a possessor of weapons of mass destruction (WMDs). Add in an administration keen to restore presidential power, and the stage was set for truly fateful decisions. All of the key variables that shape a presidency—power, authority, skills, and events—figured importantly in the major foreign policy decisions of the Bush presidency. In this realm, Bush energetically exercised and expanded his formal powers, by enunciating an ambitious foreign policy doctrine and creating new presidential clout regarding military command, homeland security, and intelligence monitoring. But Bush's managerial and heresthetic skills eventually proved deficient, contributing to a series of adverse foreign policy events during the American occupation of Iraq. The paradoxical result was a concurrent expansion of formal presidential power and shrinkage of Bush's regime authority as his informal powers of political capital withered under the foreign policy difficulties of his second term.

On September 10, 2001, political scientist Mark Rozell was quoted in the Washington Post arguing that if the new Bush administration wished to bolster its legal argument for increased executive power, it would be wise to find "something really big, like a national security issue" (Nakashima and Eggen 2001). That arrived the next day. The attack on the World Trade Center and the Pentagon inflated the president's political capital, producing strong popular support and receptivity to his leadership throughout Washington. But underneath this boon lay some strong limitations to Bush's political authority that would prove more lasting than his temporary boost in political capital. First, Bush's partisan coalition was a minority party in the Senate and held only a narrow majority in the House. Bush himself had gained office with only a minority of the popular vote. Should partisanship over foreign policy return, Bush's authority in Washington would suffer. Second, controversial foreign policies could also fall victim to "institutional thickening" in which established bureaucracies in the State and Defense Departments and Central Intelligence Agency (CIA) might "parry and deflect" the administration's efforts (Skowronek 1997, 413). In fact, the Bush administration after 2001 encountered harsh partisanship and bureaucratic resistance regarding important aspects of its foreign policy. The President's managerial, heresthetic, and rhetorical skills faced increasing challenges on these fronts, gradually but substantially depleting his informal powers of political capital and thus his regime authority. Despite this, the Bush administration was able to expand formal presidential powers in several important ways. One reason for this is the unique constitutional position of the president regarding foreign policy, which helps to explain how presidential powers could expand even as presidential authority contracted.

The President and Foreign Policy

George W. Bush's desire to expand formal presidential powers had particularly large implications for foreign policy, an area in which the president dominates processes and outcomes. The roots of formal presidential power over foreign policy lie in four general grants of authority in Article Two of the Constitution: commander in chief of the armed forces of the United States, negotiator and signer of treaties with foreign governments, conductor of diplomacy, and appointer of cabinet secretaries and ambassadors. These powers have grown in consequence as America's geopolitical role expanded after World War II. Congress responded by increasing executive branch budgets and employment for the conduct of these constitutional duties.

The White House itself became the institutional center of the foreign policy process in recent decades, resulting from the rise of "a presidential branch separate from the executive branch" (Polsby 1990, 201). Congress, in passing the National Security Act of 1947, provided the president with two new organizations, the National Security Council (NSC) and Central Intelligence Agency, to assist with broadened presidential duties. The act also created a national security advisor who reports directly to the president, along with a supporting staff now numbering about sixty. Presidents have consistently used the NSC—made up of the secretaries of Defense, State, Justice, and Treasury, and the vice president—as an arm of presidential leadership. The NSC staff works directly for the president and acts as an independent voice separate from the perspectives of the Defense and State Departments.

Presidents employ the NSC in their advisory systems on foreign policy.

The overall advisory system can include many players or the perspectives of few, depending on the temperament of the president. Bush, as we will see, relied on a "small, tightly controlled group of loyalists" regarding some critical foreign policy decisions (Haney 2005, 296). Beyond this advisory system lay the Departments of Defense and State, the former with the largest workforce of any department and the latter with a global corps of diplomats, both subject to presidential direction. The CIA and related intelligence services work for the president and their handwork appears in his daily intelligence briefings.

The military has also become an attractive and useful foreign policy tool for presidents. It had increased its power, autonomy, and legitimacy by the end of the twentieth century. Technological changes had made America's fighting forces by far the world's largest and most effective, requiring fewer people to fight major wars. The American military no longer relied on conscription. These changes increased its autonomy, in that its effective use involved fewer costs for the rest of the nation. The armed forces regularly advertise the military virtues as well, and remain very popular with the public in opinion polls. All this makes the military a handy tool for presidents to employ. And employ them George W. Bush very much did (Alasdair Roberts 2008, 106–7).

Presidents now enjoy many advantages over Congress in making foreign policy. Political scientist Stephen Hook notes that presidents have the edge in "coherence, speed, secrecy, a national constituency and control of information" whereas Congress can only claim the advantages of "deliberation, compromise and openness" (Hook 2008, 108). All this constitutes an invitation for presidents to deploy many skills—managerial, heresthetic, bargaining, rhetorical, and coalitional—on the national and international stages to great effect. Congress has operated in a largely reactive mode, able to independently shape policy only in the event of grave presidential failures. Weakened presidential authority due to foreign policy miscues, however, increases the opportunity for Congress to place its independent stamp on foreign policy. It attempted to do exactly this during the final two years of Bush's term.

Initial Bush Policy

The combination of political and institutional powers described above often leads presidents to "escape the frustrations and controversies of domestic policy making by seeking opportunities to strut their stuff in the realm of foreign and national security policy" (Rockman 1997, 26). Upon taking office, George Bush demonstrated little such inclination. The 2000 election had largely centered on domestic policy questions. Bush himself had very limited foreign policy experience as a former governor of Texas. That background figured in his early emphasis on improving relations with Mexico, choosing that nation for his first foreign visit, a month after his inauguration. Bush early on made clear his disinclination to continue the liberal multilateralism of the Clinton administration, in which America sought via treaty and multilateral military force to further human rights. The major example of that occurred in the Balkans during Clinton's second term, when the United States led a multinational military effort to curb Serbian aggression and then facilitated regional peace at a conference held at Dayton, Ohio. Bush, in contrast, indicated he was not interested in "nation building" as a major foreign policy goal. His administration initially defined its international position as a "distinctly American internationalism" with a narrower view of national interests than that of his predecessor. In particular, "hard power" would be favored over "soft power" in dealing with the international system (Bush, 1999). Hard power "refers to the utility of military capacity, sanctioning behavior, and threat behavior, among other coercive measures, as ways to influence the behavior of nations." In contrast, soft power "relies on the appeal of American culture and American values to enable the United States to influence the behavior of other states" (McCormick forthcoming, 4). Accordingly, Bush initially placed a greater emphasis on reshaping and strengthening the military than had Clinton and focused more narrowly on international involvements, eschewing efforts to create democracy in other countries.

Bush's more nationalistic view of America's international involvements appeared in his disavowal of international agreements negotiated by previous administrations. During the administration's first months, he withdrew from the Kyoto Protocol, an international agreement regarding global warming. Later that year, he withdrew from the 1972 Anti-Ballistic Missile Treaty in order to develop and deploy a missile defense system. In early 2002, Bush ordered America, alone among nations, to not recognize the jurisdiction of the International Criminal Court. As a candidate and president, he opposed a Comprehensive Nuclear Test Ban Treaty, arguing that it was not verifiable and would not ensure the safety of the US nuclear arsenal. On all of these matters, Bush disagreed with his predecessor, Bill Clinton.

The Shock of 9/11

The Islamic terrorist group Al Qaeda had a bloody history of terrorist attacks against the United States, including lethal bombings of the World Trade Center in 1993, US embassies in Kenya and Tanzania in 1998, and the US Navy ship *Cole* offshore in Yemen in 2000 (Clarke 2004, 78–79). Though the administration had received intelligence warnings during mid-2001 of increased activity by Al Qaeda, no specific dates or targets had become evident through intelligence channels. Thus the collision of two airliners into the World Trade Center and another into the Pentagon on September 11, 2001, killing 2,998 people, came as a profound shock to the administration and nation. Bush learned of the attacks while meeting with a group of school children in Florida, and then spent the remainder of the day traveling to a series of secure locations across the country while consulting with his advisors literally "on the fly." His initial reaction was visceral, telling Vice President Cheney: "We're at war, Dick. And were going to find out who did this and we're going to kick their ass" (Fleischer 2005, 42). He addressed the nation briefly twice during the day and then from the White House later in the evening. In that speech, he made a statement that would later become a central tenet of his administration's new foreign policy doctrine: "We will make no distinction between the terrorists who committed these acts and those who harbor them."

The initial challenges for the administration were in determining who planned and coordinated the attacks, whether more were imminent, and how to respond. The response would have to involve both enhanced domestic security and international diplomatic and military action to bring down the perpetrators. An advisory system based on regular meetings of the "principals"—the president, vice president, National Security Advisor Condoleezza Rice, Secretary of State Colin Powell, Secretary of Defense Donald Rumsfeld, and CIA Director George Tenet, at times accompanied by their assistants—would pilot foreign policy in the coming months.

This situation provided President Bush a rare opportunity to have an unusually large impact on foreign policy. Political scientist Glen Hastedt notes that presidents have their greatest impact under four conditions. First, when the issue is new to the agenda. Although Al Qaeda had engaged in terrorist acts against the United States for a number of years, none of them approached the scale of 9/11. A "global war on terror" was new to the agenda. Second, when the issue is addressed early in the administration, as the 9/11 response was. Third, when the issue is ongoing and deeply involves the president. The terrorism problem was ongoing and would consume Bush. Fourth, when the issue is in a state of "precarious equilibrium," meaning it could evolve in one of several possible directions. The 9/11 situation involved all of these characteristics (Hastedt 2008, 186–87). It gave George W. Bush a power few of his predecessors had to reshape American foreign and military policy.

Intelligence reports clearly indicated that Al Qaeda, based in Afghanistan, had directed the 9/11 attacks. The Taliban, a fundamentalist Islamic organization headed by Mullah Omar, had taken over the nation after the Soviet withdrawal in the 1990s. Under their harsh rule, Afghanistan had become a pariah nation, uniquely supportive of terrorism and the strictest interpretation and enforcement of Islamic law upon its citizens. The Bush administration demanded the regime turn over the Al Qaeda leaders, close their camps, protect foreign nationals in their country, and give the United States the right to inspect terrorist camps, but it was unlikely a diplomatic approach would prove effective. Bush announced these demands in a September 20 speech to Congress. The Taliban refused to speak directly with Bush, holding that talking to a non-Muslim political leader would insult Islam. Speaking through their embassy in Pakistan, they rejected the American demands.

Planning for the military option then proceeded apace. The United Nations Security Council authorized the use of its International Security Assistance Force to aid in securing Afghanistan. In the days following the 9/11 attacks, Bush had convened a meeting of the principals to discuss strategic options at Camp David. At the meeting Defense Secretary Rumsfeld and Assistant Defense Secretary Paul Wolfowitz suggested that Iraq be considered as a target for military action along with Afghanistan. Saddam Hussein, Iraq's brutal dictator, had long been a security problem for the United States. His invasion and occupation of Kuwait prompted the Gulf War of 1991, which resulted in partition of Iraq into three zones, a central region totally controlled by Hussein and northern and southern "no fly zones" patrolled by American aircraft, limiting Hussein's power over them. Postwar UN inspections had discovered an active nuclear weapons program that was close to success and large stores of chemical and biological weapons. The UN also imposed economic sanctions on Iraq, allowing oil exports only in exchange for food and medicine. The sanctions failed to dislodge Hussein. Iraq's failure to comply with UN weapons inspections led to the withdrawal of inspectors. On October 31, 1998, President Clinton signed the Iraqi Liberation Act, making it the formal policy of the United States to remove the Hussein regime. The act provided funds to Iraqi opposition groups and sought to create a democracy in Iraq. Operation Desert Fox, a four-day US bombing campaign against Iraqi military targets, occurred in December. Some intelligence reports indicated an Iraqi plot to assassinate former president George Herbert Walker Bush when he visited Kuwait in 1993, a family threat his son would later mention in a speech to the United Nations in 2002.

All this made Iraq an appealing target for American hawks, but at the time of the Camp David meeting, no intelligence clearly linked Iraq to the 9/11 attacks. Bush, Cheney, Rice, and Powell all agreed that the primary target at that time had to be Afghanistan. Still, the Iraq possibility did not leave the

THE SHOCK OF 9/11   131

president's mind. A short time later he instructed Richard Clarke, director of counterterrorism for the NSC, to scour intelligence sources for evidence of an Iraq connection to 9/11 (Clarke 2004, 30–32). By early October, another terror threat arose, as the deadly anthrax virus appeared in the mailboxes of journalists and even some senators. This led to evacuations of congressional offices and an intensive FBI search for the perpetrators, to no avail.

In this climate of national peril, Bush announced the commencement of military operations against the Taliban. 9/11 had taken the Pentagon very much by surprise, and operational planning for action in Afghanistan began almost from scratch. The administration in early September had moved toward approval of a CIA plan to provide assistance to several Afghan guerrilla organizations then challenging the Taliban regime, most prominently including the Northern Alliance, but few plans existed for large-scale military operations from Afghanistan (Woodward 2002, 35–6). Secretary Rumsfeld, a proponent of defense modernization, argued for an operation with limited American troops, coordination with Afghan guerrilla organizations, and maximum use of high tech targeting and weaponry. The general in charge, Tommy Franks, provided such a plan to Rumsfeld. The operation began with an initial deployment of CIA operatives and special forces to coordinate anti-Taliban attacks. Then came an air campaign that inflicted heavy damage on Taliban positions, which were not well fortified. As guerrillas advanced on the Taliban, American planes controlled the skies. Antigovernment guerrillas and American troops gained control of the country by early December. The American military leaders allowed guerrillas to take the lead in the final battle of Tora Bora, but their poor coordination allowed Osama Bin Laden, head of Al Qaeda, to escape.

The Afghan campaign was crowned with initial success, reinforcing the prestige of the military as an arm of presidential foreign policy. Fewer than four thousand American troops had actually been on the ground in Afghanistan during the short 2001 war (Globalsecurity.org 2008). The United States had received widespread international support for the operation; the North Atlantic Treaty Alliance (NATO) provided troops outside of the European theater for the first time in the pact's existence, in response to the attack upon a member state, the United States. Afghanistan began halting steps toward democracy, holding a constitutional convention in 2002, approving a new constitution in 2004 and also that year holding elections producing the election of Hamid Karzai as president. Despite this, Taliban guerrillas remained militarily active in several regions of the country. This led to a gradual increase in combat over several years and an increase in American and NATO troops in the country, which stood at 32,200 and 29,000 respectively in 2008 (Zakaria 2008).

The Afghan campaign produced military success with minimal American casualties. The American-led effort had received widespread international support, given the Taliban's clear link to the 9/11 attacks. Rumsfeld's battle plan, featuring much use of high-tech weaponry and limited ground troops, had proven stunningly successful. The presence of well-armed guerrillas provided the new Afghan government with indigenous military support, limiting the number of American and NATO troops necessary during an initial occupation phase once the Taliban had been overthrown. All this stoked optimism and confidence among people in the Bush administration as they contemplated their next strategic target: Iraq. The president by early 2002 enjoyed an abundance of political capital at home—high job approval (during most of the year above 65 percent in most polls), and a professional reputation as a daring and successful leader of the terror war.

A New Foreign Policy Doctrine

The administration's confidence probably contributed to its development of a new national security strategy for the nation, released in September 2002, one year after the 9/11 attacks. Much in the statement stressed continuities with previous foreign policy, such as the need for advancing democracy, working with allies, promoting economic prosperity and international trade, and solving problems of the world's trouble spots. Two new policies in the statement, however, drew much domestic and international attention and controversy. One was America's first formal statement of a policy of preemption against enemies. Given that "rogue states and terrorists" do not attack by "conventional means," "to forestall or prevent such hostile acts by our adversaries, the United States will, if necessary, act preemptively." Though the "United States has long maintained the option of preemptive action to counter a sufficient threat to our national security," the 2002 statement now made that policy official. Second, to address such threats, America must create a hegemonic superiority in its military capability: "Our military must build and maintain our defenses beyond challenge." This would require fundamental reform of America's defense posture, "transforming the way the Defense department is run," and "experimentation with new approaches to warfare" to "provide the President with a wider range of military options to discourage aggression or any form of coercion against the United States" (National Security Council 2002, 3–4).

The new strategy enhanced the president's formal powers in several ways. Military policy, legally and constitutionally directly under presidential control, became a more important element of foreign policy. The intelligence gathering capabilities of the executive branch, also under direct presidential control, played a vital role in determining preemptive threats. Preemptive action discouraged lengthy consultations with Congress over the initiation of conflict. The new policy implicitly affirmed the Bush administration's theory of the "unitary executive," which asserted presidential dominance over decisions of war and peace (Yoo et. al. 2001).

The strategy was widely recognized as a major departure in foreign policy. Harvard historian John Lewis Gaddis termed it "the most dramatic and most significant shift" in American foreign policy since 1945. Praising the policy, Gaddis argued that it appropriately suited the new circumstances of the twenty-first century: "The logic of the administration's strategy has been to say that pre-emption is necessary to deal with adversaries like the 9/11 terrorists because you not only have to find these people themselves, but you also have to either intimidate or, if necessary, take out those states which might have been supporting such terrorists in the past, the assumption being that terrorism can't succeed without some kind of state support" (Gaddis 2004). The strategy encountered a strong opponent in Senator Ted Kennedy (D-MA), who in a speech a month after it was announced found two major flaws in its approach. First: "The coldly premeditated nature of preventive attacks and preventive wars makes them anathema to well-established principles against aggression." Second: "America cannot write its own rules for the modern world. To attempt to do so would be unilateralism run amok" (Carroll 2002). Kennedy's points were shared by the policy's international critics, who argued it "flouted international laws and norms . . . reflected a degree of arrogance and hubris by suggesting no other countries could ever rival American military forces and set a dangerous precedent in international relations—after all, the logic of preemption could be used to justify aggression by any country" (Bernell 2008, 400).

The new strategy posed political problems for the administration as it sought to implement it. Reform and restructuring of the military would involve Secretary Rumsfeld in bitter battles within his own department while at the same time he was managing large overseas commitments of military forces. More importantly, military preemption carries great domestic political risks for a president. It makes military intervention heavily dependent upon the quality of intelligence reports regarding the severity of the threat meriting preemption. If those reports are inaccurate, the legitimacy of the intervention will suffer greatly, as the Bush administration would discover regarding Iraq. Also, by tilting foreign policy in the direction of military preemption, the strategy would make its success dependent on domestic political support for intervention. Thus, implementing the strategy would politicize foreign policy, because "ultimately, decisions to intervene are almost always based on tenuous coalitions—not consensus." This would require mobilizing "public and political support" that might result in the public's developing "unrealistic expectations about the nature, likely cost, and efficacy of military interventions" (Western 2004, 46). When compounded by unrealistic expectations by the president and his advisors in the run up to intervention, the result could be politically devastating for a president and impair the long-term utility of the strategy in achieving its goals. This happened to Bush in Iraq. An unpopular intervention could make the strategy a political nonstarter, effectively destroying its domestic political viability. All this meant that the new strategy creates high risks for a president's informal powers of political capital. Pursuing a strategy of preemption thus could damage a president's political authority and weaken the legitimacy of the partisan regime he seeks to maintain, making it a problematic strategy for a president over the long run. The effect of the strategy's implementation by the Bush administration, detailed next, certainly supports that view.

Into Iraq?

The 2002 Bush national security strategy appeared as the administration considered military intervention in Iraq to overthrow the regime of Saddam Hussein. Consideration was protracted over many months, from early 2002 until the invasion of Iraq on March 19, 2003. The group of principals steering the policy over these many months never formally debated the decision to go to war before the president. The process of going to war was instead an evolution shaped by intelligence about Iraq's programs regarding weapons of mass destruction, Saddam Hussein's resistance of resumed UN weapons inspections, and frustrations resulting from the decaying sanctions regime against Iraq and international discord over the maintenance of that regime.

Throughout this time, two empirical assumptions shaped administration decision making. First, they understood that Iraq would be a much more difficult project than Afghanistan. CIA director George Tenet had informed Bush that "the Iraqi opposition was much weaker, and Saddam ran a police state. He was hard to locate, and he used decoy look-alikes" (Woodward 2002, 329–30). Second, a widespread consensus existed in Washington and among the intelligence community that Saddam had active programs for creating weapons of mass destruction. Those programs were thought to include chemical, biological, and nuclear weapons. Tenet, in a crucial meeting with Bush in December 2002, termed the evidence a "slam dunk" in response to Bush's skepticism about its quality (Woodward 2004, 249).

The public argument about the war would be a discussion of hypotheticals, requiring the administration to present the Iraq threat starkly. In response to skeptics who saw no "smoking gun" in the prewar WMD evidence, Condoleezza Rice replied: "We don't want the smoking gun to be a mushroom cloud." Arguing for war from hypotheticals, however, is a politically risky enterprise for a president to undertake. Unlike Afghanistan, where the threat from the Taliban had become clear since 9/11, Iraq was a fuzzier picture. Was Saddam involved in 9/11? No evidence in 2002 clearly linked him to it. Was he building weapons of mass destruction? He had in the past, and had used chemical weapons against his own people, but it was less clear if he was still creating such weapons in 2002.

In this situation, Bush had to determine the extent of the threat and then convince the American public of the credibility of that threat and the appropriateness of his recommended response. These were the two dimensions of the administration's heresthetic strategy in arguing for war with Iraq. When Bush, with his great political capital in 2003, framed discussion of alternatives along these two dimensions, the debate tilted in the administration's direction. But long-term support for the administration's recommended response would hinge on events that were not foreseeable—discovery of Saddam's weapons capabilities, the effectiveness of diplomatic or military options against Iraq—and administration skills, political and military, in pursuing an unprecedented overturning of Iraq's regime. Risky, indeed.

Moving Toward War

In January 2002, Bush attempted to frame a credible threat in his State of the Union address, identifying an "axis of evil" including Iraq, Iran, and North Korea, and suggesting the possibility of preemption: "By seeking weapons of mass destruction, these regimes pose a grave and growing danger. They could provide these arms to terrorists, giving them the means to match their hatred. They could attack our allies or attempt to blackmail the United States. In any of these cases, the price of indifference would be catastrophic." In June, during a speech at West Point, the president first signaled a preemption doctrine: "Our security will require all Americans . . . to be ready for preemptive action when necessary to defend our liberty and defend our lives."

Involving the United States in preemptive war required not just heresthetic and rhetorical success in selling the conflict domestically, but also similar efforts to gain international support. The Bush administration spent much of 2002 attempting to win United Nations support for its efforts against Saddam and to assemble a "coalition of the willing" to participate in military action against Iraq. An early ally was British Prime Minister Tony Blair, who shared the administration's assessment of the seriousness of the threat from Iraq. Blair indicated to Bush that for the United Kingdom to participate in any military actions against Iraq, the United States would have to take its case to the United Nations Security Council. Though Rumsfeld and Cheney had voiced initial skepticism about this, Colin Powell prevailed in a private meeting with Bush in which he laid out the argument for pursuing diplomatic avenues regarding Iraq. On September 12, the president addressed the UN General Assembly, challenging the organization to enforce its many resolutions against Iraq, which required Saddam's full compliance with weapons inspectors. If the UN did not enforce its resolutions, Bush argued, the United States would have no choice but to act on its own. Five days, later, the administration released its new national security strategy document, elaborating on the doctrine of preemption.

Bush's abundant political capital was on much display in the fall of 2002. By requesting Congressional authorization for military action against Iraq, he placed the issue squarely in the middle of the 2002 election campaigns. Arguing for enhanced national security and underlining the Iraq threat, he spent much of the election campaign extolling the credibility of the Iraq threat. His high popular support and strong professional reputation in Washington moved Congress to approve a war resolution on October 11. The resolution authorized the President "to use the Armed Forces of the United States as he determines to be necessary and appropriate in order to (1) defend the national security of the United States against the continuing threat posed by Iraq; and (2) enforce all relevant United Nations Security Council Resolutions regarding Iraq." It placed no time limit on this authorization of presidential power. The resolution passed the Senate 77–23 and the House 296–133. Republicans voted for the resolution overwhelmingly but 61 percent of House Democrats (133 of 201) and 42 percent of Democratic Senators (21 of 50) voted against the resolution. Resolution opponent Senator Russ Feingold (D-WI) faulted the administration's arguments linking Saddam to global terrorism: "The facts just aren't there . . . the Administration appears to use 9/11 and the language of terrorism and the connection to Iraq too loosely, almost like a bootstrap." (Feingold 2001, 1). Despite such partisan differences, Bush cited the large margins of passage as evidence that "America speaks with one voice. The Congress has spoken clearly to the international community and the United Nations Security Council. Saddam Hussein and his outlaw regime pose a grave threat to the region, the world and the United States. Inaction is not an option, disarmament is a must."

The resolution provided leverage for the administration's efforts at the

UN. Powell worked assiduously to create unanimity in the Security Council regarding Iraq. He encountered resistance from France and Russia, both of which had long standing commercial and diplomatic links to Iraq and held veto authority over any resolution. On November 8, agreement was reached in the form of Resolution 1441, which imposed extensive new arms inspections on Iraq and precise definitions of what would constitute "material breach" of the resolution. Should Iraq violate the resolution, it would face "serious consequences" which the Security Council would then determine. This left any invocation of force under UN auspices to be determined.

Under international pressure, Saddam gave some signs of cooperation. In late November, UN inspectors returned to Iraq for the first time in five years. In early December, his regime gave the UN a twelve thousand page document asserting that it had no banned weapons. As the inspections continued, the Bush administration in late December increased American military presence in the Persian Gulf. American forces were joined by much smaller contingents of British and Australian troops. In his January 2003 State of the Union speech, Bush announced he was willing to attack Iraq even without another UN Security Council resolution. In the address, he presented a detailed case for a credible threat. He recounted the Iraq regime's flouting of previous Security Council resolutions, previous stockpiles of weapons of mass destruction, the invasion of Kuwait, and reign of terror over its own citizens. He also made controversial, much disputed claims that Iraq had tried to buy uranium from Niger and had purchased aluminum tubes "suitable for nuclear weapons production." He argued for preemption as a proper response to the credible threat: "Some have said we must not act until the threat is imminent. Since when have terrorists and tyrants announced their intentions, politely putting us on notice before they strike? If this threat is permitted to fully and suddenly emerge, all actions, all words, and all recriminations would come too late."

In February, chief UN inspector Hans Blix reported that some slight progress had been made in securing Iraq's cooperation. His report gave both pro and antiwar nations some support for their views. International peace demonstrations occurred around the world on February 15. Later in the month, Blix ordered Iraq to destroy some missiles found to have an unlawful flight range. The slow pace and indefinite results of the inspection had made the Bush administration impatient. Some 200,000 American troops were now in theater and could not be kept in their present deployments for a lengthy period. The signs of Saddam's good faith were all too fleeting for Bush and his advisors. On February 24, the United States and allies Britain and Spain proposed a Security Council resolution asking for an authorization of military force against Iraq. This time, consensus was not forthcoming. France, Germany, and Russia submitted an informal counter-resolution asking for intensified inspections and declaring that military action "should only be a last resort." As the Security Council deliberated, Iraq began destroying the missiles Blix had labeled in violation. By mid-March the United States and Britain, despite intense lobbying, had failed to win Security Council approval for the use of force. The United States decided not to call for a vote on the resolution. Two days later, President Bush in a public speech issued an ultimatum to Saddam, giving him forty-eight hours to leave the country or face attack. The president declared the beginning of military operations on March 19, 2003, and hostilities began at 5:30 A.M. Baghdad time on March 20. Thus began the first US military action of the war on terror lacking explicit United Nations support.

The Decision to Go to War

Throughout the months leading to military conflict with Iraq, the primary decision-making body regarding possible war was the group of principals— Bush, Cheney, Powell, Rice, Rumsfeld, and George Tenet, director of the CIA. The policy process Bush employed was closed, hierarchical, and relatively unstructured (Berry 2004, 1). The president did not reach out for advice and counsel beyond this group, telling journalist Bob Woodward "I have no outside advice. Anybody who says they're an outside advisor of this Administration on this particular matter is not telling the truth. The only true advice I get is from our war council. I didn't call around asking 'What in the heck do you think we ought to do?'" (Lemann 2004, 9).

This raises the question as to whether Bush's Iraq war decision making was subject to the pathology of groupthink. Groupthink is "a mode of thinking that people engage in when they are deeply involved in a cohesive in-group, when the members' striving for unanimity override their motivation to realistically appraise alternative courses of action" (Janis 1972, 9). Groupthink has been associated with several foreign policy fiascoes, such as the Vietnam War and Bay of Pigs invasion, in which events went drastically wrong in an unforeseen fashion. Groupthink involves several specific defects. Discussions are limited to a few—often only two—courses of action. The group fails to examine the preferred course of action in terms of nonobvious risks and drawbacks. Members neglect courses of action initially viewed as unsatisfactory by a group majority. Group members make little effort to obtain information from experts who can assess costs and benefits of different courses of action, and spend little time deliberating how the chosen policy can be sabotaged by bureaucratic inertia, political opponents, or accidents (1972, 10).

Some aspects of groupthink are evident in the Iraq war decision. The group of principals did not consult widely on alternative courses of action to war. Discussions were limited to a relatively small number of possible courses of action. Colin Powell, the leading principal in favor of a diplomatic solution, never presented this alternative course of action in detail to the principals. The president did not steer the group toward war, but neither did he steer them away from it. He never asked the principals to make their best arguments for or against the war (Von Drehle 2005, Woodward 2004, 268–274).

Some features of groupthink, however, are absent from administration decision making about Iraq. The group of principals did consider many drawbacks to the main option of war. Donald Rumsfeld in October 2002 presented the group with a memo listing twenty-nine possible pitfalls of going to war: "dire scenarios ranging from disasters that did not happen, such as chemical warfare and house-to-house combat with Saddam's troops in Baghdad, to bad things that did indeed come to pass, such as ethnic strife among Iraq's religious factions and the successful exploitation of the war as a public relations vehicle for the enemies of the United States" (Von Drehle 2005, W12). The memo also included the warning that WMDs might not be found, which would severely damage the administration's credibility. The memo, still classified, seems from reports to be a "realistic appraisal" of the problems with going to war. What remains unknown is how seriously Bush and the other principals took these possibilities. The actual decisions about the immediate military conquest of Iraq also did not result in adverse outcomes not foreseen by the principals, as happens in groupthink situations. The war plan devised by Rumsfeld and General Tommy Franks produced stunning success and a quick collapse of the Iraqi regime, with major combat operations ending on May 1. So though the decision to pursue war in Iraq had its structural flaws, it can not be classed as an egregious example of groupthink.

But important empirical errors accompanied the war decision. Too few troops had been employed in the invasion to prevent the looting of large numbers of stored weapons and of many neighborhoods and government offices throughout the country. The military had originally proposed 300,000 troops for the invasion, but Rumsfeld, keen to demonstrate the effectiveness of a technologically sophisticated, "lean" military, had countered that plan with a proposal of 80,000 to 100,000 troops landing in Baghdad and then fanning out to pacify the country. The compromise plan put 145,000 troops initially on the ground in Iraq. Rumsfeld's press conference response to the post invasion disorder—"freedom's untidy" and "stuff happens"—indicated a dismissal of what would become a severe security problem for the US occupation. Douglas Feith, Undersecretary of Defense for Policy from 2001 to 2005, later termed the looting a "disaster" for which the US military had not prepared (Feith 2008A). Vice President Cheney overestimated the welcome American troops would receive, arguing they would be celebrated as liberators in Iraq. After initial cheering in some sections of the country, a sullen, suspicious reception greeted the troops in the days after the liberation.

The major difference between the administration's Iraq and Afghan war decision making lay in the quality of the intelligence about likely conditions in the nation once the ruling regime suffered military defeat. A central risk of preemptive military policy, its reliance on intelligence, did not materialize in Afghanistan but proved real in Iraq. On two vital matters, intelligence was wrong: the possibility of an insurgency and the presence of weapons of mass destruction. Deputy Secretary of Defense Paul Wolfowitz recalled that war planners in the Pentagon were "clueless" on the need for counterinsurgency and slow to recognize the Iraq insurgency as it grew (Wolfowitz 2008). An extensive search for weapons of mass destruction resulted in a report in early 2004 by chief weapons inspector Charles Duelfer of the Iraq Survey Group, charged with investigation of Iraq's armaments. His findings starkly contradicted prewar intelligence reports indicating that Saddam had stockpiles of chemical and biological weapons and an active nuclear weapons program. Instead, Duelfer reported, Iraq had destroyed its illicit weapons stockpiles shortly after the end of the 1991 Persian Gulf War. Its last secret factory, producing biological weapons, closed in 1996. That did not mean, however, that Saddam had ended his threatening behavior. He had deliberately maintained ambiguity about his possession of illicit weapons in order to deter Iran. Further, he had over the years aimed at "preserving the capability to reconstitute his weapons of mass destruction when sanctions were lifted" (Jehl 2004A). Saddam thus posed a threat, but one less imminent that had been suggested by the Bush administration in its arguments for the war. The Bush administration did not challenge Duelfer's findings.

A third intelligence claim also received skeptical scrutiny after the war. The administration's prewar assertion of links between Al Qaeda and Saddam's regime received much election year criticism upon the release of a report of the 9/11 Commission in June 2004. The commission asserted that though it had found evidence of communication between them, no "collaborative relationship" or "operational" ties between Iraq and the terrorist organization existed. Vice President Cheney had claimed before the war that evidence of a link was "overwhelming" (Milbank 2004). In response, President Bush stated "This administration never said that the 9/11 attacks were orchestrated between Saddam and al Qaeda. We did say there were numerous contacts between Saddam Hussein and al Qaeda." In response, 9/11 panel chair Tom Kean confirmed "numerous contacts" between Iraq and Al Qaeda, but no evidence of any coordinated work at attacking the United States (Jehl 2004B).

Challenges also arose to the administration's prewar allegations about Saddam's attempts to purchase uranium in Niger and aluminum tubes for use in a nuclear weapons program. The Iraq Survey Group reported in 2004 that it could not conclude that a nuclear use was intended for the aluminum tubes purchased by Iraq, and American intelligence sources never confirmed the Niger story (Iraq Survey Group 2004). When doubts arose about the Niger claim, Condoleezza Rice admitted that the statement should not have been included in Bush's 2003 State of the Union speech, and George Tenet agreed it was a mistake (Risen 2003). Controversy over the Niger report led to battles between the administration and former ambassador Joseph Wilson, who had traveled to Niger to investigate the matter. Wilson's wife, CIA employee Valerie Plame Wilson, had her identity as a covert operative exposed during these battles. No one in the Bush administration was ever charged with the criminal offense of leaking her identity. A prosecution related to this incident, however, led to the resignation and eventual criminal conviction of Lewis Libby, Vice President Cheney's chief of staff, on a charge of perjury. President Bush later commuted Libby's sentence.

The political costs of military preemption based on intelligence reports thus mounted steadily for the administration in the wake of the invasion. Disclosures of intelligence flaws began to deplete Bush's political capital and invigorated his partisan opponents' attempts to challenge the administration's case for the war. As Bush's political capital shrank and the 2004 election drew near, the pre 9/11 polarization of American politics reasserted itself. The administration's heresthetic for war was under attack. The multiple intelligence failures undercut the credibility of the threat that the administration had presented to the American public and international community. The difficult Iraq occupation would also call into question the appropriateness of the administration's response to the Iraq threat. The president had not helped himself by speaking on the deck of an aircraft carrier under a banner that read "mission accomplished" the day after the invasion concluded. Subsequent months would reveal that hostilities had not concluded and that America did not have a sound occupation strategy at the conclusion of the invasion. Assaults on both dimensions of the Bush administration's heresthetic argument regarding Iraq would place the Bush White House on the permanent political defensive for the remainder of the president's time in office.

The Unforeseen Occupation

The administration's military plan for Iraq had not assumed that a large and lengthy military occupation of the country would be necessary following the invasion. An August 2002 plan for the invasion assumed "that a provisional government would be in place by 'D-Day,' then that the Iraqis would stay in their garrisons and be reliable partners, and finally that the post-hostilities phase would be a matter of mere 'months'" (Blanton 2007, 1). None of this came to pass. Military planners had devoted little attention to the occupation phase of the operation for two reasons. First, occupation and reconstruction was not a central function of the military. No major organization in the military was primarily entrusted with performing such duties. Second, the State Department was thought better able to handle the postwar situation in Iraq. General Franks told his associates in August 2002 that the State Department would take the lead once Saddam was toppled (Gordon and Trainer 2006, 68–74; Alasdair Roberts 2008, 125).

Franks' faith in the State Department was misplaced. The department's "Future of Iraq Project" began in 2001, but it was underfunded and poorly coordinated. It failed to produce an operational plan for managing postwar Iraq. The State and Defense Department bureaucracies also engaged in an extended turf war over the planned occupation, demonstrating poor cooperation (Ricks 2006, 103).

A related problem was the tension between Rumsfeld's desire for a "lighter, faster and stronger" military and the recommendations of generals for more troops on the ground once the invasion succeeded. Rumsfeld developed a reputation for being tough with his generals, engaging in "wire brushing" interrogations that produced enmity among the top ranks and discouraged candid discussions with the defense secretary. In 2001, he encountered opposition from his initial army chief of staff, Eric Shinseki, to reducing the size of the army. The initial Iraq war plan created by the uniformed military envisioned employing 500,000 troops, a number Rumsfeld thought was far too many. Eventually, the conflict erupted in public. General Shinseki in February 2003 told the Senate Armed Services committee that an occupying force of several hundred thousand troops was necessary to stabilize Iraq. In response, Assistant Defense Secretary Wolfowitz termed Shinseki "far off the mark." In April, fourteen months before Shinseki's retirement, Rumsfeld appointed his successor, an unusual move. The Defense Secretary did not attend Shinseki's retirement ceremony (O'Hanlon 2003). As instability in Iraq grew and American casualties mounted during the occupation, a group of four retired generals took the unprecedented move of speaking out against

Rumsfeld's conduct of the occupation. One of the four, Major General Paul Eaton, in charge of training Iraq forces in 2003–4, accused Rumsfeld of "ignoring the advice of seasoned officers and denying subordinates any chance for input. . . . I have seen a climate of groupthink become dominant and a growing reluctance by experienced military men and civilians to challenge the notions of the senior leadership" (Eaton 2006).

Given the administration's poor planning, it's no surprise that the initial months of the US occupation of Iraq had an air of improvisation. On April 15, 2003, while combat operations continued, General Jay Garner was appointed to run postwar Iraq until a new government was put in place. The immediate goal, consistent with prewar planning, was to create a functional government led by Iraqis as soon as possible. Garner began meetings with Iraqi leaders to establish a federal government. A dramatic change of approach occurred one month later, when Paul Bremer, a diplomat and former head of the counter-terrorism department of the State Department, replaced General Garner. Widespread violence in Iraq contributed to this change of approach. Bremer's job was to create order first, and then move toward creation of an Iraqi government. Bremer, head of the Coalition Provisional Authority, announced the dissolution of both Saddam's Baathist political party and the Iraqi military. On July 13, an interim governing council was appointed and given the power to draw up a new constitution and name government ministers.

Military action through much of 2003 focused on identifying and rounding up leaders of the previous regime, culminating in the capture of two hundred such leaders and the killings of Saddam's two sons on June 22. But members of the army and secret police began to form guerrilla organizations to combat the American presence. These units and other elements who called themselves Jihadists began using ambush tactics, suicide bombings, and improvised explosive devices, targeting coalition forces and checkpoints. In December, Saddam was captured and would be tried and executed in December 2006.

By the end of 2003, two different trajectories had been established for Iraq. The positive path involved a movement toward democracy. Creating a popular government would be difficult in a nation with strong sectarian divisions. A majority of the nation was Shia Muslim, predominately centered in the south. The minority Sunni Muslims, mainly located around Baghdad, had long benefited from the rule of Saddam, a fellow Sunni. In the north, the Kurds, a separate ethnic group, formed no natural coalition with either Shia or Sunni Muslims. In late 2003, Iraqi leaders called for elections, but the Coalition Provisional Authority preferred to delay elections and instead hand over power eventually to an interim, appointed Iraqi government. On May 28, 2004 Ayad Allawi was chosen as prime minister of the interim government, and a month later Bremer departed. The Allawi government, populated with significant numbers of holdovers from the Coalition Provisional Authority, attempted to secure control of the major cities of Iraq and of the oil infrastructure, the foundation of Iraq's currency. The continuing insurgencies, the haphazard state of the Iraqi Army and security forces, and a lack of revenue hampered their efforts to assert control. In addition, both former Baathist and militant Shia Islamic insurgent groups established their own security zones in all or part of a dozen cities.

In this unstable situation, 58 percent of eligible Iraqi voters nevertheless turned out in large numbers to elect an interim National Assembly to draft a new constitution. On October 15, 2004, the assembly's proposed constitution underwent popular ratification. The constitution required a majority of the national vote, and could be blocked by a two-thirds "no" vote in each of at least three of eighteen regions. In the actual vote, 79 percent of the voters voted in favor, and there was a two-thirds "no" vote in only two regions, both predominantly Sunni. Turnout was again high, with 63 percent of eligible voters participating. Parliamentary elections followed on December 15, featuring a strong turnout of 70 percent of those eligible. After protracted negotiations among the several political parties constituting the new permanent National Assembly, Nouri Al-Maliki, a Shia Muslim, was chosen as prime minister. The stability of Al-Maliki's government depended on a tenuous peace between Moqtada al-Sadr, who controlled one of the largest voting blocs in parliament, and two other parties, the United Iraqi Alliance and the Islamic Iraqi Supreme Council, the largest Shia party. Generations-long feuds carried over into political rivalries among Sunni and Shia factions, and their militias periodically clashed in 2005 and 2006.

The conflict among militias was evidence of a second important national trajectory that was far less promising. The nation's security situation deteriorated during the initial years of the occupation. Iraq became a violent caldron of conflict among sectarian insurgents. Though the Kurds in the north were peaceful, Shia Muslims produced several insurgent factions. Former Baathists fueled a Sunni Muslim insurgency. Al Qaeda developed a growing presence in Iraq, led by an associate of Osama Bin Laden, Abu Musab al-Zarqawi. The Iraq Health Ministry, in a study for the World Health Organization, estimated that 151,000 Iraqi civilians died between March 2003 and June 2006 (Hurst 2006). The unstable conditions prevented a large-scale withdrawal of American troops after the invasion. Instead, Americans forces worked to train the slowly forming Iraqi armed forces and maintain stability in the country. By late 2003, the Defense Department announced plans to reduce the number of American forces in Iraq to 105,000 by early 2004, but the deteriorating security situation made that impossible. By November 2006, 140,000 troops remained stationed in the nation, regularly subject to guerrilla attacks and roadside bombs.

A steady stream of American casualties ensued. Military deaths rose from 486 in the year of the invasion—only 139 in the invasion itself—to 849, 825, and 822, respectively, in 2004, 2005, and 2006 (Iraq Coalition Casualty Count 2008). The total of American forces wounded annually was four to six times the number of deaths. The American media employed the casualty count as an important indicator of the occupation's deterioration. Milestones were established in war coverage with every additional thousand US military deaths, suggesting the American occupation strategy was not working. America also suffered diplomatically when the humiliation of prisoners by rogue American soldiers at Abu Ghraib prison resulted in disturbing photographs of torture disseminated worldwide. The abuses were uncovered in April 2004.

What was the American strategy during the initial years of the occupation? Rumsfeld had remained firmly set against increasing American troop strength, and his Iraqi commander, George Casey, echoed his view. The prewar hope that Iraqis would quickly restore order after the invasion remained a core assumption behind American policy from 2003 to 2006. The strategy basically left the impetus to create order up to the Iraqis. President Bush summarized it in his public rhetoric: "As the Iraqi forces stand up, we will stand down." By limiting the American troop presence and training Iraqi forces, the plan was to exit as quickly as possible.

This proved to be a triumph of hope over experience. America had never undertaken this sort of concurrent military occupation and nation building before. There were no established roadmaps on how to proceed. By early 2006, conditions had worsened. On February 22, Sunni insurgents bombed and seriously damaged the golden dome, the Shias' most revered shrine in Iraq. This led to a surge of sectarian fighting over the next several months. At the end of April, a report by the Special Inspector General for Iraq Reconstruction revealed that oil, gas, electrical, and water reconstruction projects were lagging behind schedule. Insurgent attacks had slowed the work and security concerns had added to reconstruction costs. The previous years had seen the military and reconstruction costs of America's involvement in Iraq soar far beyond prewar estimates. Before the war, Paul Wolfowitz told a congressional hearing that a war cost estimate of $95 billion was too high, but by 2006 the cost had reached $400 billion and was climbing (Western 2005, 15; Belasco 2008, 12). The poor progress in Iraq exacted domestic political costs for Bush and the GOP as public opinion soured on the war, with majorities in several national polls terming it a mistake and Republicans losing control of the House and Senate in the November elections. The day after the election, Bush accepted Rumsfeld's resignation.

In retrospect, the Pentagon identified several errors in their approach to Iraq security during 2003 to 2006. In late 2007, Admiral Michael Mullen, chair of the Joint Chiefs of Staff, disclosed seven such mistakes. Three involved a deficient understanding and approach to the social and political complexities of Iraq and the surrounding region. The American occupiers failed to adequately engage tribal and local power structures, poorly communicated their intended goals to the Iraqi and regional audience, and did not establish dialogue with countries bordering Iraq. Four errors concerned America's military operations in the country. The various elements of US power were not well integrated during the occupation and the United States attempted "transition to stability operations with an insufficient force." Mullen identified Paul Bremer's disbanding of the Iraqi army and banning of the Baathist party as major mistakes. By dissolving the army, the United States created "a recruiting pool for extremist groups." De-Baathification "proved more divisive than helpful, created a lingering vacuum in governmental capability that still lingers, and exacerbated sectarian tensions" (Jackson 2007).

Considering a Surge

President Bush faced a very difficult situation in late 2006. The Iraq occupation had been riddled with errors, antiwar Democrats now controlled Congress, the Defense Department needed new leadership, and the public had turned against the war. There were few historical precedents in American foreign policy to draw upon in plotting the future of America in Iraq. In early December, a bipartisan commission appointed by Congress and chaired by James Baker, Secretary of State during the first Bush presidency and Lee Hamilton, a former Democratic Representative from Indiana, released a report on America's Iraq policy. The commission recommended a phased withdrawal of US combat forces from Iraq, perhaps after a temporary, small-scale surge in troops to stabilize security in the region of Baghdad. A precipitous withdrawal, they argued, would create chaos in the country. The United States should engage in direct dialogue with Syria and Iran over Iraq and the Middle East. The Pentagon, according to the commission, had underreported the extent of the violence in Iraq and had obtained sketchy information regarding the source of these attacks. The commission further described the situation in Afghanistan as unstable, suggesting a possible diversion of troops from Iraq to help stabilize the country (Baker, et. al. 2006).

As the news in Iraq remained bad in 2006, President Bush began to seek options to the present strategy. The "train and leave" approach had focused on training Iraqi troops as quickly as possible and then withdrawing American forces. It was failing because the Iraqi military was not able to contain the widespread sectarian violence plaguing the country. The security problem by 2006 no longer primarily concerned Iraqi insurgents. Instead, it involved widespread battles involving Sunni and Shia militias, exacerbated by an active Al Qaeda presence. Civilian Iraqis in this situation welcomed American troops as insurers of security. But American troops were too small in number for this task and had no orders to provide security. That would be up to Iraqi forces. Meanwhile, more than 34,000 Iraqi citizens died in the 2006 violence.

Under Iraq commander General George Casey, American forces in June attempted to secure areas of the country, acting as support for Iraqi troops. But the Iraqi troops failed to perform the missions well, and those experiments failed. Enhanced security in the short term would probably have to come from American troops themselves. Bush began querying National Security Council staffers about alternative strategies. During the last half of 2006, he engaged in meetings with a wide variety of individuals about possible strategies, including journalists, think tank scholars, uniformed military, and State and Defense Department officials. Three strategies arose from these consultations. One involved continuing "train and leave," hoping the Iraq army and government would improve its performance. Another, the "burn out" strategy, had support from the State Department. American troops would decline in number and be positioned near Iraq's borders to prevent foreign incursions as the sectarian militias fought it out in the central part of the country. Bush ultimately rejected this policy, declaring: "I don't believe you can have political reconciliation if your capital city is burning" (Barnes 2008).

The third strategy, one of "clear, hold and build," required additional American troops that would take the lead in securing areas of war-torn Iraq. With a "surge" of troops into areas of high conflict, order might be restored and political reconciliation might have its best change of reappearing. To Bush, this seemed the only strategy likely to produce victory via the development of a stable, peaceful Iraqi democracy. As he warmed to this approach, he encountered considerable resistance within the administration and executive branch. Secretary of State Condoleezza Rice favored a reduction in troops. Secretary Rumsfeld had rejected a surge plan in September 2006. The Joint Chiefs of Staff also were skeptical of the surge. In a two-hour meeting with them in December 2006, Bush cajoled them into accepting a surge strategy.

Bush had recruited a civilian and a military leader who supported the surge. Robert Gates became Rumsfeld's replacement as defense secretary. Gates had served on the National Security Council staff and as CIA director during the first Bush presidency. A member of the Baker-Hamilton commission, he had successfully advocated inclusion of a surge strategy in its final report. General David Petraeus became George Casey's successor as American commander in Iraq. Petreaus had authored the army's counterinsurgency manual. The surge would be based on that manual's tactics. The new commander asked for a minimum of five new American brigades for the surge, and Bush guaranteed those forces. Petreaus had the strong support of Vice President Cheney, who supported the change in strategy. Bush also needed to get assurances from Iraqi Prime Minister Al-Maliki that Iraq's government and armed forces would support an American-led surge strategy. He received those assurances during a series of conversations in November and December (Barnes 2008).

Adversity can alter a president's method of making decisions. In contrast to the relatively closed deliberative process about the commencement of war in Iraq, Bush consulted widely about alternative strategies when confronted with evidence that the Iraq military strategy was failing in 2006. Bush's surge decision involved widespread consultation with "experts or qualified colleagues within the organization who are not core members of the policymaking group," a useful antidote to groupthink (Janis 1972, 214). It resembles more the constructive decision making during the Cuban Missile Crisis, when those involved, including the president, "had to undergo the unpleasant experience of hearing their pet ideas critically pulled to pieces, and the acute distress of being reminded that their collective judgments could be wrong" (1972, 165). Better managerial skills by Bush in this instance, however, was no guarantee of success on the ground in Iraq.

Bush announced his surge strategy in a speech to the nation on January 10, 2007: "Our troops will have a well-defined mission: to help Iraqis clear and secure neighborhoods, to help them protect the local population, and to help ensure that the Iraqi forces left behind are capable of providing the security that Baghdad needs." Along with the surge, the president also announced a series of benchmarks of progress toward increased security and political reconciliation for the Iraqi government to meet. Democrats strongly condemned the new approach and Republicans remained largely silent. Senate Majority Leader Harry Reid and House Speaker Nancy Pelosi, in a joint statement to the president, declared: "Surging forces is a strategy that you have already tried and that has already failed. Like many current and former military leaders, we believe that trying again would be a serious mistake.... Adding more combat troops will only endanger more Americans and stretch our military to the breaking point for no strategic gain" (Baker and Wright 2007, A01).

The five additional brigades were not deployed fully around Baghdad until the early summer of 2007. Signs of progress were not immediate. A late August National Intelligence Estimate concluded that the Iraqi government had not yet quelled sectarian violence despite the recent American troop surge, but that quick American military withdrawal would erode security gains thus far achieved. In September, Bush and Petraeus announced a plan under which American troop levels in Iraq, then at 169,000, would decline to 130,000 by July 2008 if the surge succeeded. By the end of 2007, Petraeus was able to report a 60 percent decline in car bombs and suicide attacks in Iraq. By early 2008, multiple signs of the surge's success were evident. Iraqi civilian casualties dropped from over 3,500 in September 2007 to just over 500 by January 2008. Enemy initiated attacks against American troops fell by two-thirds during that period, as the number of American/Iraqi security patrols tripled. American military casualties fell to the lowest levels since the initial invasion of the country. Some political reconciliation occurred, with progress evident on a majority of American benchmarks (O'Hanlon and Campbell 2008, 4, 8, 9, 15, 17, 19). America, however, was increasingly on its own in Iraq during this time as Prime Minister Blair withdrew thousands of British troops from Iraq in 2007.

As the surge took hold, Bush fought a series of battles with the Democratic Congress over war funding. In February 2007, the House in a predominately partisan 246–182 vote passed a nonbinding resolution criticizing the surge, and the Senate fell four votes short of sixty votes needed for cloture on a measure to begin a wide-ranging Iraq war debate. The 56–34 vote failed due to GOP support for Bush. In May, Bush vetoed a $124 million spending bill for Iraq and Afghanistan passed by Congress; the bill required a fixed timeline for troop withdrawal, to be determined by Iraqi attainment of American-specified benchmarks. Yielding to Bush's veto threats, Congress passed a 2008 funding bill for Iraq and Afghanistan on December 20, 2007 that provided the White House's requested amount but included no withdrawal timetable. During these battles, Bush was able to wield the power of the veto successfully, despite his diminished political capital. In the absence of much political authority, Bush relied on his formal powers. That, coupled with just enough partisan support from minority GOP lawmakers, allowed the surge policy to continue.

Losing the Argument over Iraq

By 2008, the situation in Iraq was improving, but President Bush's popular support and professional reputation was not. The long years of policy mistakes and adverse news from Iraq had taken their toll, producing a permanent decline in the president's political fortunes. The public and a majority in Congress by 2008 had rejected both aspects of Bush's heresthetic argument about the Iraq war. The Iraq threat now seemed less credible. The stream of disclosures revealing errors in prewar intelligence that had exaggerated the threat led many Americans to doubt any relationship between the Iraq occupation and the broader war on terror. For the public, a key turning point occurred during the 2006 Iraq violence, when for the first time polls reported that a majority agreed that the Iraq involvement had no relationship to the war on terror (Hulse and Connelly 2006). By then, majorities in most polls also viewed the decision to go to war as a mistake. This was followed by the election of a Congress ruled by Democrats, most of whom shared that view. The second dimension of the administration's heresthetic argument, the credibility of their response to the threat, also became less believable as violence mounted during the 2003 to 2006 period. By the time of the surge, Bush was not a trusted messenger for it. The surge's success gradually led Americans to perceive improvement in conditions in Iraq, but the decision to go to war was no more popular than before the surge. Before the war began, strong partisan divisions had existed about the possibility of attacking Iraq. That meant the president never had a large political margin for error in the war's conduct. When mistakes occurred, the die was cast.

The rhetorical strategy of the Bush administration in this difficult environment was a curious one. Prior to the war, the administration touted intelligence indicating a sizeable threat from Iraq. Though the president himself had not called the threat "imminent," the constant talk of peril from the administration suggested to many an imminent threat. A commission headed by former Virginia Senator Charles Robb (D-VA) and Federal Judge Lawrence Silberman reported in 2005 that it had found no evidence the administration had distorted prewar intelligence to suit their political agenda, but also noted that "intelligence analysts worked in an environment that did not encourage skepticism about the conventional wisdom," (Purdum 2005). An ongoing battle between the intelligence and military communities and the Bush administration had erupted during the Iraq occupation. Intelligence leaks and anonymous criticism from the uniformed military impugned the competence of the administration, a stark instance of "permanent Washington" striking back at its elected masters (Alasdair Roberts 2008, 151–58).

In a divided political climate amidst an unpopular war, partisan charges of administration manipulation of intelligence inevitably ensued. But the Bush White House retreated from challenging such arguments. As the occupation proceeded and intelligence mistakes became clear, the administration changed its rhetorical focus.

Douglas Feith, Undersecretary of Defense for Policy from 2001 to 2005, examined presidential speeches and found a great shift in emphasis during the years of Iraq involvement. From 2002 to September 2003, the president primarily focused on the threat posed by Saddam. Beginning in late 2003, the emphasis shifted to the goal of bringing democracy to the Iraq and the Arab world (Feith 2008B, 475–76). This shift was particularly evident in Bush's second inaugural address, in which he proclaimed: "So it is the policy of the United States to seek and support the growth of democratic movements and institutions in every nation and culture, with the ultimate goal of ending tyranny in our world." Feith views the president's failure to challenge critics of prewar Iraq intelligence as a mistake that "aggravated the damage to the administration's credibility" by making it seem that the president was shifting his argument for the war "without forthrightly explaining the change." Further, "political opponents quickly came to realize that if they attacked the administration for its prewar analyses and other prewar work, they would not be refuted" (Feith 2008B, 477). This rhetorical failure to engage war critics combined with adverse events in Iraq to shrink the administration's credibility during the Iraq occupation. The administration's emphasis on democratization encountered a chilly reception from an American public that ranked promoting democracy in other nations quite low as a foreign policy priority (Pew Center 2004B). The attendant damage to Bush's political authority and to his GOP electoral coalition was severe.

Relations around the Globe

America's Iraq involvement became a central issue in the Bush administration's relations with nations around the world. The invasion and occupation proved internationally unpopular. One aspect of American power suffered as a result. That is "soft power" defined by Joseph Nye: "If my behavior is determined by an observable but intangible attraction—soft power is at work. Soft power uses a different type of currency—not force, not money—to engender cooperation. It uses an attraction to shared values, and the justness and duty of contributing to the achievement of those values" (Nye 2004, 7). Fewer citizens of other countries were attracted to America via "shared values" as a result of the Iraq occupation.

Foreign policy scholar James McCormick notes that "any goodwill created after 9/11 among the European public, for example, quickly dissipated in the run-up to the Iraq War, and it has largely not rebounded" (McCormick 2008, 229). In March 2003, at about the start of the Iraq War, only 48 percent of the public in Britain, 34 percent in Italy, 25 percent in Germany, 31 percent in France, and 14 percent in Spain expressed a favorable view of the United States (Pew Global Attitudes Project 2003, 19). Three years later, and more than a year into President Bush's second term (April 2006), the favorable percentages of the United States had improved only slightly among key European allies. By 2006, 56 percent of Britons, 39 percent of the French, 37 percent of the Germans, and 23 percent of the Spanish expressed favorable opinions of the United States. Skepticism or downright opposition was hardly confined to Europe. In a 2006 Pew survey which included ten countries outside Europe, a majority of the publics in only three viewed the United States favorably. These countries were Japan, India, and Nigeria. The rest—Russia, Indonesia, Egypt, Pakistan, Jordan, Turkey, and China—had favorability ratings of the United States ranging from 12 percent positive in Turkey to 47 percent positive in China (Pew Global Attitudes Project 2006, 1). President Bush's personal unpopularity probably contributed to America's image problems. In a BBC World Service Poll (2005), in only three of twenty-two countries did a majority or a plurality view Bush's reelection positively. The rest, including five European countries, viewed his reelection as "negative for peace and security for the world." Majorities in only India and the Philippines and a plurality in only Poland viewed the Bush administration positively.

What difference did global unpopularity mean for the Bush administration? In 2003, Bush's unpopularity in their countries gave two European leaders who prominently opposed the Iraq invasion—German Chancellor Gerhard Schroeder and French President Jacques Chirac—domestic support for their resistance to American policy. Later, America's unpopularity put pressure on sympathetic leaders, who grew in number during Bush's second term to include German Chancellor Angela Merkel, French President Nicolas Sarkozy, and Italian Prime Minister Silvio Berlusconi. When asked by Condoleezza Rice in 2007 how she could help him, Sarkozy relied: "Improve your image in the world. It's difficult when the country that is the most powerful, the most successful—that is, of necessity, the leader of our side—is one of the most unpopular countries in the world. It presents overwhelming problems for you and overwhelming problems for your allies. So do everything you can to improve the way you're perceived—that's what you can do for me" (Gopnik 2007).

Relations between governments, however, are not totally dictated by global public opinion. In this regard, the Bush administration did make some progress. Despite strong support for Pakistan in its efforts to assist with combating terrorism, the administration was able to improve relations with India. America in 2006 agreed to sell nuclear materials to India in return for India's opening its nuclear programs to international inspection (Bumiller and Sengupta 2006). The breakthrough with India occurred while the administration also maintained good relations with China, a regional rival of India. Relations with most Asian governments were quite sound despite the Iraq war (Green 2008). Ties with the Japanese and Australian governments grew closer during the Iraq war, as both nations sent troops and civilian assistance during the occupation.

Relations with Russia, however, were strained by Prime Minister Vladimir Putin's increasingly authoritarian rule and by the Bush administration's successful attempts to expand NATO. During Bush's presidency, Croatia, Albania, Slovenia, Estonia, Latvia, Lithuania, Bulgaria, and Romania joined NATO.

In August 2008, Russia invaded South Ossetia, a region claiming independence from the surrounding nation of Georgia, in response to a military incursion into the area by the Georgian government. Georgia, a democratic nation, sought membership in NATO. A negotiated cease-fire initially left Russian troops free to patrol South Ossetia, which soon after received diplomatic recognition from Russia, as did another breakaway Georgian region, Abkhasia. The United States continued to assert that these regions remained part of Georgia. The invasion prompted Poland, a NATO member wary of Russia, quickly to sign a missile defense treaty with the United States. Strong U.S.-Russian tensions suddenly characterized international politics. In early 2008, former Secretary of State Henry Kissinger described diplomatic relations between the United States and most European states as "adequate," those with China "good," and those with India "excellent" (Kissinger 2008). Relations with Latin American nations did not fare so well. Estrangement with Mexico increased when its government expressed disapproval of the Iraq invasion and as the American debate over illegal immigration intensified. Popular reaction against the economic costs of neoliberal policies helped to produce the election of several left-leaning Latin American governments, all of whom voiced opposition to the Iraq war. The most outspoken was the left populist leader of Venezuela, Hugo Chavez, who rhetorically assaulted American foreign policy on a regular basis.

The Bush administration courted domestic and international controversy in its approach to the United Nations. The Iraq war commenced without Security Council approval. Bush's 2005 appointment of John Bolton as UN ambassador provoked widespread opposition in Congress because of "Bolton's previous criticism of multilateral diplomacy in general and of the UN in particular" (Hook 2008, 112). When the Bolton nomination was blocked by Senate Democrats and a few GOP dissenters, Bush resorted to a recess appointment, which under the constitution allows a president to temporarily install political appointees when Congress is not in session. The new ambassador's abrasive style at times impeded his effectiveness at the UN. Bolton remained as UN ambassador until January 2007, after the newly elected Democratic Senate failed to approve his nomination.

The Iraq war's most immediate impact was in the Middle East, upon the long-standing Israeli-Palestinian problems and the challenge of addressing an aggressive Iran. Prior to the Iraq war, Secretary of State Colin Powell dispatched Assistant Secretary of State William Burns and Special Envoy Anthony Zinni to seek diplomatic resolution of the violence between Israel and Palestinians. They made little headway. By early 2002, Palestinian attacks on Israel continued, and Israel had Palestinian leader Yasser Arafat's compound under siege. The Bush administration sought to promote democratization of the Palestinian Authority in order to promote new Palestinian leadership as a way toward peace. The death of Yasser Arafat in late 2004 raised hopes for this strategy, but it suffered a setback with the victory of radical Islamic group Hamas—labeled by the United States a terrorist organization—in parliamentary elections in early 2005. In this instance, democratization, extolled as a pacifier by Bush, had not moved the region toward peace. The relatively moderate Mahmoud Abbas had won election as Palestinian president that same month, but repeated attempts by the Bush administration to further peace produced few results in the ensuing years.

Israel's situation was complicated by the presence of heavily armed troops of Hezbollah, a Shia terrorist organization supported by Syria and Iran, on their northern border. A several-week war erupted during mid-2006 as Israel, with limited success, sought to defang the threat in response to border violations by Hezbollah guerrillas. By the end of Bush's second term, peace remained as elusive as ever. The Iraq war had removed one hostile regime from Israel's security concerns, but had not alleviated more pressing threats. Nor had the war weakened the terrorist organizations of Hamas and Hezbollah.

Behind these terrorist organizations was a member of Bush's "axis of evil," Iran. Iran's military and diplomatic support of both Hamas and Hezbollah served to frustrate American interests regarding Israel and Palestine, and Iran supported Shia terrorists in Iraq during the American occupation. Under the bellicose leadership of Mahmoud Ahmadinejad, the nation's ruling theocracy saw great opportunities to extend its regional power with the removal of its long-time rival Saddam Hussein. Intelligence reports indicated that the regime was pursuing nuclear weapons technology, prompting the Bush administration to seek ways to contain Iran's ambitions.

Though America's armed forces were heavily involved in Iraq and Afghanistan, any comparable military effort was not possible with Iran. America lacked the military capacity to invade, international opinion would not tolerate it, and the Iraq war had demonstrated the great costs of such intervention. The Bush White House instead engaged in multilateral attempts to contain Iran. Russia supplied Iran with nuclear technology and was a reluctant participant in such efforts. Over several years, Iran jousted with the International Atomic Energy Agency's attempt to inspect its nuclear facilities. Their behavior proved belligerent enough to prompt the UN Security Council in late 2006 to impose sanctions on trade with Iran regarding sensitive nuclear-related technologies. An American intelligence report in late 2007 indicated that Iran's nuclear weapons program was not as active as previously thought. Bush remained emphatic in his rhetoric toward Iran, calling the nation in early 2008 "a threat to world peace." Still, the administration lacked effective means of countering Iran's support for terrorism throughout the Middle East.

The third nation in the administration's evil axis, North Korea, also produced recurrent problems regarding nuclear weaponry. President Clinton had negotiated a closing of North Korea's plutonium-based nuclear reactor and had eased economic sanctions against the regime, but in 2002 US diplomats learned that the nation had continued a uranium enrichment program. North Korea restarted a plutonium-based reactor in 2003, and in 2005 announced they had nuclear weapons. The Bush administration pursued a multilateral solution, seeking to involve other nations in the region, most notably China, in six-party talks to curtail North Korea's nuclear programs. Initial signs were far from promising, and North Korea exploded a small nuclear device in 2006. In the summer of 2008, however, a breakthrough, seemingly at least, resulted. America removed North Korea from a list of states that sponsor terrorism and lifted some trade sanctions once the nation delivered to China extensive details on its nuclear program. North Korea destroyed a nuclear cooling tower, suggesting good faith compliance with disarmament. By the end of the Bush presidency, North Korea had dropped from the evil axis, an apparent testament to effectiveness of the administration's multilateral negotiations. Its involvement in international terrorism was vastly smaller than that of Iran during the Bush presidency (Tanter and Kersting 2007, 223).

The multilateral approach to Iran and North Korea is just one of several largely unnoticed continuities between the foreign policy of George

W. Bush and Bill Clinton. Both used the military in the name of American values, though Bush's pursuit of democracy in Iraq and Afghanistan was far more aggressive than Clinton's bombing of Serbia. Both emphasized free trade, with Clinton signing the North American Free Trade Agreement with Mexico and Canada, and Bush obtaining free trade agreements with Jordan, Morocco, Australia, Bahrain, and the Central American region. Both focused on African problems, making successful tours of the continent and obtaining new forms of development and humanitarian assistance for countries there. Still, Bush's more unilateral and preemptive approach to security threats provides a contrast with Clinton's policies that overshadows these continuities.

Conclusion

The central fact of the Bush administration's foreign policy is its involvement in Iraq. The war and occupation greatly exceeded the White House's predicted cost in lives, time, treasure, and attention. America's Iraq occupation is the major reason for the decline of Bush's informal powers of political capital—his popular support and professional reputation—over the course of his presidency. A 2008 poll sought to examine the sources of widespread popular disapproval of Bush's conduct of office. Fully half of those surveyed who disapproved of Bush's governance cited the Iraq war as the reason, far more than those naming any other reason (Goeas and Nienaber 2008). Political costs extended beyond Bush to his GOP regime coalition in the 2006 elections. As Bush's political capital and partisan regime declined, his political authority became ever smaller. His energetic assertion of the presidency's formal powers over military and defense policy paradoxically shrank his informal powers. Persistent endogenous problems within his partisan coalition and exogenous challenges from partisan opponents were the inevitable result.

Why were the political costs of the Iraq involvement so large? The casualty count is vastly lower than those of the controversial Korean and Vietnam wars. Three reasons account for Bush's Iraq problems. First, the Iraq war began in a political environment featuring much more partisan polarization than was evident in the Korea and Vietnam cases. When the Iraq occupation went wrong, the partisan knives came out. Second, the war was uniquely preemptive and justified primarily by intelligence reports. When those reports proved wrong, a central justification for the war disappeared. Third, the Iraq involvement proved to be far more costly in time and treasure than originally predicted. The Vietnam involvement lasted ten years, Korea three. Note that the longer involvement—Vietnam—ended with a precipitous withdrawal. Impatience with a war's progress makes such ventures difficult to sustain; it made itself felt over Iraq and cost Bush and his party.

In retrospect, it seems implausible that America would have invaded Iraq in 2003 if we had known then what we learned subsequently about the threat posed by Saddam Hussein's regime. The domestic and international problems engendered by the Iraq war are now clear. That said, some benefits have resulted from America's military involvements in Iraq and Afghanistan. Political liberty, however fragile, is now enjoyed by 27 million Iraqis and 32 million Afghans, in two new Middle East regimes now friendly to America's strategic interests. Al Qaeda has suffered great reversals in both nations. America has suffered no major terrorist attacks since September 11, 2001.

Despite clear progress, final success in Iraq, however, had not arrived by 2008. A stable, representative regime that controls its borders and internal security may take several more years to create. The American military is also sorely pressed by the large and long deployment in Iraq (Snow 2008, 131). The situation in Afghanistan is also fraught with uncertainties. "Without question, additional US troops would be helpful in 2009," according to American General Dan McNeill, commander of coalition forces in Afghanistan (Ignatius 2008). Both Iraq and Afghanistan are undergoing counterinsurgencies driven by a "clear and hold" surge strategy. Both still have weak governments threatened by corruption. The future of these missions is far from clear, and on that much of the legacy of the Bush presidency depends.

The political risks of preemptive conflict, however, are quite evident at the end of the Bush presidency. The costs proved particularly high for Bush because the intelligence proved incorrect and he pressed the conflict in a polarized political environment in which his public support was likely to dwindle. But international costs, in estranged allies and hostile public opinion in other nations, also appeared in the war's wake. Hard power in this case did not supplement, but instead diminished, America's soft power. Future presidents are likely to consider the Iraq case carefully and weigh such potential costs thoroughly. Future military involvements will require better evidence of threats, a more promising theory of victory, and less partisan political style than was evident during the Bush presidency. The ironic consequence of George W. Bush's foreign policy may well be fewer preemptive military actions in the future.

6 LEGACIES

Take your pick:

1. George W. Bush is the worst president in American history. His administration's lies about the terrorist threat led us into an unnecessary Iraq war, while his White House gave inadequate attention to our military involvement in Afghanistan. His Patriot Act placed civil liberties under assault. Bush responded abysmally to Hurricane Katrina, showing appalling insensitivity to the African American residents of New Orleans. His tax cuts have mortgaged the nation's future, mushrooming the national debt and threatening the living standards of future generations. The Bush administration has failed to address severe problems of health care access and costs. Bush's insensitivity to global warming threatens planetary peril. He coddled the bigoted religious right. History will scorn him.

2. George W. Bush will go down in history as a great president. He is currently underappreciated because several of his important and necessary decisions are temporarily unpopular. He has not shied away from directly addressing tough issues. American military action promises to transform Iraq and Afghanistan into stable, moderate democracies in the heart of the Middle East. After 9/11, he prevented additional attacks on America while keeping domestic civil liberties secure. His No Child Left Behind education reform brought test-based accountability to the elementary and secondary education establishment. The Medicare prescription drug bill improved health care for millions of senior citizens. His tax cuts spurred economic revival from recession. By addressing the problems of Social Security, he paved the way for sorely needed restructuring of the program in the future. History will vindicate him.

The truth surely lies somewhere in between these assessments. The simple terms, "failure" or "success" cannot summarily describe such an eventful presidency. Sorting through the specific events of the Bush administration, however, does reveal some lessons for future presidents and lasting legacies of this presidency. It also raises important questions about the relationship of formal presidential powers to presidential authority in contemporary American politics.

Lessons for Future Presidents

The Bush presidency's successes in popular politics underscore the need for presidents to seek heresthetic command of political discussion. By credibly framing the dimensions of public debate, a president can keep momentum behind his initiatives. The key term in this is "credibly." Finding believable arguments and presenting them with rhetorical effectiveness is not easy, but remains essential work. It is also important for a president to keep his partisan base enthusiastically behind him. Constant attention to the technology of politics—microtargeting, fundraising, web networking, and voter turnout efforts—also must receive careful White House attention, because political rivals will keep innovating on these fronts. Presidents also cannot avoid "going public" on a regular basis, not so much because doing so produces great gains, but rather because not doing so risks strong political reversals.

The Bush White House's political reversals also hold their share of lessons. There is no higher risk than pressing for partisan advantage with an issue that is hostage to immediate events. The Iraq war was such an issue, and the political costs of adverse events proved enormous. Bush also discovered that the endogenous costs of GOP coalition maintenance created substantial exogenous costs among other voters. A limited focus on one's partisan base has two possible downsides. First, it can provide partisan activists with a sense of hubris and entitlement regarding their pet issues, as the Bush White House discovered regarding immigration reform. Second, a base focus diverts attention from efforts to expand that base and attend to the concerns of moderate, independent, and swing voters. By 2008, the Bush presidency had become unpopular with all three of these groups. Able electoral tactics and technologies cannot save a party when adversities mount, as was evident in the 2006 elections. Overreaching costs popular support. The unsuccessful fate of highly ambitious initiatives regarding Iraq and Social Security illustrates that point.

The Bush presidency's successes in Washington governance, however, also present several useful lessons for successors. Presidential powers are now massive and provide handy tools for inducing change. Executive orders, signing statements, management initiatives, judicial appointments, and direction of the military constitute an array of powers unrivaled by most previous presidents. Appointments and management reforms are underappreciated means that can be effectively employed to pursue presidential goals. It's particularly important to identify key agencies—such as the Office of Information and Regulatory Affairs of OMB—and use them resolutely to pursue the president's agenda. A president can most effectively restructure government on his own, via executive orders. Partisan rule in Congress can also be surprisingly advantageous, even with small majorities, if a president's party stays unified. Fellow congressional partisans can effectively override hostile Supreme Court decisions, as happened in the *Hamdan* case. Careful attention to judicial appointments can provide a powerful presidential legacy lasting far beyond an administration's time in the White House.

Difficulties in Washington governance encountered by Bush also provide lessons for his successors. The use of presidential power invites its challenge, from litigation in federal courts, partisan opponents in Congress, estranged allies, and hostile global public opinion. A president thus should make enemies only when he must, not via an aggressive and partisan governing style that routinely creates them. "Institutional thickening" has created relatively secure bulwarks from which permanent Washington can work to undercut presidential initiatives. The revolt of the intelligence community during the Iraq occupation is a striking example of that. Unified, majority partisan support for major court nominees is imperative in a time of congressional polarization. Its absence cost Bush some appointments. Quick and personal presidential responses to major domestic crises are essential to successful presidential leadership. Bush's 9/11 response boosted his informal powers of political capital, but the sluggish Katrina reaction shrank that capital. Pushing big policy changes costs political capital. It's important to not overestimate one's political capital and thus spend it too freely, as Bush did regarding Social Security.

In domestic policy, Bush's triumphs provide advice for future presidents as well. Presidents must find efficient means to achieve their major domestic goals. Tax cuts were such a means for Bush. They stimulated the economy, rewarded partisan constituencies, created pressure against increasing government spending, and enhanced the president's popular support and professional reputation. It's also important, when possible, to attempt to take issues away from partisan opponents. No Child Left Behind sought to reduce the Democrats' popular edge in education policy. The prescription drug reforms attempted the same regarding health care. Guiding concepts like "compassionate conservatism" and "ownership society" can be invaluable in shaping a domestic agenda, because they help in setting priorities among policy initiatives. On the other hand, taking issues away from opponents may not always prove politically successful. The prescription drug plan and No Child Left Behind policies did not improve the public's perception of the GOP regarding health care and education, and encouraged Democrats to direct a barrage of criticisms at both policies. Such initiatives also conflicted with the administration's avowed commitment to spending restraint, producing strains within its own partisan coalition.

The Bush foreign policy record contains a mix of positive and negative lessons for successors. Large international threats require a disciplined deployment of all presidential skills—managerial, rhetorical, heresthetic, coalitional, and bargaining—in order to address crises well and thus enhance popular support and professional reputation. In the initial months after 9/11, the Bush White House largely succeeded at this. Partisan polarization, however, serves to challenge and weaken presidential authority over time, making the use of presidential powers increasingly conflictual and subject to challenge and reversal. The president's abundant foreign policy powers, however, can allow a chief executive to maintain a policy in the face of popular and congressional opposition, as Bush did regarding Iraq in 2007 and 2008. The military is a powerful international tool for a president, but its attractiveness as an implement poses a problem. Troops are easily deployed and can win immediate conflicts, but long-term commitments can prove costly diplomatically and politically, as the Iraq experience shows.

Major foreign policy decisions require wide consultation and consideration of multiple alternatives. Bush accomplished this with the surge but not with his decision to invade Iraq in the first place. Delegating major policy authority to subordinates, as Bush did to Secretary Rumsfeld, can be quite risky. When policies are failing, it is essential to consult widely and rethink them, as Bush did with the Iraq surge. Hard, military power can prove useful to presidents in some situations, but Iraq demonstrates that costs in soft power—global goodwill—can result from the use of hard power. Presidential foreign policy power can seem an attractive refuge from a president's domestic frustrations, but success in foreign policy may produce little domestic political benefit, beyond perhaps a boost in a president's professional reputation. Bush's increasing focus on foreign policy in 2007 and 2008 earned him little political capital.

What Lasts and What Doesn't Last

Some of George W. Bush's accomplishments will have lasting effects in future years, while the effects of others will vanish with his presidency. Which are lasting legacies and which are not? The tax cuts are one important lasting legacy, affecting the future course of the economy and the national budget. The cuts placed pressure on future spending while boosting the economy in the short term. In 2008, politicians of both parties continued to attest to the popularity of tax cuts. Democratic nominee Barack Obama proposed tax cuts aimed at the middle class. GOP nominee John McCain pledged to make the Bush tax cut permanent. Another initiative likely to last is the Medicare prescription drug program, which costs less than projected and is popular with seniors. It is likely a permanent addition to entitlement programs. The Department of Homeland Security and terrorism alerts are also likely to persist for many years, given the increased incidence of and national consciousness about international terrorism.

The Bush administration's domestic "war footing" regarding terrorism, however, seems unlikely to persist across future presidencies. A strong commitment to unilateralism and secrecy prevented the administration from building lasting bipartisan support in Congress and retaining public support for its policies through accurate information and credible arguments (Heclo 2003, 249–50). A Democratic president would surely deemphasize domestic surveillance programs, and frequent court challenges may weaken the reach of such programs over time. Attentiveness to the agenda of social conservatives—opposition to euthanasia, gay marriage, and abortion—also seems likely to fade as the percentage of Americans holding these views continues to decrease. Such issues are moving from "wedge" issues that draw voters to the GOP to "base" issues that appeal mainly to GOP social conservatives. Bush's opposition to certain environmental policies, particularly a "cap and trade" approach to addressing global warming, seems unlikely to survive his presidency. Both GOP and Democratic presidential nominees in 2008 support "cap and trade," which sets limits for emissions and then allows the sale of limited pollution rights within that cap, and vow to address global warming as a top priority.

Will the "Bush doctrine" formally embracing military preemption remain at the center of American foreign policy? Yes and no. Yes, in that American presidents before Bush often used the military for preemptive purposes and probably will again in the future. These incursions, however, usually involved military actions of short duration, as in Grenada (under Reagan), Panama and Kuwait (both under George H. W. Bush), Somalia and Haiti (both under Clinton). No, in that future presidents are unlikely to draw attention to the American military option as conspicuously as does the 2002 Bush doctrine. The most ambitious application of that doctrine, the Iraq occupation, has also produced such problems for Bush that it is unlikely that his successors will be inclined to apply the doctrine in a similar way. The Bush doctrine was not quite as dramatic a departure from previous practice as it seemed at the time of its announcement, but is also not likely to be a formal guidepost for future US foreign policy.

Presidential Power and Presidential Authority

A striking aspect of the regime ambitions of the Bush presidency is how much they depended upon the presidency and the president himself. Domestic political strategy originated in the White House, with the national party organization and congressional party performing strictly subservient roles. The domestic policy agenda strongly relied on presidential executive branch management and the deployment of presidential skills. Foreign policy doctrine and execution rested solely within White House control. This placed the project to create a lasting GOP regime in national politics on a treacherously narrow footing. As Bush fared, so would his party's regime project.

Bush ended up not faring well by the end of his presidency, and the GOP's regime project became impossible. Aggressive use of his formal powers did not help the president retain political authority enhancing his partisan regime. This raises a broader question about presidential powers and presidential authority. Does the vast array of formal presidential powers now serve to enhance presidential authority? In the past, the great reconstructive presidents, particularly Lincoln and FDR, expanded the reach of formal presidential powers and also built new claims to political authority with lasting partisan regimes (Skowronek 1997, 198–227, 287–324). But the expansion of presidential powers by the more recent "orthodox innovators" Truman and Johnson did not enhance regime authority (Skowronek 1997, 325–60). Both waged unpopular wars that shriveled the popularity of their partisan regimes and damaged their party's brand. George W. Bush seems to be a similar case.

It may well be that contemporary presidents find the energetic use of their expansive formal powers so inviting that the challenges of maintaining their informal powers of political capital become secondary concerns. The George W. Bush presidency was willing to let the chips fall where they may regarding Iraq without foreseeing the great threat to their political capital and political authority in the enterprise. The Bush experience may not just be another example of an "orthodox innovator" walking a tightrope to preserve an established regime, but rather the norm for all future presidents. "Political time" demarcated by the persistence of political regimes may well have disappeared. Presidents may be losing their ability to create lasting political regimes, as Stephen Skowronek argues (1997). Presidents also may have, in practice, lost that aspiration. Why? First, a stable era dominated by one party seems unlikely to evolve in a time of evenly balanced partisan polarization. Second, institutional thickening has created a permanent Washington of interest groups, bureaucrats, and congressional specialists that often resist broad, regime-building initiatives in policy. Third, presidents now find so many formal powers at their command that concerns about regime maintenance can be displaced by the immediate attractiveness of exercising those powers. George W. Bush has expanded presidential powers regarding executive secrecy, domestic surveillance, use of military force, executive orders, signing statements, management initiatives, and congressional relations. Yet his regime-building efforts, a central aspect of a "presidency of achievement," have failed. Formal presidential powers, now, may be the enemy of presidential authority. In practice, contemporary presidents may inevitably be poor at regime maintenance. If true, that is a Bush legacy with grand implications for the American political system.

APPENDIX: EVENTS OF THE GEORGE W. BUSH PRESIDENCY

Events are included if they appeared in two of three sources: *World Almanac* (New York: World Almanac Books), *New York Times Almanac* (New York: Penguin Books), *Time Almanac* (Chicago: Encyclopedia Britannica). Events positively affecting the president in the short term are coded P, events negatively affecting the president in the short term are coded N. Events over which "the surface impression suggested some control by the president or occurrence of the event" are coded D; events over which the president appeared to have no discretion are coded ND. Three researchers independently coded the event data. The Index of Agreement among the three coders was 95.7 percent. The few differences in coding regarding disputed cases were easily resolved in subsequent discussions among the coders. Event coding follows procedures in Paul Brace and Barbara Hinckley, *Follow the Leader* (New York: Basic Books, 1993, 183–88).

2001

1/22	Bush bans overseas abortion aid	P-D
1/28	Bush announces faith-based initiative	P-D
2/1	John Ashcroft approved as attorney general	P-D
3/20	Bush meets with Sharon	P-D
3/30	Bush abandons global warming treaty	P-D
4/1	Chinese plane collision incident	P-ND
4/23	Bush offers weapons to Taiwan	P-D
5/1	Bush proposes US-Russia missile shield	P-D
5/16	Bush energy plan announced	P-D
5/23	Senator Jeffords abandons GOP	N-ND
5/26	Bush tax cuts pass	P-D
6/12	Bush's first European trip	P-D
6/14	Vieques bombing stopped	P-D

6/26	Bush meets with Sharon	P-D
7/5	New FBI director announced	P-D
7/22	Bush agrees to arms control with Putin	P-D
7/23	Bush meets with Pope re embryonic research	P-D
8/9	Bush gives stem-cell speech	P-D
9/11	Bombing of Pentagon and World Trade Center	P-ND
9/14	Bush visits New York City	P-D
9/20	Bush seeks Bin Laden in public remarks	P-D
9/24	Bush seizes Taliban assets	P-D
9/30	Bush approves aid to Taliban foes	P-D
10/10	DC anthrax scare	P-ND
10/26	Bush signs Patriot Act	P-D
11/2	Unemployment reaches five year high	N-ND
11/13	Bush and Putin agree to nuclear weapons cuts	P-D
12/13	US withdraws from ABM treaty	P-D
12/17	US prevails in Afghanistan	P-D

2002

1/8	Bush signs education bill	P-D
2/14	Bush offers antipollution plan	P-D
2/22	Bush changes toxic waste policy	P-D
2/23	GAO sues Cheney over energy task force	N-ND
2/29	Bush welcomes Saudi peace offer	P-D
3/5	Bush imposes steel tariffs	P-D
4/4	Bush sends Powell to Mideast	P-D
4/18	Senate rejects ANWR drilling	N-D
5/3	Unemployment reaches eight year high	N-ND
5/13	Bush signs farm bill	P-D
5/15	White House admits pre 9/11 CIA warning	N-D
5/24	Bush and Putin sign nuclear weapons treaty	P-D
6/6	Bush proposes cabinet homeland security department	P-D
6/10	DOJ says dirty bomb plot foiled	P-D
6/24	Bush announces new Mideast policy	P-D
7/10	Bush speaks out on corporate malfeasance	P-D
7/12	Bush announces deficits are back	N-D
8/6	Bush signs fast-track trade bill	P-D
8/13	Bush hosts Texas economic forum	P-D
9/4	Bush will seek Congressional approval re Iraq war	P-D
9/5	Senate rejects Priscilla Owens for US appeals court	N-D

9/10	Bush places country on high alert on 9/11 anniversary	P-D
10/8	Bush invokes Taft-Hartley to end dock strike	P-D
10/10	Congress approves Bush Iraq resolution	P-D
11/8	UN Security Council approves Iraq resolution	P-D
11/25	Homeland Security Department approved by Congress	P-D
12/6	Economic team shakeup	N-D
12/17	Bush announces missile shield program	P-D

2003

1/7	Bush proposes tax cut legislation	P-D
2/1	Space shuttle explodes	P-ND
2/15	International antiwar demonstrations	N-ND
3/20	Iraq War begins	P-D
5/1	Mission Accomplished speech by Bush	P-D
5/6	Bremer appointed to oversee Iraq	P-D
5/28	Tax cut bill signed	P-D
6/1	Bush at international summit	P-D
6/6	Unemployment at nine year high	N-ND
7/3	Unemployment rises again	N-ND
7/7	Bush administration admits flawed intelligence re Iraq	N-D
7/15	Administration projects largest deficit in US history	N-D
9/4	Miguel Estrada court nomination withdrawn	N-D
9/7	Bush seeks $87 billion for Iraq	P-D
9/23	Bush speaks to UN	P-D
9/23	David Kay reports Iraq Survey Group draft finds no WMD in Iraq	N-ND
9/27	Putin rebuffs Bush on Iran reactor	N-ND
9/29	Justice department begins White House leak investigation	N-ND
10/16	UN Security Council passes Iraq resolution	P-D
11/3	Congress passes $87 billion for Iraq	P-D
11/6	Bush gives major Iraq speech	P-D
11/25	Congress passes Medicare prescription drug bill	P-D
11/27	Bush makes Thanksgiving visit to Iraq troops	P-D
12/4	Bush lifts steel tariffs he previously imposed	N-D

2004

1/7	Bush announces immigration reform plan	P-D
1/13	Paul O'Neill attacks Bush in book and media	N-ND

1/28	David Kay congressional testimony on no WMD	N-ND
1/29	Cost of drug benefit escalates dramatically	N-ND
2/6	Bush appoints 9/11 Commission	N-D
2/24	Bush announces Constitutional amendment on gay marriage	P-D
3/24	Richard Clarke attacks Bush in book and media	N-ND
4/1	9/11 commission presses administration re confidentiality	N-ND
4/8	Rice testifies before 9/11 Commission	N-ND
4/14	Bush for Israeli settlements	P-D
4/29	Bush/Cheney 9/11 testimony	N-D
5/3	Abu Ghraib scandal breaks	N-ND
6/11	9/11 commission finds no Iraq link to 9/11	N-ND
6/28	Supreme Court rebukes administration in Hamdi case	N-ND
7/22	Final 9/11 Commission report issued	N-ND
8/2	Bush calls for national intelligence director	P-D
8/11	Bush appoints Goss CIA director	P-D
8/23	Bush asks for an end to independent political ads	P-D
9/8	CBS news report of Bush national guard service	N-ND
9/15	Grim intelligence report from Iraq	N-ND
11/8	Cabinet shakeup	N-D
11/14	Big battle for Falluja in Iraq	N-D
12/10	Kerik withdraws as homeland security nominee	N-D

2005

1/11	Bush nominates Chertoff homeland security secretary	P-D
2/2	Bush announces Social Security plan	P-D
2/9	Cost of Medicare prescription drug plan up again	N-ND
2/17	Bush nominates Negroponte intelligence czar	P-D
3/7	Bush nominates John Bolton as UN ambassador	N-D
3/16	Bush nominates Wolfowitz to World Bank	P-D
3/31	Intelligence commission report on Iraq failures	N-ND
4/11	Bush meets with Sharon	P-D
4/25	Bush meets with Saudi leader	P-D
4/28	Bush defends Social Security plan at news conference	N-D
5/10	Supreme Court supports Cheney energy task force	P-ND
6/28	Major Bush Iraq speech	P-D
6/29	Bush proposes intelligence overhaul	P-D
7/14	Karl Rove implicated in Plame case	N-ND
7/19	Roberts nominated to Supreme Court	P-D

8/1	Bush appoints John Bolton, defying Senate	N-D
8/8	Bush signs energy and transport bills	P-D
8/29	Hurricane Katrina wreaks havoc	N-ND
9/5	Bush nominates John Roberts chief justice	P-D
9/13	Bush takes responsibility for Katrina debacle	N-D
10/3	Bush nominates Harriet Miers to Supreme Court	N-D
10/15	Iraqis vote on Constitution	P-ND
10/19	Trial of Saddam Hussein starts	P-ND
10/27	Harriet Miers withdraws nomination	N-D
10/28	Lewis Libby indicted	N-ND
10/30	Samuel Alito nominated to Supreme Court	P-D
11/11	Bush gives speech on Iraq	P-D
11/15	Senate debates Iraq War	N-ND
11/16	Bush tours Asian countries	P-D
11/30	Bush gives speech on Iraq	P-D
12/2	Ten U.S soldiers killed in Iraq	N-ND
12/15	Patriot Act stalls in Congress	N-ND
12/15	Bush agrees to McCain amendment re torture	N-D
12/17	Bush continues controversial wiretap program	N-D
12/18	Bush gives speech on Iraq	P-D

2006

1/7	DeLay steps down as House majority leader	N-ND
1/24	Bush administration refuses to turn over Katrina documents to Congress	N-ND
1/31	Samuel Alito confirmed to Supreme Court	P-D
2/6	Attorney General Gonzales in hearing on wiretaps	N-ND
2/9	Former FEMA head Brown attacks White House in hearings	N-ND
2/16	UN calls for closure of Guantanamo	N-ND
2/16	Dubai ports controversy erupts	N-ND
2/22	Golden Dome destroyed in Iraq	N-ND
3/1	Bush visits Pakistan and Afghanistan	P-D
3/2	Bush announces India nuclear agreement	P-D
3/9	Patriot Act renewed	P-D
3/9	Dubai ports deal collapses	N-ND
4/3	DeLay resigns from House	N-ND
4/6	Libby says Bush authorized his leaking	N-ND
4/13	Retired generals call for resignation of Rumsfeld	N-ND

4/26	Karl Rove testifies in Libby case	N-ND
5/10	Congress passes tax bill	P-D
5/11	*USA Today* report on wiretap surveillance	N-ND
5/15	Bush gives speech introducing immigration proposal	P-D
5/23	Bush meets with Olmert	P-D
6/7	Same sex marriage constitutional amendment fails in Senate	N-D
6/8	Zarquari, Al-Qaeda leader in Iraq, killed	P-ND
6/13	Bush visits Iraq	P-D
6/20	OMB official Safavian convicted	N-ND
6/22	Congress debates Iraq	N-ND
6/29	Supreme Court *Hamdan* decision challenges administration	N-ND
7/13	Bush allows secret court review of wiretaps	N-D
7/19	Bush's first veto, of stem cell research bill	N-D
8/3	US general gives bleak Iraq assessment	N-ND
8/17	US district judge rules against administration wiretapping	N-ND
9/11	Bush gives 9/11 fifth anniversary speeches	P-D
9/23	National Intelligence Estimate negative	N-ND
9/27	Congress approves terrorist detainee bill	P-D
10/19	Military admits failure in Iraq security campaign	N-ND
11/8	Rumsfeld resigns	N-D
12/4	John Bolton, UN ambassador, resigns	N-D
12/6	Iraq Study Group report issued	N-ND
12/30	Saddam Hussein executed	P-D

2007		
1/5	White House staff changes	P-D
1/10	Bush announces Iraq surge strategy in speech	P-D
1/17	Administration ends wiretapping	N-D
1/24	Senate Foreign Relations Committee votes anti-Iraq resolution	N-ND
3/2	Walter Reed hospital scandal emerges	N-ND
3/6	Lewis Libby convicted	N-ND
3/13	Gonzales US attorney controversy begins	N-ND
4/18	Large cab bomb in Baghdad	N-ND
4/19	Gonzales testifies before Congress	N-ND
5/1	Bush vetoes funding bill with Iraq withdrawal	N-ND
5/3	Rice at Cairo summit	P-D

5/15	Testimony about administration wiretapping policy	N-ND
5/17	Wolfowitz resigns at World Bank	N-ND
5/24	Bush signs Iraq bill with no timetable	P-D
5/28	Bush announces Sudan sanctions	P-D
6/5	Lewis Libby sentenced	N-ND
6/7	Administration-backed immigration bill fails in Senate	N-D
6/8	Peter Pace not reappointed Joint Chiefs chair	N-D
7/2	Bush commutes Libby sentence	N-D
7/20	Bush executive order on new CIA interrogation procedures	N-D
8/5	Bush signs warrantless surveillance bill	P-D
8/22	Bush speech defending war policy	P-D
8/27	Gonzales resigns	N-D
9/3	Bush visits Iraq	P-D
9/10	Petraeus reports Iraq progress	P-ND
9/13	Bush speech endorses Petraeus approach	P-D
9/17	Bush nominates Mukasey as Attorney General	P-D
9/17	Greenspan criticizes Bush in book	N-ND
10/3	Bush vetoes child health bill	N-D

BIBLIOGRAPHY

Aberbach, Joel D. 2007. "Supplying the Defect of Better Motives? The Bush II
Administration and the Constitutional System." In *The George W. Bush Legacy*,
edited by Colin Campbell, Bert A. Rockman and Andrew Rudalvige, 112–34.
Washington, D.C.: Congressional Quarterly Press.

Abramowitz, Alan I. and Kyle L. Sanders. 1998. "Ideological Realignment in the U.S.
Electorate." *Journal of Politics* 60 (3): 634–52.

Abramowitz, Alan I. and Walter J. Stone. 2006. "The Bush Effect: Polarization,
Activism and Turnout in the 2004 Presidential Election." *Presidential Studies
Quarterly* 36 (1): 141–54.

Abramowitz, Alan. 2007. "Disconnected, or Joined at the Hip?" In *Red and Blue Nation
Volume One*, edited by Pietro S. Nivola and David W. Brady, 72–84. Washington,
D.C.: Brookings Institution Press.

Abramson, Paul R., John H. Aldrich and David W. Rohde. 2003. *Change and Continuity
in the 2000 and 2002 Elections.* Washington, D.C.: Congressional Quarterly Press.

Abramson, Paul R., John H. Aldrich and David W. Rohde. 2007. *Change and Continuity
in the 2004 and 2006 Elections.* Washington, D.C.: Congressional Quarterly Press.

Addicot, Jeffrey. 2006. "The Military Commissions Act: Congress Commits to the
War on Terror." *Jurist: Legal News and Research.* 9 October. http://jurist.law.pitt.edu/
forumy/2006/10/military-commissions-act-congress.php (accessed July 2008).

Ahern, William. 2004. "Comparing the Kennedy, Reagan and Bush Tax Cuts."
Washington, D.C.: Tax Foundation.

Allen, Mike. 2005. "Semantics Shape Social Security Debate." *Washington Post.*
January 23.

Aristotle. 2007. *Aristotle's Rhetoric.* http://www.public.iastate.edu/~honeyl/Rhetoric/
oneindex.html (accessed July 2008).

Auletta, Ken. 2004. "Fortress Bush," *New Yorker.* January 19, 52–57.

Baker, James A., Lee H. Hamilton and the Iraq Study Group. 2006. *The Iraq Study
Group Report: The Way Forward—A New Approach.* New York: Vintage Books.

Baker, Peter. 2007A. "Looking Past Disputes, Sides Join Together to Enact Energy
Bill." *Washington Post.* December 20, A18.

Baker, Peter. 2007B. "In Bush's Final Year, The Agenda Gets Greener." *Washington
Post.* December 29, A1.

Baker, Peter A. and Robin Wright. 2007. "Pelosi, Reid Urge Bush to Begin Iraq
Pullout." *Washington Post.* January 6, A1.

Balz, Dan and Jon Cohen. 2007. "Independents' Day." *Washington Post National Weekly
Edition.* July 16–22, 11–14.

Balz, Dan. 2006. "Rove Offers Republicans a Battle Plan for the Election." *Washington Post.* January 21, A1.

Barnes, Fred. 2006. *Rebel in Chief: Inside the Bold and Controversial Presidency of George W. Bush.* New York: Three Rivers Press.

Barnes, Fred. 2008. "How Bush Decided on the Surge." *Weekly Standard.* February 4, 6–10.

Barnes, Robert and Juliet Eilperin. 2007. "High Court Faults EPA Inaction on Emissions." *Washington Post.* April 3, A1.

Barone, Michael. 2006. "2006 Realignment? No." October 16. http://www.realclearpolitics.com/articles/2006/10/competence_in_2006_ideology_in.html (accessed July 2008).

Barringer, Felicity and William Yardley. 2007. "Bush Splits With Congress and States on Emissions." *New York Times.* April 4.

Barshay, Jill. 2002. "Bush Starts a Strong Record of Success with the Hill." *CQ Weekly,* January 12, 110–12.

Bartels, Larry M. and John Zaller. 2001. "Presidential Vote Models: A Recount." *PS: Political Science and Politics* 34 (1): 9–20.

Bartlett, Bruce. 2006. *Impostor: How George W. Bush Bankrupted America and Betrayed the Reagan Legacy.* New York: Doubleday.

BBC World Service Poll 2005. http://www.worldpublicopinion.org/pipa/articles/views_on_countriesregions_bt/117.php?nid=&id=&pnt=117 (accessed July 2008).

Becker, Elizabeth. 2001. "Big Visions for Security Post Shrink amid Political Drama." *New York Times.* May 2, A1.

Becker, Elizabeth and Elaine Scolino. 2001. "A New Federal Office Opens Amid Concerns That Its Head Won't Have Enough Power." *New York Times.* October 9, B11.

Belasco, Amy. 2008. *The Cost of Iraq, Afghanistan and Other Global War on Terror Operations Since 9/11.* Washington: Congressional Research Service. April 11.

Benson, Clea. 2008. "The Power of No." *CQ Weekly.* January 14, 132–39.

Bernell, David. 2008. *Readings in American Foreign Policy: Historical and Contemporary Problems.* New York: Pearson Longman.

Berry, Nicholas. 2004. "Bush's Foreign Policy Process is the Big Problem. Coalition for a Realistic Foreign Policy. April 23. http://www.realisticforeignpolicy.org/archives/2004/04/_iraqs_future_s.php (accessed July 2008).

Best, Samuel J. 2006. "Scandals Scorch House GOP." November 8. http://www.cbsnews.com/stories/2006/11/08/politics/main2161340.shtml (accessed July 2008).

Bettelheim, Adriel. 2002. "Impatient Senate Drafts Its Own Homeland Security Plan." *CQ Weekly.* May 25, 1387.

Birnbaum, Jeffrey H. and Thomas B. Edsall. 2004. "At the End, Pro-GOP '527s' Outspent Their Counterparts." *Washington Post.* November 6, A6.

Black, Amy E., Douglas L. Koopman and David K. Ryden. 2004. *Of Little Faith: The Politics of George W. Bush's Faith-Based Initiatives.* Washington, D.C.: Georgetown University Press.

Blanton, Thomas. 2007. "Top Secret Polo Step." George Washington University. National Security Archive. February 14. http://www.gwu.edu/~nsarchiv/NSAEBB/NSAEBB214/index.htm (accessed July 2008).

Bosso, Christopher J. and Deborah Lynn Gruber. 2006. "Maintaining Presence: Environmental Advocacy and the Permanent Campaign." In *Environmental Policy: New Directions for the Twenty-First Century,* edited by Norman J. Vig and Michael E. Kraft, 78–99. Washington, D.C.: CQ Press.

Boumediene v. Bush 553 U.S. (2008).

Brace, Paul and Barbara Hinckley. 1993. *Follow the Leader: Opinion Polls and the Modern Presidents.* New York: Basic Books.

Breul, Jonathan D. 2007. "Three Bush Management Reform Initiatives: The President's Management Agenda, Freedom to Manage Legislative Proposals, and the Program Assessment Rating Tool." *Public Administration Review* 67 (1): 21–26.

Brinkley, Douglas. 2006. *The Great Deluge: Hurricane Katrina, New Orleans, and the Mississippi Gulf.* New York: Morrow.

Brinkley, Joel. 2004. "Out of Spotlight, Bush Overhauls U.S. Regulations." *New York Times.* August 14, A1.

Brody. Richard A. 1991. *Assessing the President: The Media, Elite Opinion and Public Support.* Stanford, California: Stanford University Press.

Brownstein, Ronald. B. 2007. *The Second Civil War.* New York: Penguin.

Bumiller, Elizabeth and Somini Sengupta. 2006. "Bush and India Reach Pact that Allows Nuclear Sales." *New York Times.* March 3, A1.

Burke, John P. 2004. *Becoming President: The Bush Transition, 2000–2003.* Boulder, Colorado: Lynne Rienner.

Busch, Andrew E. 1999. *Horses in Midstream: U.S. Midterm Elections and Their Consequences.* Pittsburgh: University of Pittsburgh Press.

"Bush Finds Ways to Win." 2005. *2004 CQ Almanac,* B3–B7. Washington: Congressional Quarterly Press.

Bush v. Gore 531 U.S. 98 2000.

Bush, George W. 1999. *A Charge to Keep: My Journey to the White House.* New York: William Morrow.

Bush, George W. 2002. "Statement on Signing of the Homeland Security Act." *Weekly Compilation of Presidential Documents.* 25 November.

Bush, George W. 2003. "Statement on Signing the Vision 100–Century of Aviation Reauthorization Act." *Weekly Compilation of Presidential Documents.* December 22.

Cable News Network. 2000. "Exit Poll Results National." http://www.cnn.com/ELECTION/2000/results/index.epolls.html (accessed July 2008).

Cable News Network. 2004. "U.S. President/National/Exit Poll." http://www.cnn.com/ELECTION/2004/pages/results/states/US/P/00/epolls.0.html (accessed July 2008).

Cable News Network. 2005. "Transcripts: CNN Late Edition with Wolf Blitzer." June 12. http://transcripts.cnn.com/TRANSCRIPTS/0506/12/le.01.html (accessed July 2008).

Cable News Network. 2006. "U.S. House of Representatives/National/Exit Poll." http://www.cnn.com/ELECTION/2006/pages/results/states/US/H/00/epolls.0.html (accessed July 2008).

Cable News Network. 2006. "Bush: CIA Holds Terror Suspects in Secret Prisons." September 7. http://www.cnn.com/2006/POLITICS/09/06/bush.speech/ (accessed July 2008).

Campbell, James E. 2001. "The Curious and Close Presidential Campaign of 2000."

In *America's Choice 2000,* edited by William Crotty, 115–37. Boulder, Colorado: Westview Press.

Campbell, James E. 2005. "Why Bush Won the Presidential Election of 2004: Incumbency, Ideology, Terrorism and Turnout." *Political Science Quarterly* 120 (2): 219–41.

Campbell, James E. 2007. "Presidential Politics in a Polarized Nation: The Reelection of George W. Bush." In *The George W. Bush Legacy,* edited by Colin Campbell, Bert A. Rockman and Andrew Rudalvige, 21–44. Washington, D.C.: Congressional Quarterly Press.

Carney, James. 1999. "Why Bush Doesn't Like Homework." *Time,* 15 November.

Carp, Robert A., Kenneth L. Manning, and Robert Stidham. 2004. "The decision-making behavior of George W. Bush's judicial appointees: Far-right, conservative, or moderate?" *Judicature* 88 (1): 20–29.

Carroll, James. 2002. "Antiwar Then, Antiwar Now." *Boston Globe.* October 8, A16.

Ceaser, James W. and Andrew E. Busch. 2001. *The Perfect Tie: The True Story of the 2000 Presidential Election.* Lanham, Maryland: Rowman and Littlefield.

Ceaser, James W. and Andrew E. Busch. 2005. *Red over Blue: The 2004 Elections and American Politics.* Lanham, Maryland: Rowman and Littlefield.

Center for Media and Public Affairs. 2006. "Covering Bush—The Same Old Story." *Media Monitor* 20 (2): 1–5.

Center for Responsive Politics. 2000. "2000 Presidential Race Total Raised and Spent." http://www.opensecrets.org/races/summary.php?id=PRES&cycle =2000.

Center for Responsive Politics. 2004. "527 Committee Activity: The Top 50 Federally Focused Organizations." http://www.opensecrets.org/527s/527cmtes.asp?level-C&cycle=2004 (accessed July 2008).

Center on Budget and Policy Priorities. 2004. "Tax Returns: New Report Questions Effectiveness, Design of Bush Tax Cuts through 2004 and Beyond." Washington, D.C.: Center on Budget and Policy Priorities.

Centers for Medicare and Medicaid Services. 2008. "Medicare Prescription Drug Benefit's Projected Costs Continue to Drop." Washington, D.C.: Department of Health and Human Services. January 31.

Clarke, Richard A. 2004. *Against All Enemies: Inside America's War on Terror.* New York: Free Press.

Clayton, Cornell. 2005. "Introduction: The Bush Presidency and the New Right Constitutional Regime." *Law and Courts* 15 (1): 6–12.

Congressional Budget Office. 2004. "Effective Federal Tax Rates Under Current Law, 2001–2014." Washington, D.C.: Congressional Budget Office.

Congressional Record. 2001. U.S. House. October 12.

Conley, Patricia Heidotting. 2001. *Presidential Mandates: How Elections Shape the National Agenda.* Chicago: University of Chicago Press.

Cook, Charles E. 2005. "A Summer of Discontent." *Washington Quarterly* 28 (4): 173–77.

Cook, Daniel M. and Andrew J. Polsky. 2005. "Political Time Reconsidered: Unbuilding and Rebuilding the State under the Reagan Administration." *American Politics Research* 33 (4): 577–605.

Cook, Timothy E. 1998. *Governing with the News: The News Media as a Political Institution.* Chicago: University of Chicago Press.

Cooper, Phillip J. 2005. "George W. Bush, Edgar Allen Poe and the Use and Abuse of Presidential Signing Statements." *Presidential Studies Quarterly* 35 (3), 515–532.

Dahl, Robert. 1957. "Decision-Making in a Democracy: The Supreme Court as a National Policy-Maker." *Journal of Public Law* 6 (2): 279–95.

Dilulio, John J. 2002. "The Dilulio Letter." *Esquire.* October, 1–7. http://www.esquire.com/features/dilulio (accessed July 2008).

Dinan, Stephen. 2007. "Immigration Bill Quashed." *Washington Times.* June 29, A1.

Dionne, E. J. 2002. "What Matters on Election Day." *Washington Post.* October 11, A18.

Dowd, Matthew. 2006. "Campaign Organization and Strategy" In *Electing the President 2004: The Insiders' View,* edited by Kathleen Hall Jamieson, 21–28. Philadelphia: University of Pennsylvania Press.

Drucker, Peter F. 1995. "Really Reinventing Government." *Atlantic Monthly* (February): 49–61.

DuHaime, Michael. 2006. "Maintaining our majorities is more important than ever— it will determine where American is heading." Washington, D.C.: Republican National Committee.

Dunham, Richard S. 2005. "The Patriot Act: Business Balks." *Business Week.* November 10. http://www.businessweek.com/bwdaily/dnflash/nov2005/nf20051110_9709_db016.htm?chan=search (accessed July 2008).

Economic Report of the President 2008. Washington, D.C.: Government Printing Office.

Eaton, Paul D. 2006. "A Top-Down Review for the Pentagon." *New York Times.* March 19, A20.

Edsall, Thomas B. 2002A. "GOP Touts War as Campaign Issue." *Washington Post.* January 19, A2.

Edsall, Thomas B. 2002B. "GOP Wins Race for Cash, Too." *Washington Post.* November 7, A37.

Edsall, Thomas B. 2006. *Building Red America.* New York: Basic Books.

Edsall, Thomas B. and James V. Grimaldi. 2004. "On Nov. 2, GOP Got More Bang For Its Billion, Analysis Shows." *Washington Post.* December 30, A1.

Edwards, George C. III. 2007. *Governing by Campaigning: The Politics of the Bush Presidency.* New York: Pearson Longman.

Edwards, George C. III. 2008. *Power as Persuasion.* Princeton, N.J.: Princeton University Press.

Electronic Frontier Foundation. 2008. "Let the Sun Set on Patriot." http://w2.eff.org/patriot/sunset/ (accessed July 2008).

Epstein, Lee and Jeffrey Segal. 2005. *Advice and Consent.* New York: Oxford University Press. Updated Bush appointee scores located at http://ws.cc.stonybrook.edu/polsci/jsegal/qualtable.pdf (accessed July 2008).

Executive Order 12498. 1985. 50 Federal Register 1036.

Farnsworth, Stephen J. and Robert Lichter. 2006. *The Mediated Presidency: Television News and Presidential Governance.* Lanham, Maryland: Rowman and Littlefield.

Feingold, Russell. 2002. "Why I Oppose Bush's Iraq War Resolution." October 11. http://www.antiwar.com/orig/feingold1.html (accessed July 2008).

Feingold, Russell. 2001. "Statement of U.S. Senator Russell Feingold On the Anti-Terrorism Bill From The Senate Floor." http://feingold.senate.gov/speeches/01/10/102501at.html (accessed July 2008).

Feith, Douglas J. 2008A. Comments at Hudson Institute Forum on Douglas J. Feith's book, *War and Decision*. Washington, D.C. April 28. Televised by C-SPAN.

Feith, Douglas J. 2008B. *War and Decision: Inside the Pentagon at the Dawn of the War on Terrorism*. New York: Harper Books.

"FEMA the feeble cost lives; Brown, other political appointees must answer for historic failure after Katrina." *Buffalo News*. September 9, 2005 A8.

Fiorina, Morris P. and Matthew S. Levendusky. 2006. "Disconnected: The Political Class versus the People." In *Red and Blue Nation Volume One*, edited by Pietro S. Nivola and David W. Brady, 49–71. Washington, D.C.: Brookings Institution Press.

Fleischer, Ari. 2005. *Taking Heat: The President, The Press and My Years in the White House*. New York: William Morrow.

Fletcher, Michael A. 2006. "Bush Warns of Enduring Terror Threat." *Washington Post*. September 6, A1.

Foreman, Christopher J. 2007. "The Braking of the President: Shifting Context and the Bush Domestic Agenda." In *The George W. Bush Legacy*, edited by Colin Campbell, Bert A. Rockman and Andrew Rudalvige, 265–87. Washington, D.C.: Congressional Quarterly Press.

Gaddis, John Lewis. 2004. "Gaddis: Bush Preemption Doctrine The Most Dramatic Policy Shift Since Cold War." Interview with Bernard Gwertzman. Washington, D.C.: Council on Foreign Relations, February 6. http://www.cfr.org/publication.html?id=6755 (accessed July 2008).

Geer, John G. 1996. *From Tea Leaves to Opinion Polls: A Theory of Democratic Leadership*. New York: Columbia University Press.

Gerson, Michael. 2008. *Why Republicans Need to Embrace America's Ideals (And Why They Deserve to Fail If They Don't)*. New York: HarperCollins.

Globalsecurity.org. "US Forces Order of Battle." http://www.globalsecurity.org/military/ops/iraq_orbat.htm (accessed July 2008).

Goeas, Ed and Brian Nienaber. 2008. "Key Findings of a National Survey of Likely Voters." Alexandria, Virginia: Tarrance Group. http://www.tarrance.com/Nat'l-poll-overview-Mar-08.pdf (accessed July 2008).

Goldsmith, Stephen. 2000. "What Compassionate Conservatism Is—And Is Not." *Hoover Digest* 4: 1–5.

Gopnik, Adam. 2007. "Letter from France: The Human Bomb." *New Yorker*. August 27, 38–42.

Gopoian, David. 2005. "Kerry's 2004 ANES Thermometer Ratings: The Least-Liked Democratic Candidate since McGovern?" http://www.thedemocraticstrategist.org/donkeyrising/2005/02/kerrys_2004_anes_thermometer_r.html (accessed July 2008).

Gordon, Michael R. and Bernard E. Trainor. 2006. *Cobra II: The Inside Story of the Invasion and Occupation of Iraq*. New York: Pantheon.

Gorman, Siobhan. 2004. "White House Calculus." *National Journal*, December 11, 3666.

Government Accountability Office. 2006. "Health Savings Accounts: Early Enrollee Experiences with Accounts and Eligible Health Plans." September 26. Washington: Government Accountability Office. http://www.gao.gov/new.items/d061133t.pdf (accessed July 2008).

Government Accountability Office 2007. "B-308603, Presidential Signing Statements Accompanying the Fiscal Year 2006 Appropriations Acts, June 18, 2007." http://www.gao.gov/decisions/appro/308603.htm (accessed July 2008).

Green, Michael J. 2008. "The Iraq War in Asia: Assessing the Legacy." *Washington Quarterly* 31 (2): 181–200.

Greenberg, Karen J. and Joshua L. Dratel. 2005. *The Torture Papers: The Road to Abu Ghraib.* New York: Cambridge University Press.

Greenhouse, Linda. 2008. "Detainees in Cuba Win Major Ruling in Supreme Court." *New York Times.* June 13, A1.

Greenstein, Fred I. 2004. "The Leadership Style of George W. Bush." In *The George W. Bush Presidency: An Early Assessment,* edited by Fred I. Greenstein, 1–17. Baltimore: Johns Hopkins University Press.

Groeling, Tim and Samuel Kernell. 1998. "Is Network News Coverage of the President Biased?" *Journal of Politics* 60 (4): 1063–1087.

Grunwald, Michael. 2006. "Programation: Why Hurricane Katrina was a man-made disaster." *New Republic.* August 14 and 21, 32–37.

Gwertzman, Bernard. 2004. "Gaddis: Bush Preemption Doctrine the Most Dramatic Policy Shift Since Cold War." Council on Foreign Relations. http://www.cfr.org/publication.html?id=6755 (accessed July 2008).

Hacker, Jacob S. and Paul Pierson. 2007. "Tax Politics and the Struggle over Activist Government." In *The Transformation of American Politics: Activist Government and the Rise of Conservatism,* edited by Paul Pierson and Theda Skocpol, 256–80. Princeton, N.J.: Princeton University Press.

Halperin, Mark. 2006. "Ace of Base." *New York Times.* October 1, section 4, 11.

Hamburger, Tom and Peter Wallstein. 2006. *One Party Country.* New York: Wiley.

Hamdan v. Rumsfeld 126 S. Ct. 2749 (2006).

Hamdi v. Rumsfeld 542 U.S. 507 (2004).

Hamilton, Alexander, John Jay and James Madison. 1961. *The Federalist.* Middletown, Connecticut: Wesleyan University Press.

Hamilton, Laura S., Brian M. Stecher, Georges Vernez, and Ron Zimmer. 2007. "Passing or Failing? A Midterm Report Card for 'No Child Left Behind.'" *RAND Review.* Fall, 1–6.

Haney, Patrick J. 2005. "Foreign-Policy Advising: Models and Mysteries from the Bush Administration." *Presidential Studies Quarterly* 35 (2): 289–302.

Hargrove, Erwin C. 1998. *The President as Leader: Appealing to the Better Angels of Our Nature.* Lawrence: University Press of Kansas.

Hargrove, Erwin C. and Michael Nelson. 1984. *Presidents, Politics and Policy.* New York: McGraw-Hill.

Harvey, Diane Hollern. 2000. "The Public's View of Clinton." In *The Postmodern Presidency: Bill Clinton's Legacy in U.S. Politics,* edited by Steven E. Schier, 124–42. Pittsburgh: University of Pittsburgh Press.

Hastedt, Glen P. 2008. *American Foreign Policy: Past, Present and Future.* Seventh edition. Washington, D.C.: Congressional Quarterly Press.

Heclo, Hugh. 1977. *A Government of Strangers: Executive Politics in Washington.* Washington: Brookings Institution Press.

Heclo, Hugh. 2003. "The Political Ethos of George W. Bush." In *The George W. Bush Presidency: An Early Assessment,* edited by Fred I. Greenstein, 245–59. Baltimore: Johns Hopkins University Press.

Heil, Emily. 2004. "Medicare Actuary Details Threats Over Estimates." *CongressDaily.* March 25.

Herz, Michael. 1993. "Imposing Unified Executive Branch Statutory Interpretation." *Cardozo Law Review* 15 (1–2): 240–61.

Hetherington, Marc J. and Michael Nelson. 2003. "Anatomy of a Rally Effect: George W. Bush and the War on Terrorism." *PS: Political Science & Politics* (2003), 36: 37–42.

Holland, Robert. 2004. "No Child Left Behind Fuels Fierce Debate." *School Reform News,* March 1. Chicago: Heartland Institute.

"Homeland Security Employees Rank Last In Job Satisfaction Survey." 2008. ABC, Incorporated, WLS Television. February 8. http://abclocal.go.com/wls/story?section=nation_world&id=5017688 (accessed July 2008).

Hook, Steven W. 2008. *U.S. Foreign Policy: The Paradox of World Power.* Washington, D.C.: Congressional Quarterly Press.

Howell, William G. 2003. *Power without Persuasion: The Politics of Direct Presidential Action.* Princeton: Princeton University Press.

Hulse, Carl. 2006. "House Plans National Hearings before Changes to Immigration." *New York Times.* June 21, A1.

Hulse, Carl and Marjorie Connelly. 2006. "Poll Shows a Shift on Iraq War." *New York Times.* August 31, A2.

Hurst, Steven R. 2006. "Iraqi Official: 150,000 Dead." Associated Press. November 10.

Ignatius, David. 2008. "What Petraeus Would Face in Afghanistan." *Washington Post.* April 27, A16.

Investment Company Institute. 2006. *401 (k) Plans: A 25-Year Retrospective.* Washington, D.C., ICI. http://www.ici.org/stats/res/arc-ret/per12-02.pdf (accessed July 2008).

Iraq Coalition Casualty Count. 2008. "Military Deaths by Year/Month." http://www.icasualties.org/oif/ (accessed July 2008).

Iraq Survey Group. 2004. "Iraq Survey Group Final Report." http://www.globalsecurity.org/wmd/library/report/2004/isg-final-report/isg-final-report_v012_nuclear-05.htm (accessed July 2008).

Jackson, Derrick Z. 2007. "Admiral Mullen Reports for Duty." *Boston Globe.* October 2, A24.

Jacobs, Lawrence R. and Robert Y. Shapiro. 2000. "Conclusion: Presidential Power, Institutions, and Democracy." In *Presidential Power: Forging the Presidency for the Twenty-First Century,* edited by Robert Y. Shapiro, Martha Joynt Kumar and Lawrence R. Jacobs, 489–508. New York: Columbia University Press.

Jacobson, Gary C. 2003. "Terror, Terrain and Turnout: Explaining the 2002 Midterm Elections." *Political Science Quarterly* 118 (1): 1–22.

Jacobson. Gary C. 2007A. "Referendum: the 2006 Midterm Congressional Elections." *Political Science Quarterly* 122 (1): 1–24.

Jacobson, Gary C. 2007B. *A Divider, Not a Uniter: George W. Bush and the American People.* New York: Pearson Longman.

Jacobson, Gary C. 2008. *A Divider, Not a Uniter: George W. Bush and the American People: The 2006 Election and Beyond.* New York: Pearson Longman.

Jakes Jordan, Lara. 2006. "Credit Card Fraud at DHS." *Homeland Security Weekly.* July 19. http://www.homelandsecurityweekly.com (accessed October 2007).

Janis, Irving L. 1972. *Victims of Groupthink.* Boston: Houghton Mifflin.

Jehl, Douglas and Andrew C. Revkin. 2001. "Bush, in Reversal, Won't Seek Cut in Emissions of Carbon Dioxide." *New York Times.* March 14.

Jehl, Douglas. 2004A. "The Issue of War: Inspector's Judgment: U.S. Report Finds Iraqis Eliminated Illicit Arms in 90's." *New York Times.* October 7, A1.

Jehl, Douglas. 2004B. "Threats and Responses: the Context." *New York Times,* A12.

John Doe and ACLU v. Ashcroft, 2004 WL 2185571 (S.D.N.Y) (Sept. 28, 2004).

Johnson, Bertram. 2004. "A Stake in the Sand: George W. Bush and Congress." In *High Risk and Big Ambition: The Presidency of George W. Bush,* edited by Steven E. Schier, 167–88. Pittsburgh: University of Pittsburgh Press.

Johnson, Doug and Tristan Zajonic. 2006. "Can Foreign Aid Create an Incentive for Good Governance? Evidence from the Millennium Challenge Corporation." April 11. http://www.ssrn.com/abstract=896293 (accessed July 2008).

Johnston, David and Eric Lipton. 2007. "'Loyalty to Bush and Gonzales Was a Factor in Prosecutors' Firings." *New York Times,* March 14, A1.

Jones, Charles O. 2005. *The Presidency in a Separated System.* Second edition. Washington: Brookings Institution Press.

Jones, Charles O. 2007A. "Governing Executively: Bush's Paradoxical Style." In *Second-Term Blues: How George W. Bush Has Governed,* edited by John C. Fortier and Norman J. Ornstein, 109–30. Washington, D.C.: American Enterprise Institute and Brookings Institution Press.

Jones, Charles O. 2007B. "The U.S. Congress and Chief Executive George W. Bush." In *The Polarized Presidency of George W. Bush,* edited by George C. Edwards III and Desmond S. King, 387–418. New York: Oxford University Press.

Jones, Jeffrey M. 2004. "Views of Bush Reach New Heights of Polarization." http://www.gallup.com/poll/13735/Views-Bush-Reach-New-Heights-Polarization.aspx (accessed July 2008).

Jurkowitz, Mark. 2003. "Playing Second Fiddle: Political Ads, International Newsmakers Bury Election Coverage." In *Midterm Madness: The Elections of 2002,* edited by Larry J. Sabato, 47–56. Lanham, Maryland: Rowman and Littlefield.

Justice, Glenn. 2004. "Advocacy Groups Reflect on Their Role in the Election." *New York Times.* November 5, A18.

Kamen, Al. 2007. "Recess Appointments Granted to 'Swift Boat' Donor, Two Other Nominees." *Washington Post.* April 8, A6.

Kelley, Christopher S. 2005. "Rethinking Presidential Power—The Unitary Executive and the George W. Bush Presidency." A paper presented at the Annual Meeting of the Midwest Political Science Association, April 7–10.

Kelley, Christopher S. and Bryan W. Marshall. 2007. "Going It Alone: The Politics of Signing Statements from Reagan to Bush II." A paper presented at the Annual Meeting of the American Political Science Association, August 30–September 2.

Kelley, Christopher S. and Ryan J. Barilleaux. 2006. "The Past, Present and Future of the Unitary Executive." A paper presented at the Annual Meeting of the American Political Science Association, September 1–3.

Kennedy, Anthony. 2008. "From Justice Kennedy." *New York Times.* June 13, A20.

Kenski, Kate and Russell Tisinger. 2006. "Hispanic Voters in the 2000 and 2004 Presidential General Elections." *Presidential Studies Quarterly* 36 (2): 189–202.

Kern, Montague. 2001. "Disadvantage Al Gore in Election 2000: Coverage of Issue and Candidate Attributes, including the Candidate as Campaigner, on Newspaper and Television News Web Sites." *American Behavioral Scientist* 44 (12): 2,125–39.

Kernell, Samuel. 2007. *Going Public: New Strategies of Presidential Leadership.* Fourth edition. Washington, D.C.: Congressional Quarterly Press.

Kessel, John H. 2001. *Presidents, the Presidency, and the Political Environment.* Washington, D.C.: Congressional Quarterly Press.

Kettl, Donald F. 2003. *Team Bush: Leadership Lessons from the Bush White House.* New York: McGraw-Hill.

King, Anthony. 1993. "Foundations of Power." In *Researching the Presidency: Vital Questions, New Approaches,* edited by George C. Edwards III, John H. Kessel and Bert A. Rockman, 415–52. Pittsburgh: University of Pittsburgh Press.

Kirkpatrick, David D. 2004. "Churches See an Election Role and Spread the Word on Bush." *New York Times.* August 9, p A1.

Kissinger, Henry. 2008. Interview. "Uncommon Knowledge," Television program hosted by Peter Robinson. April 21.

Knapp, Bill. 2006. "Advertising." In *Electing the President 2004: The Insiders' View,* edited by Kathleen Hall Jamieson, 39–83. Philadelphia: University of Pennsylvania Press.

Kogan, Richard. 2008. "Federal Spending, 2001–2008: Defense Is a Rapidly Growing Share of the Budget, While Domestic Appropriations Have Shrunk." Washington, D.C.: Center for Budget and Policy Priorities.

Kraft, Michael E. 2006. "Environmental Policy in Congress." In *Environmental Policy: New Directions for the Twenty-First Century,* edited by Norman J. Vig and Michael E. Kraft, 124–47. Washington, D.C.: CQ Press.

Kriz, Margaret. 2008. "Vanishing Act." *National Journal.* April 12, 18–23.

Krugman, Paul. 2008. "Federal Spending Mythology." *New York Times.* February 2, A14.

Kumar, Martha Joynt. 2004. "News Organizations as a Presidential Resource in Governing: Media Opportunities and White House Organization." In *New Challenges for the American Presidency,* edited by George C. Edwards and Philip John Davies, 65–84. New York: Pearson Longman.

Kumar, Martha Joynt. 2007. "Managing the News: The Bush Communications Operation." In *The Polarized Presidency of George W. Bush,* edited by George C. Edwards III and Desmond S. King, 351–86. New York: Oxford University Press.

Labaton, Stephen. 2008. "Paulson, at Talks on Regulation, Suggest Pendulum Has Swung Too Far." *New York Times,* March 13.

Lane, Charles. 2007, "Narrow Victories Move Roberts Court to Right." *Washington Post.* June 29, A4.

Lemann, Nicholas. 2004. "Remember the Alamo: How George W. Bush Reinvented Himself." *New Yorker.* October 18, 37–42.

Lichtblau, Eric. 2008. "Senate Approves Bill to Broaden Wiretap Powers." *New York Times.* July 10, A1.

Lieberman, Robert C. 2000. "Political Time and Policy Coalitions: Structure and

Agency in Presidential Power." In *Presidential Power: Forging the Presidency for the Twenty-First Century,* edited by Robert Y. Shapiro, Martha Joynt Kumar and Lawrence R. Jacobs, 274–310. New York: Columbia University Press.

Light, Paul C. 1983. *The President's Agenda: Domestic Policy Choice from Kennedy to Carter.* Baltimore, Maryland: Johns Hopkins University Press.

Lightman, David. 2007. "Bush is the Biggest Spender since LBJ." McClatchy Newspapers: McClatchy Washington Bureau, October 24.

Lipton, Eric. 2006. "Homeland Security Department is Accused of Credit Card Misuse." *New York Times.* July 19, A16.

Lizza, Ryan. 2005. "Legal Theory." *New Republic,* August 1, 12.

Lochhead, Carolyn. 2005. "Republicans Broaden Strategies for Overhauling Social Security." *San Francisco Chronicle.* April 30, A6.

Locke, John. 1965. *Two Treatises of Government.* New York: New American Library.

Magnet, Myron. 1993. *The Dream and the Nightmare: The Sixties' Legacy to the Underclass.* New York: William Morrow.

Mann, Thomas E. 2000. "The 2000 Election Transition." Panel transcript, Brookings Council Retreat. November 16. Washington, D.C.: Brookings Institution. http://www.brookings.edu/events/2000/1116elections02.aspx (accessed July 2008).

Mann, Thomas E. and Norman J. Ornstein. 2006. *The Broken Branch: How Congress Is Failing America and How to Get It Back on Track.* New York: Oxford University Press.

Maveety, Nancy. Forthcoming. "Low Risk but Big Ambition: the Politics of George W. Bush's Judicial Appointments." In *Ambition and Division: The George W. Bush Presidency and U.S. Politics,* edited by Steven E. Schier, 1–34. Pittsburgh: University of Pittsburgh Press.

Mayer, Jeremy D. 2004. "The Presidency and Image Management: Discipline in Pursuit of Illusion." *Presidential Studies Quarterly* 34 (3): 620–31.

Mayhew, David R. 2002. *Electoral Realignments: A Critique of an American Genre.* New Haven: Yale University Press.

Mayhew, David R. 2005A. "Wars and American Politics." *Perspectives on Politics* 3 (3): 473–94.

Mayhew, David R. 2005B. *Divided We Govern: Party Control, Lawmaking and Investigations, 1946–2002.* Second edition. New Haven: Yale University Press.

Mayhew, David R. 2008. "Updates to *Divided We Govern.*" http://pantheon.yale.edu/~dmayhew/data3.html (accessed July 2008).

McCarty, Nolan, Keith T. Poole and Howard Rosenthal. 2006. *Polarized America: The Dance of Ideology and Unequal Riches.* Cambridge: Massachusetts Institute of Technology Press.

McCormick, James M. Forthcoming. "The Foreign Policy of the George W. Bush Administration: A Focus on Terrorism and the Promotion of Democracy." In *Ambition and Division: The George W. Bush Legacy in U.S. Politics,* edited by Steven E. Schier, 211–40. Pittsburgh: University of Pittsburgh Press.

Meece, Mickey. 2008. "With Stimulus Package, Big Winner Could Be Small Business." *New York Times,* February 13, B1.

Milbank, Dana. 2004. "9/11 Panel's Findings Vault Bush's Credibility to Campaign Forefront." *Washington Post.* June 20, A1.

Miller, Gary J. 1993. "Formal Theory and the Presidency." In *Researching the Presidency:*

Vital Questions, New Approaches, edited by George C. Edwards III, John H. Kessel and Bert A. Rockman, 289–336. Pittsburgh: University of Pittsburgh Press.

Mooney, Chris. 2005. *The Republican War on Science.* New York: Basic Books.

Morris, Dick. 2005. "With Deft Roberts Choice, Bush Plays Judicial Jujitsu." *The Hill,* July 28, 16.

Mucciaroni, Gary and Paul J. Quirk. 2004. "Deliberations of a 'Compassionate Conservative': George W. Bush's Domestic Presidency." In *The George W. Bush Presidency: Appraisals and Prospects,* edited by Colin Campbell and Bert A. Rockman, 158–90. Washington, D.C.: Congressional Quarterly Press.

Mycoff, Jason D. and Joseph A. Pika. 2008. *Confrontation and Compromise: Presidential and Congressional Leadership 2001–2006.* New York: Rowman and Littlefield.

Nagourney, Adam, Janet Elder and Fred Backus. 2004. "The 2004 Campaign: Surveys, Polls Show Tie; Concerns Cited on Both Rivals." *New York Times.* October 19, A1.

Nakashima, Ellen, and Dan Eggen. 2001. "White House Seeks to Restore Its Privileges; Congress Finding Bush Administration Strongly Resists Some Requests for Internal Documents." *Washington Post.* September 10, A2.

National Security Council. 2002. *The National Security Strategy of the United States of America.* Washington, D.C.: National Security Council.

Natural Resources Defense Council. 2006. "White House Forest Fire Plan Will Increase Risk of Fire, Says NRDC." May 30. Washington, D.C.: Natural Resources Defense Council. http://www.nrdc.org/media/pressreleases/030530.asp (accessed July 2008).

Neustadt, Richard E. 1990. *Presidential Power and the Modern Presidents.* New York: Free Press.

"New Majority Struggles To Turn Pledges into Law." 2008. *CQ Weekly.* January 7, 62–70.

Niven, David. 2001. "Bias in the News: Partisanship and Negativity in Media Coverage of Presidents George Bush and Bill Clinton." *Harvard International Journal of Press/Politics* 6 (3): 31–46.

Norquist, Grover G. 2008. *Leave Us Alone: Getting the Government's Hands Off Our Money, Our Guns, Our Lives.* New York: William Morrow.

Nye, Joseph S., Jr. 2004. "The Benefits of Soft Power." *Compass: A Journal of Leadership.* Spring, 7–10. Published by the John F. Kennedy School of Government, Harvard University.

O'Brien, David M. 2004. "Ironies and Disappointments: Bush and Federal Judgeships." In *The George W. Bush Presidency: Appraisals and Prospects,* edited by Colin Campbell and Bert A. Rockman, 133–57. Washington, D.C.: Congressional Quarterly Press.

O'Hanlon, Michael E. 2003. "History Will Credit Shinseki." *Japan Times.* June 19.

O'Hanlon, Michael E. and Jason H. Campbell. 2008. *Iraq Index: Tracking Variables of Reconstruction and Security in Post-Saddam Iraq.* Washington, D.C.: Brookings Institution. http://www.brookings.edu/saban/iraq-index.aspx (accessed July 2008).

Olasky, Marvin. 1997. *Renewing American Compassion: How Compassion for the Needy Can Turn Ordinary Citizens into Heroes.* Washington, D.C.: Regnery Publishing.

Olson, Theodore B., et al. 2004. Brief for Petitioners, *Cheney v. U.S. District Court for the District of Columbia.* U.S. Supreme Court case 03–475. April.

On Message, Incorporated. 2006. "MRI of the Republican Meltdown: Memo 3 Diagnosis A Shattered Brand." November 20. Crofton, Maryland: On Message, Incorporated.

Ornstein, Norman. 2003. "Filibuster Redux: Reform Is Needed, but Tread Carefully." *Roll Call*, May 21, 16.

Orren, Karen and Stephen Skowronek. 2004. *The Search for American Political Development*. New York: Cambridge University Press.

Orzag, Peter R. 2001. "The Bush Tax Cut is now about the Same Size as the Reagan Tax Cuts." Washington, D.C.: Center for Budget and Policy Priorities.

Owens, John. 2006. "American-Style Party Government: Delivering Bush's Agenda, Delivering Congress's Agenda." In *Right On? Political Change and Continuity in George W. Bush's America*, edited by Iwan Morgan and Philip Davies, 131–60. London: Institute for the Study of the Americas.

Parks, Daniel J. and Mary Dalrymple. 2002. "New Pot of Federal Dollars Has Admirers From All Over." *CQ Weekly*. 27 April, 1066.

Parsons, Claudia. 2005. "Study Shows U.S. Election Coverage Harder on Bush." Reuters News Service. March 14. http://www.freerepublic.com/focus/f-news/1362474/posts (accessed July 2008).

"Partisan Votes Echo Electoral Themes." 2005. *2004 CQ Almanac*, B8-B13. Washington: Congressional Quarterly Press.

Passel, Jeffrey S. 2006. "Size and Characteristics of the Undocumented Migrant Population in the United States." Washington, D.C.: Pew Hispanic Center. http://www.pewhispanic.org/reports/report.php?ReportID=61 (accessed July 2008).

Pear, Robert. 2007. "Bush Directive Increases Sway on Regulation." *New York Times*. January 30, A6.

Perlez, Jane. 2001. "U.S. Sanctions on Islamabad will be Lifted." *New York Times*, 22 September, A1.

Peterson, Mark A. 2007. "Still a Government of Chums: Bush, Business, and Organized Interests." In *The George W. Bush Legacy*, edited by Colin Campbell, Bert A. Rockman and Andrew Rudalvige, 288–324. Washington, D.C.: Congressional Quarterly Press.

Pew Global Project Attitudes. 2003. "Views of a Changing World June 2003." Washington, D.C.: The Pew Research Center for the People & the Press.

Pew Global Project Attitudes. 2006. "America's Image Slips, But Allies Share U.S. Concerns Over Iran." Washington, D.C.: The Pew Research Center for the People & the Press.

Pew Research Center for the People and the Press. 2004A. "The State of the News Media 2004." http://www.stateofthenewsmedia.com/narrative_overview_author.asp?media=1 (accessed December 2007).

Pew Research Center for the People and the Press. 2004B. "Foreign Policy Attitudes Now Driven by 9/11 and Iraq Part Three: Foreign Policy Priorities." http://people-press.org/report/?pageid=866 (accessed June 2008).

Pew Research Center for the People and the Press. 2007. "Trends in Political Values and Core Attitudes: 1987–2007: Political Landscape More Favorable to Democrats." http://www.pewresearch.org/pubs/434/trends-in-political-values-and-core-attitudes-1987–2007 (accessed July 2008).

Pfiffner, James P. 2007. "The First MBA President: George W. Bush as Public Administrator." *Public Administration Review* 67 (1): 6–20.

Pfiffner, James P. 2005. "Presidential Leadership and Advice About Going to War." Paper presented at the Conference on Presidential Leadership, Richmond, Virginia, September 9–10.

PollingReport.com. 2005. CBS/New York Times poll. June 10–15, and CNN/USA Today/Gallup poll, May 20–22. http://www.pollingreport.com/bush2.htm (accessed July 2008).

POLO STEP planning group briefing for Central Command. 2002. National Security Archive Briefing Book No. 214. http://www.gwu.edu/~nsarchiv/NSAEBB/NSAEBB214/index.htm (accessed July 2008).

Polsby, Nelson W. 1990. "Congress, National Security, and the Rise of the 'Presidential Branch.'" In *The Constitution and National Security: A Bicentennial View,* edited by Howard E. Schuman and Walter R. Thomas, 201–10. Washington, D.C.: National Defense University Press.

Pomper, Gerald M. 1999. "Parliamentary Government in the United States?" In *The State of the Parties: The Changing Role of Contemporary American Parties,* edited by John C. Green and Daniel M. Shea, 251–70. Lanham, Maryland: Rowman and Littlefield.

Pomper, Gerald M. 2003. "Parliamentary Government in the United States: A New Regime for a New Century?" In *The State of the Parties.* Edited by John C. Green and Rick Farmer, 267–86. Fourth Edition. Lanham, Maryland: Rowman and Littlefield.

Pomper, Gerald M. 2005. "The Presidential Election: The Ills of American Politics after 9/11." In *The Elections of 2004,* edited by Michael Nelson, 42–68. Washington, D.C.: Congressional Quarterly Press.

Poole, Isiah J. 2006. "Two Steps Up, One Step Down." *CQ Weekly,* January 9, 80–90.

Poole, Keith T. and Howard Rosenthal. 2007. *NOMINATE Data.* http://www.voteview.com/dwnl.htm (accessed July 2008).

Project for Excellence in Journalism. 2000. "The Last Lap: How the Press Covered the Final Stages of the Campaign." October 31. http://www.journalism.org/node/309 (accessed July 2008).

Purdum, Todd. 2005. "A Final Verdict on Prewar Intelligence Is Still Elusive." *New York Times.* April 1, A1.

Rasmussen, Scott. 1997. "People Who Work for the Government Are More Likely to Be Democrats." Rasumussen Reports. http://www.rasmussenreports.com Cited in Norquist 2008, 343.

Rauch, Jonathan. 1999. *Government's End: Why Washington Stopped Working.* New York: PublicAffairs.

Renshon, Stanley A. 2004. *In His Father's Shadow: The Transformations of George W. Bush.* New York: Palgrave Macmillan.

Reuters. 2007. "Colin Powell Says Guantanamo Should Be Closed." June 10. http://www.reuters.com/article/newsOne/idUSN1043646920070610 (accessed July 2008).

Ricks, Thomas E. 2006. *Fiasco: The American Military Adventure in Iraq.* New York: Penguin.

Riedl, Brian M. 2007. "Ten Myths about the Bush Tax Cuts." Washington, D.C.: Heritage Foundation.

Riedl, Brian M. 2008. "Federal Spending By the Numbers 2008." Washington, D.C. Heritage Foundation.

Riker, William. 1986. *The Art of Political Manipulation*. New Haven: Yale University Press.

Risen, James. 2003. "After the War: Congress; A Democrat is Wary of Appearing Too Partisan over White House Handling of Iraq." *New York Times*. June 19, A12.

Roberts, Alasdair. 2008. *The Collapse of Fortress Bush: The Crisis of Authority in American Government*. New York: New York University Press.

Roberts, John. 2008. "From Chief Justice Roberts." *New York Times*. June 13, A20.

Rockman, Bert A. 1997. "The Presidency and Bureaucratic Change after the Cold War." In *Change in U.S. Foreign Policy after the Cold War: Processes, Structures and Decisions*, edited by Randall B. Ripley and James M. Lindsay, 21–41. Pittsburgh: University of Pittsburgh Press.

Rockman, Bert A. 1984. *The Leadership Questions: The Presidency and the American System*. New York: Praeger.

Roe v. Wade 410 U.S. 113 (1973).

Roll Call. 2002. September 26, 13.

Roosevelt, Theodore. 1925. *An Autobiography*. New York: Charles Scribner's Sons.

Rosen, Jeffrey. 2006. "Power of One." *New Republic*. July 24, 8–10.

Rothenberg, Stuart. 2007. "The Fight for the Senate." In *The Six Year Itch: The Rise and Fall of the George W. Bush Presidency*, edited by Larry Sabato, 65–82. New York: Pearson Longman.

Rowley, James. 2006. "Congress Supports Military Tribunals for Suspected Terrorists." Bloomberg News. Abstract available at SSRN (http://papers.ssrn.com/s013/papers.cfm?abstract_id=1068402) (accessed July 2008).

Rozell, Mark J. 2006. "Executive Privilege in an Era of Polarized Politics." In *Executing the Constitution: Putting the President Back into the Constitution*, edited by Christopher S. Kelley, 91–108. Albany: State University of New York Press.

Rubenzer, Steven J. and Thomas R. Faschingbauer. 2004. *Personality, Character and Leadership in the White House: Psychologists Assess the Presidents*. Washington, D.C.: Brassey's Incorporated.

Rudalvige, Andrew. 2005 *The New Imperial Presidency: Renewing Presidential Power after Watergate*. Ann Arbor: University of Michigan Press.

Rudalvige, Andrew. 2007. "'The Decider' Issue Management and the Bush White House." In *The George W. Bush Legacy*, edited by Colin Campbell, Bert A. Rockman and Andrew Rudalvige, 135–63. Washington, D.C.: Congressional Quarterly Press.

Ryan, James E. 2004. "The Perverse Incentives of the No Child Left Behind Act." *New York University Law Review*, Spring. http://www.ssrn.com/abstract=476463 (accessed July 2008).

Saad, Lydia. 2008. "Disapproval of Bush Spans the Issues." Washington, D.C.: Gallup Poll.

Sabato, Larry J. 2003A. "The George W. Bush Midterm: From Popular-Vote Loser to Political Colossus in Two Not-So-Easy Election Steps." In *Midterm Madness: The Elections of 2002*, edited by Larry J. Sabato, 1–34. Lanham, Maryland: Rowman and Littlefield.

Sabato, Larry J. 2003B. "A Final Look in the Rearview Mirror for 2002: The Midterm

Map of America." In *Midterm Madness: The Elections of 2002,* edited by Larry J. Sabato, 263–66. Lanham, Maryland: Rowman and Littlefield.

Seelye, Katherine Q. 2001. "Bush Picks Insiders to Fill Environmental Posts." *New York Times.* May 12, A8.

Schier, Steven E. 1992. *A Decade of Deficits: Congressional Thought and Fiscal Action.* Albany, New York: State University of New York Press.

Schier, Steven E. 2004. "Introduction: George W. Bush's Project." In *High Risk and Big Ambition: The Presidency of George W. Bush,* edited by Steven E. Schier, 1–16. Pittsburgh: University of Pittsburgh Press.

Schier, Steven E. 2005. "Bush is Parliamentary, not Bipartisan." *The Hill.* July 12, 16.

Schweers, Maureen. 2003. "U.S. House Races: Republican Resurgence after Eight Lean Years." In *Midterm Madness: The Elections of 2002,* edited by Larry J. Sabato, 67–76. Lanham, Maryland: Rowman and Littlefield.

Shane, Scott and Ron Nixon. 2007. "In Washington, Contractors Take on Biggest Role Ever." *New York Times.* February 4, A1.

Sherman, Amy L. 2002. "Tracking Charitable Choice: A Study of the Collaboration between Faith-Based Organizations and the Government in Providing Social Services in Nine States." *Social Work and Christianity* 27 (2): 112–29.

Shull, Steven A. and James M. Vanderleeuw. 1987. "What Do Key Votes Measure?" *Legislative Studies Quarterly* 12 (4): 573–82.

Simon, Roger. 2004. "High Stakes Numbers Game." *U.S. News and World Report.* May 2. http://www-origin.usnews.com/usnews/news/articles/040510/10notes.htm (accessed July 2008).

Sinclair, Barbara. 2007. "Living (and Dying?) by the Sword: George W. Bush as Legislative Leader." In *The George W. Bush Legacy,* edited by Colin Campbell, Bert A. Rockman and Andrew Rudalvige, 164–87. Washington, D.C.: Congressional Quarterly Press.

Singel, Ryan. 2007. "Court Strikes Down 2 Key Patriot Act Provisions." *Wired GQ.* September 26. http://blog.wired.com/27bstroke6/2007/09/court-strikes-2.html (accessed July 2008).

Singer, Paul. 2005. "By the Horns." *National Journal.* March 26, 898–905.

Skowronek, Stephen. 1997. *The Politics Presidents Make: Leadership from John Adams to Bill Clinton.* Cambridge: Harvard University Press.

Skowronek, Stephen. 2001. "The Setting: Change and Continuity in the Politics of Leadership." In *The Elections of 2000,* edited by Michael Nelson, 1–26. Washington: Congressional Quarterly Press.

Skrzycki, Cindy. 2007. "Bush Order Limits Agencies' 'Guidance,'" *Washington Post,* January 30, D1.

Snow, Donald M. 2008. *What After Iraq?* New York: Longman.

Tanner, Michael. 2007. *Leviathan on the Right: How Big-Government Conservativism Brought Down the Republican Revolution.* Washington, D.C.: Cato Institute.

Tanter, Raymond and Stephen Kersting. 2007. "Grand Strategy as National Security Policy: Politics, Rhetoric and the Bush Legacy." In *The George W. Bush Legacy,* edited by Colin Campbell, Bert A. Rockman and Andrew Rudalvige, 213–38. Washington, D.C.: Congressional Quarterly Press.

Tatalovich, Raymond and Thomas S. Engeman. 2003. *The Presidency and Political*

Science: Two Hundred Years of Constitutional Debate. Baltimore: Johns Hopkins University Press.

Tax Policy Center. 2008. "The Tax Policy Briefing Book." Washington, D.C.: Urban Institute and Brookings Institution.

Timberg, Craig. 2008. "African AIDS Crisis Outlives $15 Billion Bush Initiative." *Washington Post.* February 20, A9.

Todd, Chuck. 2003. "Air Force Won." In *Midterm Madness: The Elections of 2002,* edited by Larry J. Sabato, 35–46. Lanham, Maryland: Rowman and Littlefield.

Toner, Robin. 2005. "It's 'Private' vs. 'Personal' in Social Security Debate." *New York Times.* March 22, A8.

Toner, Robin. 2002. "Welfare Chief Is Hoping to Promote Marriage." *New York Times,* February 19, A1.

Toner, Robin and Neil A. Lewis. 2001. "A Nation Challenged: House Passes Terrorism Bill Much Like Senate's but with 5-Year Limit." *New York Times.* October 13, A1.

Towers Perrin. 2007. "Without the Correct Approach and Implementation, Long-Term Effectiveness of Account-Based Health Plans Could Be Undermined, Towers Perrin Research Shows" May 22. Stamford, Connecticut: Towers Perrin. http://www.towersperrin.com/tp/showdctmdoc.jsp?url=HR_Services/United_States/Press_Releases/2007/20070522/2007_05_22.htm&selected=press&language_code=global (accessed July 2008).

U.S. v. Nixon 418 U.S. 683 (1974).

Union of Concerned Scientists. 2004. "Scientific Integrity in Policymaking: Further Investigation of the Bush Administration's Misuse of Science" July. http://www.ucsusa.org/scientific_integrity/interference/scientific-integrity-in-policy-making-204.html (accessed July 2008).

Vig, Norman J. 2006. "Presidential Leadership and the Environment." In *Environmental Policy: New Directions for the Twenty-First Century,* edited by Norman J. Vig and Michael E. Kraft, 102–23. Washington, D.C.: CQ Press.

Viguerie, Richard A. 2006. *Conservatives Betrayed: How George W. Bush and Other Big Government Republicans Hijacked the Conservative Cause.* Santa Monica, California: Bonus Books.

Von Drehle, David. 2005. "Wrestling with History." *Washington Post.* November 13, W12.

Waas, Murray. 2006. "What Bush Was Told about Iraq." *National Journal.* March 4, 40–42.

Warshaw, Shirley Anne. 2004. "Mastering Presidential Government: Executive Power and the Bush Administration." In *Transformed by Crisis: The Presidency of George W. Bush and American Politics,* edited by Jon Kraus, Kevin J. McMahon and David M. Rankin, 101–18. New York: Palgrave Macmillan.

Wasserman, David. 2007. "The 2006 House Midterm Maelstrom: From 'The GOP's to Lose' to a 'House of Blues.'" In *The Six Year Itch: The Rise and Fall of the George W. Bush Presidency,* edited by Larry Sabato, 97–134. New York: Pearson Longman.

Weisberg, Herbert and Clyde Wilcox. 2003. *Models of Voting in Presidential Elections: The 2000 U.S. Election.* Palo Alto, California: Stanford University Press.

Weisman, Jonathan. 2006. "Senate Pact Offers Permits to Most Illegal Immigrants." *Washington Post.* April 7, A1.

Weisman, Jonathan and Amit R. Paley. 2007. "Dozens in GOP Turn against Bush's Prized 'No Child' Act." *Washington Post.* March 15, A1.

West, William F. 2005. "The Institutionalization of Regulatory Review: Organizational Stability and Responsive Competence at OIRA." *Presidential Studies Quarterly* 35 (1): 76–93.

Western, Jon. 2004. "Doctrinal Divisions: The Politics of US Military Interventions." *Harvard International Review.* Spring, 46–50.

Western, Jon. 2005. *Selling Intervention and War: The Presidency, the Media and the American Public.* Baltimore: Johns Hopkins University Press.

Whelan. Ed. 2007. "The Record-Slow Pace of Judicial Confirmations." *Bench Memos.* http://bench.nationalreview.com/post/?q=MjJhZDllOWRmYmZiMjUxOWFj NTllZGI5ZTNmYTU4NGU= (accessed July 2008).

White House. 2003. "Fact Sheet: Guidance Released on Health Savings Accounts (HSAs)." News release. December 22.

White House. 2005. "Fact Sheet: Securing America Through Immigration Reform." Immigration Reform." News release. November 28.

White House. 2005. "President Bush Signs into Law a National Energy Plan." News release. August 8.

Wolfensburger, Donald R. 2005. "A Reality Check on the Republican House Reform Revolution at the Decade Mark." Introductory essay for Congress Project Roundtable on "The Republican Revolution at 10: The Lasting Legacy or Faded Vision?" Washington, D.C.: Woodrow Wilson International Center for Scholars, January 24.

Wolfowitz, Paul. 2008. Comments at Hudson Institute Forum on Douglas J. Feith's book, *War and Decision.* Washington, D.C. April 28. Televised by C-SPAN.

Woodward, Bob. 2002. *Bush at War.* New York: Simon and Schuster.

Woodward, Bob. 2004. *Plan of Attack.* New York: Simon and Schuster.

Woodward, Bob. 2006. *State of Denial.* New York: Simon and Schuster.

Wooldridge, Adrian and John Mickelthwait. 2004. *The Right Nation: Conservative Power in America.* New York: Penguin Press.

Yalof, David A. 2007. "In Search of a Means to an End: George W. Bush and the Federal Judiciary." In *The George W. Bush Legacy,* edited by Colin Campbell, Bert A. Rockman and Andrew Rudalvige, 188–212. Washington, D.C.: Congressional Quarterly Press.

Yoo, Christopher S., Steven G. Calabresi and Anthony Colangelo. 2001. "The Unitary Executive in the Modern Era, 1945–2001." Nashville: Research Paper Program, Vanderbilt University Law School.

Zacher, Alfred J. 1996. *Trial and Triumph: Presidential Power in the Second Term.* Fort Wayne, Indiana: Presidential press.

Zakaria, Tabassum. 2008. "Afghan Challenge Romantic–Bush." Reuters News Service. March 13. http://www.reuters.com/article/politicsNews/idUSN13331111 20080313?feedType=RSS&feedName=politicsNews (accessed July 2008).

Zandi, Mark M. 2004. "Assessing President Bush's Fiscal Policies." *The Dismal Scientist,* June, 1–11. West Chester, Pennsylvania: Economy.com.

Zelinsky, Edward A. 2007. *The Origins of the Ownership Society: How The Defined Contribution Paradigm Changed America.* New York: Oxford University Press.

INDEX

ABOUT THE AUTHOR

Steven E. Schier is Dorothy H. and Edward C. Congdon Professor of Political Science at Carleton College, where he has directed the college's off-campus program in Washington since 1983. He has written or edited ten books and composed numerous scholarly articles on topics including the presidency, Congress, political parties, and elections. His edited volume *The Postmodern Presidency: Bill Clinton's Legacy in U.S. Politics* received an "outstanding academic book" award from *Choice* magazine in 2001. Opinion pieces by Schier have appeared in the *New York Times, Washington Post, Los Angeles Times, USA Today,* and other papers.